Endorsements

I thank God for calling Nancy Petrey to be a "mizpah for Israel" and using her in such powerful ways. In this book she gives the exciting account of how God awakened her to the Jewish roots of our faith and how it changed her life. Interwoven with her testimony are many nuggets of precious truths about Israel. There is an awesome power in the truth.

There is a spiritual battle raging today over Israel and the Jewish people. Satan is making a final attempt to wipe out the chosen people, like he has tried so many times before in history. It is the 1930s all over again, and we must not be silent but speak out on behalf of Israel. Experts predict that the young generation of Christians in America will take the side of the Palestinians in the conflict in the Middle East. May God use this book to open the eyes of many people and raise up hundreds of mizpahs for Israel to undo that prediction!

Blessings in abundance!
Lars Enarson
Founder of *The Watchman International* (www.thewatchman.org).
Founder of *The Elijah Prayer Army* (A Worldwide Network of Prayer for Israel and the Middle East)

In her *Memoirs of a Mizpah*, Nancy Petrey combines stories from her personal journeys to Israel and around the United States with the knowledge of Israel's biblical and modern history she has gained through study to provide an account of her understanding of God's coming redemption. Inspired by Corrie ten Boom and Lydia Prince, this book is a passionate retelling of her personal encounters with the God of Israel, the Messiah of Israel and the People of Israel and her God given passion for the Jewish people. Through sharing these experiences she hopes to inspire and encourage her readers to become "watchmen on the walls of Jerusalem" and connect to the Jewish roots of the Christian faith. Read her memoirs and be encouraged by what God has done and continues to do in Israel and within the body of Messiah.

Avi & Chaya Mizrachi
Directors of *Dugit Messianic Outreach Centre*
Dugit, PO Box 11174, Tel Aviv 61111, Israel (www.dugit.org)
(www.adonairoi.com)

Nancy Petrey is one of the most exuberant and enthusiastic people I know who is involved with the Israel work. She loves the country, the State of Israel, the history of the Jewish people, and with her marvelous gifts of music and radiant worship, she is able to reach many people with her influence. Israel is truly blessed to have a friend like Nancy.

Pamela Suran
Licensed Israeli tour guide
Ministry of *Chazon Yerushalayim*
with husband, Pastor Shmuel Suran
Prophetic artist - "Pamela Suran, Biblical Artist"
(www.pamelasuran.com)

It is a delight for us to recommend the reading of this book by our friend, Nancy Petrey. Mary and I always enjoy our encounters with her and her husband Curtis, when he is with her. We consider it an honor to be mentioned several times in the recounting of her memories in and out of Israel. Come and join Nancy on a journey. Yes, the physical journey of her life and times since discovering the incredible reality of God. But even more than that, a journey of amazing learning and understanding of how God shows us, like a time-released capsule, His reality through the Land and People of Israel.

Each chapter is like sitting down with a cup of coffee or tea and listening as Nancy shares with you the wonderful things she has seen and learned. I particularly enjoyed the story of her encounter with a sparrow while she was playing the piano and singing, "His Eye is on the Sparrow." As you follow along with her on this journey, you will also learn as she did so many incredible truths about God's love story in His Word, and how that relationship is available to us today. You'll even get practical advice about "Mr Expert Guide" and wild taxi rides! The Appendix section of this book alone, along with the richness of the memoirs of Nancy Petrey, will make this book a treasure in your home.

Roy and Mary Kendall
Directors, *School of Worship*
SOW in Jerusalem
(www.sowij.com)

Jewish Roots Journey

Memoirs of a Mizpah

Nancy Petrey

Energion Publications
Gonzalez, Florida
2012

Contact the author via Energion Publications, P. O. Box 841, Gonzalez, FL 32560, pubs@energion.com, http://energionpubs.com.

Cover Images: Nancy walking down the Jewish Cardo, an old Roman street, in the heart of the Old City of Jerusalem.

Wailing Wall, © Jeremy Wee | Dreamstime.com, Used by Permission

The Hebrew word on the front cover is "Mizpah," meaning "watchtower" in Hebrew. For a more detailed explanation of this word, see pages 1-6.

ISBN10: 1-938434-05-6
ISBN13: 978-1-938434-05-1
Library of Congress Control Number: 2012941663

Dedication

In deeply felt gratitude, I dedicate this book
to my husband, Curtis Petrey.
He is my best friend, the love of my life, and
the "wind beneath my wings."
He has walked alongside me in the majority of my
experiences as a Mizpah for Israel.
His support, patience, wisdom and advice
have been invaluable.

"Do not boast against the branches.
But if you do boast,
remember that you do not support the root,
but the root supports you" (Rom. 11:18).

Acknowledgments

First of all, I wish to acknowledge the God of Abraham, Isaac, and Jacob (Ex. 3:15), who is also the God and Father of our Lord Jesus Christ (Eph. 1:3). He has empowered the writing of this book through His Holy Spirit. My gratitude and love know no bounds as I ponder the sacrifice of Yeshua, the Lamb of God on the cross, who took away my sins, paid for my sicknesses, filled me with His Spirit, gave me blessings untold in my family and friends, and called me to minister His truth concerning Israel and the Jewish people! Hallelujah! What a privilege to serve Him by writing this book about the experiences and understanding He has given me.

So many of the people in this book have been my teachers, and I am indebted to them. God has used them to open my eyes to precious truths in His Word, as they have ministered and modeled a biblical life style. I feel so privileged and blessed that God brought these "cream-of-the-crop" people into my life! This book would not have been written without them. Some of them were gracious enough to proofread the parts about themselves and offer corrections. Their contributions to the book are obvious within the following chapters, but I will acknowledge a few of them here.

To those who wrote the endorsements – Lars (& Harriet) Enarson, Avi (& Chaya) Mizrachi, Pamela (& Shmuel) Suran, and Roy (& Mary) Kendall, I say, "Thank you from the bottom of my heart for endorsing my book and for your friendship and mentoring!"

To Janice Bell, my ministry partner and best friend (see Chapter 12), I say, "Finding you was like finding a gold mine for friendship and ministry! Sharing in your Jewish life and in our trips to Israel have been priceless gifts. I thank you and love you."

I am especially grateful to Hannah May (see Chapter 28), whose book inspired me to write this book. She recommended me to her publisher, Energion, and she encouraged me throughout the process. "I love you, Hannah May!"

A big thanks is also due to Henry and Jody Neufeld, the publishers of Energion. "Thank you for believing in me and for helping my dream come true, to be a published author!"

I also want to acknowledge the people to whom I am leaving this book as the primary recipients of my legacy as a Mizpah for Israel – my children, grandchildren, and their descendants. Mine and Curtis' four children are all Petreys – Perry, Susan, Jim, and Bert. Perry's wife is Liv, and their child is David. Perry's other children are Franco, Joshua, P.J. (Perry Jr.) & his wife Kelly, Anna & her husband Nate Duhe, Isaiah, and Zoe. Susan's son is Zach Zwerg. Jim's children are Taylor, Hannah, Madeline, and Trey. I dearly love and treasure my wonderful family. They light up my life! It is my prayer that they will carry the torch of God's Word relating to the Jewish people and Israel.

Table of Contents

INTRODUCTION

My "Jewish roots journey" actually began when I gave my life to Jesus at a Lay Witness Mission in Tupelo, Mississippi, in March of 1968. I received the Lord's clarion call to salvation upon really hearing this verse: "Jesus said to him, 'I am the Way, the Truth, and the Life. No one comes to the Father except through Me'" (John 14:6). My life was totally changed and given new meaning. It was a joy to see how my personal Savior would lead me each day, and on this journey I eventually realized His Jewishness.

When I started out on the journey, I had no idea that my Lord and Savior had the Hebrew name, Yeshua, meaning "salvation." I had never noticed His words to the Samaritan woman, "Salvation is from the Jews" (John 4:22). I also had no idea that the Church I was involved in began on a Jewish feast day called Shavuot, "Feast of Weeks" (Acts 2). Neither did I realize that the Bible I so adored had been written by all Jewish or Hebrew authors except for Luke.

Of course, I knew Jesus and most of the Bible characters were Jewish, but it had not registered on my mind the **significance** of that fact. I eagerly embraced the Gentile version of Jesus I had grown accustomed to throughout my church-saturated life. I was oblivious to the Jewishness of Jesus. As He so often does, however, the Lord led me gently and gradually along the journey, until He could reveal Himself to me more fully. When the time came, He opened my eyes to see His Jewish identity as Messiah and to see the Jewish roots of the Church.

He showed me His priority of ministry, to the Jews first. Jesus sent His disciples out, saying, "Do not go into the way of the

Gentiles … but go rather to the lost sheep of the house of Israel" (Matt. 10:5-6). He told the Canaanite woman, "I was not sent except to the lost sheep of the house of Israel" (Matt. 15:24). Peter preached to the Jews after the Day of Pentecost (Shavuot), "**To you first,** God, having raised up His Servant Jesus, sent Him to bless you, in turning away every one of you from your iniquities" (Acts. 3:26).

The Apostle Paul had the same priority of ministry, going to the Jews first. He said, "For I am not ashamed of the gospel of Christ, for it is the power of God unto salvation for everyone who believes, for **the Jew first** and also for the Greek" (Rom. 1:16). You may say that God called him to be the Apostle to the Gentiles. That is true, but Paul always went to the Jewish synagogue first in every city he visited.

Before Jesus ascended back to heaven, He commissioned His disciples to go into all the world and preach the gospel, but surely the priority of Jew, then Gentile would continue. Sadly, most mission agencies today have little to do with Jewish evangelism.

Another new focus Jesus gave me on my Jewish roots journey was that He was born King of the Jews, died as King of the Jews, and will come back to the Jewish capital of Jerusalem as King of the Jews and King over all the earth. The last title for Jesus in the Bible is "Root and the Offspring of **David**, the Bright and Morning Star" (Rev. 22:16). King David was the greatest King that Israel ever had. Jesus was called "the Son of David, the Son of Abraham" (Matt. 1:1). Can there be any greater Jewish identity than that?

In this very personal account of my growing understanding of the place in God's end-time plans of redemption which center on the Jewish people and the nation of Israel, I wanted to add my voice to the increasing number of voices, urging the Church to get back to her Jewish roots.

The Church, made up mostly of Gentiles, has a Jewish Savior, but we Christians down through the centuries have either ignored or sought to harm Jewish people simply for being Jews. Anti-

Semitism originated in the Church, of all places, and it led right to the Holocaust!

In my Jewish Roots Journey, God revealed to me some of these shocking truths. He also gave me wonderful experiences on the journey, introducing me to some of His choice servants, His Holy Land, and His holy language, Hebrew. As these experiences accumulated over nearly 36 years, I knew I had to share these things on paper for all who may have either curiosity or a hunger to know more about God's ancient people and Land.

In the ongoing Middle East conflict between Israel and her hostile neighbors it is incumbent on Bible believers to understand the history of this conflict as recorded in the Holy Scriptures and in the modern history of the State of Israel. This book is not an academic study on the subject, but, using the Word of God, it does cast light on the causes and the solution to the conflict over the Land. One thing is for sure, God guarantees the continuing existence of His chosen nation Israel. His promise can be depended on just as surely as the earth revolving around the sun. He declares, "If this fixed order [the sun, moon, and stars] departs from before Me," declares the Lord, "then the offspring of Israel also shall cease from being a nation before me forever" (Jer. 31:36). In the light of God's immutable Word, how can anyone argue against Israel's right to her inherited Land?

My prayer is that all who read my *Memoirs of a Mizpah* will join the ranks of "watchmen on the walls of Jerusalem" (Isa. 62:6) and will "pray for the peace of Jerusalem" (Ps. 122:6). Christians need to take a supportive stand for the physical nation of Israel. Also, watchmen need to help the Church reconnect with her Jewish roots – first, realizing the Jewishness of her Messiah, and then the Jewishness of the Bible written by Jewish authors, the Jewishness of the Apostles, and the Jewishness of the first Church! This is the way we prepare for the coming of the Lord to Jerusalem, the Jewish capital, from where He will rule and reign over all the earth!

This narrative is not strictly chronological, but it moves along in a semi-chronological and topical fashion, if that makes sense! My six trips to Israel were in 1994, 1996, 1998, 2002, 2003, and 2007. This book is my "witness" as a "watchman," and I hope you are inspired and entertained and educated by it.

May God be glorified in the accomplishments set forth. He planned it all, and I can never thank Him enough for these awesome experiences, for the knowledge I have gained, and the giants of the faith He has introduced me to! It has been an exciting and fulfilling journey.

Shalom and love,
Nancy Petrey
Petrey, Alabama

1

Mizpah? What's That?

I was almost through writing this book when I happened to see a note I wrote to myself on the back of my prayer list. It pays to write things down, because we all tend to forget. This note was meant to be in my journal, I could see, but somehow didn't make it there. The "seed" planted in that note had germinated into this book without my realizing it!

Here is the note: "July 24, 2011. Seeking God for direction – what area to concentrate on. Turned to AMOS, name means 'burden bearer,' first of WRITING prophets – God is telling me to WRITE – carry His burden – as a Mizpah? – through a burden give birth to a prophet? Hannah birthing Samuel? Write 'Memoirs of a Mizpah' and give to Evan Kohen? Is this wild?"

It may have been a "wild" word from God, but it did happen! Evan Kohen was the Minister of Music at our church, South Luverne Baptist, in Luverne, Alabama, from November 7, 2010 until January 1, 2012. Soon after he came to the church, I asked him if he was Jewish. I knew the answer would be yes, because Kohen is a Jewish name. It is Hebrew for "priest." The Kohanim (plural) are from the tribe of Levi, one of the twelve tribes of Israel. Evan was glad to say he was Jewish. I was impressed that God had sent a Jewish man to our church to lead us in worship. What could be more appropriate?

I began to wonder if Evan fully appreciated his Jewish roots. I also wondered if he understood the importance of knowing about the Jewish roots of the church. Perhaps God had placed him right in front of me – especially since I am the church pianist – in order that I might share with him the things God had been teaching me. After all, he not only led our choir and congregation in singing to God. He also preached. And he was planning to go to seminary after graduating from college. Maybe he was the "prophet" referred to in my journal entry! He would be in a position to influence many people. This stayed in the back of my mind for some time.

I also thought about the fact that I had not passed on to my children and grandchildren very much of what I had learned and experienced since the Lord had called me to be a Mizpah for Israel. I had made a recording of some of my favorite piano pieces, primarily as a legacy for them. So I had shared **that** part of my life, but what about the Mizpah message? Maybe now was the time to write down the Jewish roots message and give it to them before I got much older.

This unformulated vagueness about passing on a message both to Evan and to my children and grandchildren was the **kindling that ignited** when I read my friend Hannah May's book, *Operation Olive Branch*. I was astounded to find out she was so much like me, and we had the same heart for the Jewish people and Israel! (See Chapter 28.) I loved writing, so that was all it took to "launch out into the deep" (Luke 5:4) and try my hand at writing a book, telling about the things I had learned and experienced ever since God called me to be a Mizpah for Israel in 1995.

For years I immersed myself in so many activities connected with Israel and the Jewish people, that my family and friends must have rolled their eyes and thought, "Oh, this is just a phase she is going through. She'll get over it." But over 16 years have passed, and my passion to be a Mizpah for Israel has not waned. God let me know He wanted me to teach the church about her Jewish roots and, hopefully, show the Jewish people their Jewish Messiah. I have tried to be true to His calling.

"Well, get to the point!" you may say. "What is a Mizpah?" The word "Mizpah" appears in the Bible many times. In Haifa, I met Hannah, a Jewish lady who had taught English in Israel for 20 years. She said "mizpah" or "mitzpeh" means "overseer" or "watchtower." The "mitzpim" (plural) are villages in northern Galilee that "overlook" Israel. Jews are encouraged to settle there and "stand guard" over the land. They let everyone know what is going on. She had hit the nail on the head for me! That was exactly what I felt called to do – let the church know what is going on with Israel and the Jewish people, to be a "lookout," so to speak.

You may remember that after King Nebuchadnezzar and the Babylonians took the Jews captive and burned the Temple in 586 B.C., the king left Gedaliah as the governor of the poor people remaining in the land.

The seat of government was at Mizpah (II Kings 25:23), about seven miles northwest of Jerusalem. That location was an ideal vantage point for the government to watch over Israel.

I have been to that Mizpah! I actually climbed the steep steps inside the watchtower and walked on top, surveying the Land for miles around. There was a young Jewish man there who stuck out his chest, jubilantly waved his arm over the Land we were viewing, and boastfully declared, "This belongs to us!" Our group held hands and prayed for the peace of Jerusalem. Later

Ancient Mizpah ("watchtower") at Arab village of Nabi Samwil ("Prophet Samuel") (Nancy and Randy peering out the windows and Frank on top) – 1996

that day as we enjoyed a Shabbat[1] meal in the home of Roy and

Mary Kendall, we met a friend of theirs who was stranded from her home because of a forest fire in the very area we were surveying. Who knows how God may have used our prayers at that God-appointed time?

Samuel's tomb is housed in a cellar in the watchtower at Mizpah, which is part of the old Crusader church building and monastery now incorporated into the village mosque. The Jews have a synagogue adjacent to the mosque. Mizpah is a place of pilgrimage today for Jews, Muslims, and Christians. A village of 20 Muslim families, approximately 220 inhabitants, beside the mosque is called Nabi Samwil ("prophet Samuel"). Samuel was buried in his hometown of Ramah in Benjamin (I Sam. 25:1), but his bones were found by a Crusader and reburied at ancient Mizpah.

The mountain of Mizpah was named Montjoie (mountain of joy), because it was from this spot that pilgrims coming from the foothills had their first sight of Jerusalem. It truly was a joyful experience for us on the mountain at the top of the watchtower as we looked out over the Holy City of Jerusalem.

Out of my six trips to Israel, this was the second one in September of 1996. We had been supporting Christian Friends of Israel (CFI)[2] in Jerusalem for some time. They are an outreach ministry to Israel and educational resource for the Church. They had assigned me the village of Nabi Samwil to pray for. Since then I have been praying that Nabi Samwil will be like a "city set on a hill," with the light of Yeshua shining out, that it will be a place of refuge for persecuted Jews. What a miracle that will take, since this "West Bank" town of Muslims would normally be hostile to Jews. The last thing they would want to do is provide a safe haven to people the Koran describes as their enemies. Besides that, "collaborating" with the Jews is declared by Muslim leaders as a crime punishable by death. The power of prayer, however, can overcome the power of Islam! So I will continue to "watch and pray" for Nabi Samwil.

On that trip in 1996, I was determined to see the ancient site of Mizpah, but it wasn't easy to arrange. Since it is in a Muslim area, we had to find an Arab taxi driver to take us there. This wasn't a tourist site. When we got there, IDF (Israeli Defense Force) soldiers were standing around the mosque. Feeling no fear, we proceeded to go inside, noted the tomb of Samuel, and some of us climbed to the top. There I was, **literally "watching"** over the Land as a Mizpah for Israel! This was real, not a spiritual fantasy. What an exciting adventure God blessed us with. It was truly a "God thing!"

But, let me go back to the meaning of "Mizpah." I'll never forget the day – it was August 18, 1995, and I was at home in Columbus, Mississippi. My husband Curtis, pastor of Trinity Church, called me from his office and announced, "God said you are a Mizpah for Israel." "Oh! Really?" I answered excitedly. "What's that?"

Curtis replied, "I don't know. I'm just telling you what God said." It was not a common thing for Curtis to prophesy. I had seen him do it at the altar on occasion, but he had never before given a "word from the Lord" to his wife. I knew this had to be a genuine word from the Lord.

At the time, I was in the middle of studying Hebrew, so I looked in my Hebrew dictionary. I couldn't find it. Then I called a friend, Joyce, and asked her. She didn't know, but she said her husband Ken would surely know the meaning. She asked him and reported back to me that Ken said the word "Mizpah" was found in Genesis 31:49, where it is recorded that Jacob and his father-in-law Laban made a covenant at Mizpah with stones heaped up to serve as a *witness*. The name Mizpah (meaning "watchtower") was given to these stones, because Laban said, "May the Lord watch between you and me when we are absent one from another." In essence Laban was saying, "If you cross this line and try to harm me, you better watch out, or I'll kill you!" Not very spiritual, huh? Anyway, I understood that God was calling me to be a **witness** and a **watchman** about things pertaining to Israel and the Jewish people.

The word "mizpah" can be found on headstones in cemeteries and on other memorials. Also, this word is found on jewelry which is worn to signify friendship, according to Genesis 31:49, it is claimed. However, looking more carefully at this covenant Jacob and Laban made with each other, it doesn't seem very friendly. Their covenant was more like a peace treaty between hostile partners.

Regardless of Laban's and Jacob's motives, the **intended** meaning for "mizpah" in the case of jewelry is that of an emotional bond between people who are separated, either physically or by death. As a Mizpah for Israel, I see my role as helping to heal the separation between Jews and their Messiah and the separation between Gentile Christians and their Jewish roots. I had two outstanding role models for this new calling God had given me.

2

Righteous Gentiles

My fascination with the Jews actually began back around 1975, when I read the book, The Hiding Place[3] by Corrie ten Boom. This woman, who called herself "tramp for the Lord," became my role model as a Mizpah. The ten Boom family worked in the Dutch underground during World War II. Because of their Christian faith and the history of a 100-year-long prayer meeting in their home, praying for the peace of Jerusalem and God's chosen people, the Jews, they saved an estimated 800 Jews and protected many Dutch underground workers from the clutches of Hitler. The ten Booms paid the price for their courageous defiance of the Nazis, when they were arrested and sent to concentration camps.

In the camp at Ravensbruck, Corrie's sister Betsie lay on a stretcher, dying. Corrie leaned over to hear her faltering voice, "... must tell people what we have learned here. We must tell them that **there is no pit so deep that He is not deeper still.** They will listen to us, Corrie, because we have been here."[4] That was the message that Corrie would take to the world. After a year in prison, she was released on a clerical error at the age of 51. Her ministry lasted 33 years and took her to 60 countries. Corrie's story instilled in me a desire to emulate her and stick my neck out for the Jews, should I ever be called on to do so.

There were two incidents in Corrie's life that made a special impact on me. One took place in Ravensbruck, when Corrie and Betsie discovered fleas in the barracks where they were assigned. Corrie expressed her utter disgust at the situation, but Betsie gently persuaded Corrie to simply praise God for the fleas, because His Word says "In everything give thanks." They proceeded to hold

Bible studies in those flea-infested barracks, and many lives were given hope. Later, Corrie and Betsy saw God's wisdom in allowing the fleas to co-occupy their quarters. The Nazi guards would not even get close to those barracks because of the fleas, and the Bible studies could continue unabated!

The other incident happened after Corrie's release, when she was going around the country speaking about forgiving your enemies. At the conclusion of one of her talks, the church was emptying, and a man approached her, smiling, and bowing. Corrie was shocked as she recognized the former Nazi guard. He said, "How grateful I am for your message, Fraulein. To think that, as you say, He has washed my sins away!"[5] Corrie recoiled as the man extended his hand. Anger and unforgiveness boiled inside her, but she knew Jesus had died for this man and had forgiven him. She silently prayed that He would help her forgive the man, too. Corrie struggled to raise her hand. As soon as their hands touched, a warmth spread from her shoulder down to her hand, and a current passed between them. Then a love sprang into her heart that almost overwhelmed her. She explained it thus: "When He tells us to love our enemies, He gives, along with the command, the love itself."[6]

It was some time later that my husband Curtis was asked by the Billy Graham Association to head up the committee for the World Wide Pictures' showing of the *The Hiding Place* movie in Tupelo, Mississippi. I was honored to assist in this evangelistic outreach by serving as a counselor.

Corrie ten Boom was truly my hero, and I prayed that God would prepare me to act as she did in the event of a second Holocaust. The State of Israel recognizes the contributions that Gentiles have made to their survival as Jews and as a nation in their Holocaust museum in Jerusalem, Yad VaShem.[7] In 1968, Corrie was asked by the museum to plant a tree in their Garden of Righteousness where hundreds of Righteous Gentiles have been honored. On a trip to Israel in 2003, my Jewish friend, Janice

Horowitz Bell, and I visited Yad Vashem, and we saw the memorial to Corrie ten Boom.

It was on an earlier visit to Israel in 1998, when I went by myself and had a seven-and-a-half hour layover in Amsterdam, that I was able to visit the ten Boom house in Haarlem, a suburb of Amsterdam. I walked out of the airport terminal to the first bus stop and waited for the bus that would take me there, a 20-minute ride. As I stood there, I was approached by a young man who immediately asked me if I was going to the ten Boom house. I was shocked! I said, "How did you know?" He introduced himself as Daniel, and he was from Chicago. At that moment he looked like an "angel" God sent to help me find the way. We soon became friends, as we had much in common, including music. Daniel had been employed by Rabbi Ekstein in his International Fellowship of Christians and Jews. He discovered he was a descendant of King David through King Zedekiah's daughter, Tea Tephi, so that made him Jewish. This discovery was now sending him to a kibbutz near Jerusalem to learn Hebrew and get involved with the Boaz ministry to the homeless. He also hoped to work with an underground ministry which was preparing to hide Jews in Bozrah, near Petra. Daniel was a person of many accomplishments, as he had just written a book and made a recording of his songs. He wanted to make a recording also in Jerusalem. He told me many fantastic things, and I wondered if it all was true. What a colorful character God had introduced me to!

Daniel had a one-way ticket to Israel, because he was "making aliyah" (immigrating to Israel). We stayed together during our visit to Haarlem and also at the airport, sharing our songs and our lives. When we got off the plane at the Ben Gurion Airport in Tel Aviv, my hosts, Roy and Mary Kendall, were waiting for me, but they were surprised I had brought someone else along! It was a blessing for me to be able to guide Daniel to a bed & breakfast place where I had stayed two years before, the Allenby 2, and help him get a room. Of course, the Kendalls graciously detoured so I could accomplish that!

Back to the bus ride. Daniel and I were the only ones on the bus. Truly, this had to be God's doing. We had quite a way to walk after the bus let us off, and it was very windy. Having a companion alleviated my fears of finding the place, so I was thankful for God's provision. Finally, there it was, the Béjé (bay-yay). This was the ten Boom clock and watch shop, which served as a place of refuge for Jews and resistance workers during World War II. People were standing around outside, waiting for the next tour.

I started a conversation with a couple, Harry and Jamie Brown, who were Methodists from Sylacauga, Alabama. I had been a Methodist most of my life and was born and bred in Alabama. Small world, as they say. They had also been members of Frazer Memorial United Methodist Church in Montgomery, close to Petrey, Alabama, my husband's hometown. But it gets better than that. In Tuscaloosa a year later I learned while talking with a new friend, Karen Thompson, that the Browns were old friends of hers, and Jamie was in her wedding! If there had been any doubt before, there was none now – God had truly orchestrated my steps and encounters on that solo trip to Israel.

Finally, the Browns, Daniel, and I entered the Béjé. Right away I spotted a piano, and it had a piece of sheet music on it. I walked over and saw that it was a beloved song with a title befitting the home, "You Are My Hiding Place." As I sat down and began to play and sing, others gathered around and sang with me. What a blessing.

Another blessing is that I just happened to be there during the tenth anniversary of the establishment of the Béjé as the Corrie ten Boom Museum. The guide got caught up in her story, telling us that the whole ten Boom family was a prophetic family. Corrie's grandfather William had prayed, with other men in this medieval home, for the peace of Jerusalem in 1844, and the prayer group continued their praying over the years. One hundred years later in 1944, Corrie realized there were Jews living in peace in this home, an answer to William ten Boom's prayers!

    The most thrilling part of the tour was going to the top floor of the Béjé where Corrie's bedroom was. Behind a false wall was "the hiding place." Seeing that brought tears to my eyes, as I visualized the frantic people fleeing there to hide, when the Nazis came to arrest the ten Booms that fateful day on February 28, 1944. Thirty people were taken into custody by the Gestapo, but the hidden Jews were nowhere to be found. There were six people – two Jewish men, two Jewish women, and two resistance workers – who hid in that tiny secret place for 47 hours with no water and little food. The Gestapo stayed in the house for days, hoping to starve out the refugees, but the Resistance managed to liberate them and take them to "safe houses."

    The wall to the hiding place was cut out, so tourists could see inside. I stepped inside the hiding place, but, unfortunately, I did not bring a camera with me. A young missionary couple saw my plight and offered to photograph me and mail the picture to me, which they did. God always provides!

    Little did I know what God had in store for me, when 23 years ago I had read the book about Corrie ten Boom's courageous life as

Nancy en route to Israel via Amsterdam – in Corrie Ten Boom's "Hiding Place" at the Beje

a Righteous Gentile. From that time on I prayed that I would be worthy of the title of Righteous Gentile, one who would be willing to risk my life on behalf of God's chosen people, the Jews.

Another book I read around the same time as *The Hiding Place* was *Appointment in Jerusalem*[8] by Lydia Prince. Curtis and I had

the opportunity to meet her and her husband Derek Prince in Oxford, Mississippi, where they were holding a meeting, in the early 1970s. Her story greatly impacted my life and gave me a yearning to go to Jerusalem like she did.

Lydia and Corrie had a similar background. Lydia was born in 1890, and Corrie was born in 1892. Both were from northwest Europe

Corrie ten Boom

and within about 400 air miles of each other, Corrie from Amsterdam and Lydia from Denmark. They were both spinsters, except that Lydia finally married at the age of 56 to Derek Prince at the end of World War II. Corrie started working in the Dutch underground when she was 50. Lydia was 38 years old when she set out for Jerusalem. These two courageous women were driven by the same passion for God.

Lydia Prince

At a mature age, Lydia had everything that a woman in her position could normally desire – affluence, professional success as a teacher, a luxurious apartment, the esteem and affection of her colleagues. Still she felt incomplete. One day alone in her apartment she knelt and prayed, "God, if you will show me Jesus as a living reality, I will follow Him."[9] The next moment she was conscious of Jesus standing over her with His arms outstretched in the attitude of blessing! Weeks later she was filled with the Holy Spirit and given a vivid, detailed vision of the land and the people to whom God would later send her.

Lydia took the unheard of action of being baptized, and it was done in a bath tub in the kitchen of the local Pentecostal pastor! This stirred the whole of Denmark. She was a teacher, and the state schools were under the Lutheran State Church. Her bold action violated Lutheran doctrine. This controversy was fueled by the newspapers, and the subsequent litigation went all the way to the national parliament. The ruling was in Lydia's favor. She could keep her teaching position.

However, the Lord led her to give up teaching and go to Jerusalem in October of 1928. She went without anyone supporting her, taking only $200 in traveler's checks. Two months after her arrival she was asked to take a dying Jewish baby girl named Tikva ("hope") into her stark basement apartment. By then Lydia was down to her last dollar. Through much prayer the child lived, and through much prayer Lydia continued to survive in Jerusalem and take in more destitute children. She did all this without supporters! She had given her inheritance from her father to the Lord's work before she came to Jerusalem.

During the next twenty years Lydia cared for about seventy children, mostly girls. The majority were Jewish, but there were Arabs, Armenians and Europeans. She felt the Lord had given her eight of the children for her own. Prayer to the Father was her method of operation, and every need was supplied.

The adventures Lydia had in primitive Jerusalem during the opening battles of the long war between Jew and Arab that are continuing today was a story that powerfully gripped my heart. She risked her life many times, but in the midst of it all she had peace and perfect security in the Lord.

Now I had two heroines, Corrie ten Boom and Lydia Prince, and they both saved the lives of Jewish people and made an enduring contribution to the state of Israel as Righteous Gentiles. I felt the pull to visit Israel, the homeland of my Jewish Messiah and the birthplace of His church. But there were other influences God placed in my life as a Christian to point me to my Jewish roots.

3

Back to My Roots

Curtis was appointed by the United Methodist Church in 1979 to pastor a fledgling church in Southaven, Mississippi, a "suburb" of Memphis, Tennessee. The church was named Faith United Methodist, and we were there until another appointment came in 1988 to Central UMC in Columbus, Mississippi. As the pianist and song leader for Faith UMC, I chose a lot of Jewish-flavored music for our congregational singing, and people loved it. My repertoire grew.

The proximity of Southaven to Memphis afforded us the opportunity to have guest preachers who were "big names," you might say. Three of them were Messianic Jewish leaders – Dr. Michael Brown, Dan Juster, and Sid Roth. Most people will recognize the name of Sid Roth as the host of the television show, "It's Supernatural." Dr. Brown is a Messianic Jewish apologist and scholar, founder of the FIRE school of ministry, and author of the book series, *Answering Jewish Objections to Jesus*[10]. Dan Juster is founder of Union of Messianic Jewish Congregations and current director of Tikkun Ministries. What a blessing and what a privilege I had to sit under the preaching and teaching of these men of God.

Dr. Brown had prophecies for our church that proved to be true, and he was also used by the Lord to settle the controversy we were having about the use of drums in the church. No one had told him about this controversy, so it came as quite a surprise to the congregation when at the conclusion of his sermon that fateful Sunday morning, he asked permission to play the drums! He explained that before his conversion he was a rock drummer. Then

Dr. Brown asked me to lead the congregation in a Jewish praise song we had sung earlier in the service. I began to play the piano and sing, and Dr. Brown really tore up those drums! From then on there were no more complaints about the drums.

Dr. Michael Brown, speaker at "Let the Thirsty Come" outreach conference in Tel Aviv – 2002

As for Sid Roth, I asked him to go with me to visit a Jewish lady who lived right by the church. He did so, and we witnessed to the lady about her Jewish Messiah. That was a bold adventure for me. Looking back on this experience, I marvel that God gave me such nerve.

Added to these blessings was our involvement with a Messianic Jewish Church in Memphis named B'rit Hadashah (Hebrew for "New Testament"). One of our members was their pianist, and a couple who attended our church also attended B'rit Hadashah regularly. This couple, Bill and Sally, always spent the Sunday school hour in a small room, praying. Looking back, I know part of their prayers surely must have centered on our church reconnecting with her Jewish roots. It is true that so much good can be attributed to secret prayer warriors which we only recognize by hind sight.

Curtis and I received an invitation to B'rit Hadashah to attend their Passover Seder[11] one spring. That was our first Seder, and it was quite an eye opener. Jesus was demonstrated in the ritual foods of the service, much to our delight. Curtis determined to have a Seder at the church. This didn't happen until several years later, however, and it was in a different church.

While pastoring Central United Methodist Church in Columbus, Mississippi, Curtis was given a vision from God to build a church in the Golden Triangle area – Columbus, Starkville, and West Point. We left the Methodist church in 1991 to seek fulfillment of the vision with others who had a similar vision. The church was named Trinity Church of the Golden Triangle. It was to this church that B'rit Hadasha brought a team on two occasions and hosted the Passover Seders for us.

Our congregation at Trinity was growing in the knowledge of the Jewishness of Christianity. Curtis presented the idea of traveling to the Holy Land. Everyone was excited, and many signed up. However, as the time for the tour approached, people began to drop out. Only six of us were left – Curtis and me, Frank and Esther, and Ken and Joyce.

The day finally arrived on February 2, 1994, for this glorious sight-seeing tour of Israel. How wonderful it was. It became apparent to me later that I had just taken a tour of my own real estate, my inheritance! Paul declared, "And if you are Messiah's, then you are Abraham's seed [even though I am a Gentile], and heirs according to the promise" (Gal. 3:29). Yeshua, the Jewish Messiah, gave His life for me, and the Father adopted me into the family. When Curtis and I received Jesus as our Savior in March of 1968, we "received the Spirit of adoption by whom we

First trip to Israel with Troskeys and Lintons – February 1994

cry out, 'Abba, Father,'" and we became "heirs of God and joint heirs with Messiah" (Rom. 8:15, 17). My inheritance of the Holy Land is what God promised Abraham and his descendants through Isaac and Jacob. The first description of this Land in the Bible is found in Genesis 15:18, and it stretches from the Nile River to the Euphrates. Wow! At the conclusion of the tour, I said more than once, "I am coming back here!" I was prophesying without knowing it.

Upon our return to Columbus, I wrote a report entitled, "Back to Our **Roots**." Little did I know that the Jewish **Roots** Movement would soon be opened up to me and literally change my life. I began to share with others the realization that Jesus is Jewish, the Apostles were Jewish, the Bible has all Jewish authors (except Luke), and the early church was all Jewish for at least the first ten years. As I studied in the years to come, I discovered that the first 15 bishops of the church were Jewish. Yes, the Church needs to get back to her roots, I strongly declared.

Lars Enarson, a Swedish intercessor, was the first person to help me fully understand the rightful place of the church as she relates to her Jewish roots. Lars and Harriet and their three children, Josefin, Johanna, and John, moved to Columbus from Sweden in the fall of 1992. Curtis helped them renew their visa as guests of Trinity

Lars, Harriet, John, Johanna, and Josefin Enarson at the Petreys' – Christmas, 1995

Church, so they could stay in the United States. Lars had been a translator for a Columbus pastor who was a popular evangelist in Sweden, so the Enarsons moved to Columbus to help this pastor translate his book into Swedish. Lars, himself a pastor in Sweden, was used mightily of God in our area to form prayer groups and to teach on prayer. He and Harriet had always felt they would eventually move to Israel, and they did in 1997, where they more fully developed their world-wide prayer ministry, The Watchman International.[12]

Lars influenced my life in a profound way, as I heard his teachings and participated in his prayer groups. The 11th chapter of Romans came alive to me, as Lars explained that we Gentiles were wild branches grafted into the Jewish olive tree and received nourishment from the Jewish root. We are not to boast against the natural branches that were cut off, which were the unbelieving Jews, because God is able to graft them in again. Indeed, all Israel, though partially blinded now, will be saved, and it is the responsibility of the Gentile Christians to provoke the Jews to jealousy with our love for **their** Messiah. The church should not be haughty, but remember we don't support the root. The root supports us. The church has been joined with the Jewish people but has not replaced them, as I would more fully understand in the next few years.

Unfortunately, the church throughout history has disregarded Paul's admonition to provoke the Jews to jealousy so they can be saved. Instead, the church has provoked the Jews to a stubborn resistance to the gospel, causing them to perceive Jesus as the cause of their troubles. After all, in committing atrocities against the Jews, the Nazi guards claimed they were giving the "Christ killers" what was due them. Many of these Nazis faithfully attended church.

My passion was to show the church that because of her Jewish Messiah and her Jewish Bible, she has Jewish roots. The implications of our Jewish identity should affect our lives as Christians in many ways. I began to explore those many ways, but prayer was the backbone of it all. "Yes," I would say, "We should get back to our roots. They are Jewish roots!"

4

Pray for the Peace of Jerusalem

Because of Lars Enarson's having moved to Columbus, we were blessed with his teachings on prayer, but also we were blessed by prayer conferences he set up. Lars' friend and an outstanding man of prayer, Rolland Smith, came to Trinity Church and led a Concert of Prayer in February of 1993, in which 500-plus people came together from more than 15 churches. That was just the beginning of other outstanding people and events God brought to us through Lars.

My corporate and private prayer life was growing, and I was learning about the priority of prayer for the Jewish people. I learned that God's admonition to "Pray for the peace of Jerusalem" (Psalm 122:6) not only meant to pray for the actual city but to pray for the salvation of the Jewish people. Upon my return from the Holy Land, I arose for prayer at 5:00 a.m. and afterward recorded this in my journal on February 14, 1994: "Centered in on Jews, claiming Isaiah 46:13, "... I will place salvation in Zion, for Israel My glory." and Isaiah 62, especially verse 11, "... say to the daughter of Zion, 'Surely your salvation is coming ...'"

My journal entries also indicated that I prayed for Lars Enarson, read his Elijah Prayer Army alert at that time about fasting, and felt God was calling me to fast. Later I prayed for the upcoming prayer conference in April of 1994 at Lake Tiak-O'Khata outside Louisville, Mississippi. I prayed that the conference would have a mix of leaders, across lines of denomination, economic status, and race. How thrilling it was to see how my prayer had been answered, because the whole conference was about racial reconciliation!

Some local Indians sang for us. Along with others of Indian descent in the room, they received our apology on behalf of the white men who had persecuted their ancestors and stolen their land. A black lady from Washington, D.C. spoke powerfully concerning persecution. We were given an opportunity to participate in "identificational repentance," a type of prayer which identifies with and confesses before God the corporate sins of one's nation, people, church, or family. We did this through a prayer drama, taking the part of Jacob, who represented the Jews, as he asked forgiveness of Esau, who represented the Arabs. Identifying with Jacob, we repented for tricking Esau out of his birthright and stealing his blessing. This conference had a powerful effect on me.

Lars Enarson was heavily involved, along with Curtis and others from Columbus, in planning the conference. It was another benchmark in my life, as I soaked up the messages from Frances Frangipane, Kjell Sjoberg (a Swedish intercessor, the "prayer father" of Europe), Lars, and others. But the person who influenced me the most was not one of the speakers, but a lady who was enlisting everyone she could to take a time slot each week to pray for Israel and the Jewish people. Her name was Bessie Honeysucker, an imposing, tall, black lady from Carthage, Mississippi. I signed up on her Israel Prayer Chain to pray 15 minutes each Friday.

Bessie had a supernatural call from God for her unique ministry. She and her pastor husband Percy became world travelers in pursuing this call. When I was with Bessie, I knew I was in the presence of greatness. She had a deep, rich singing voice, and hearing her rendition of Israel's national anthem, "Hatikva" (the hope), was a stirring experience.

I will never forget the time when we were in Israel in 1996, and I knew Bessie and Percy were there at the same time, attending the Jerusalem House of Prayer for All Nations Convocation. Our group of six had just been enlisted by another ministry to take a three-hour watch at an around-the-clock Prayer and Praise ministry in a room at the Mt. Zion Hotel. We didn't realize that was the meeting place for Bessie's conference, but when we arrived there, we saw her on the roof of the hotel! She and Percy were joining in the singing as the conference was in full swing. We got a good hug and continued on to the designated room to fulfill our prayer and praise assignment. She later came by to join in with us. What a privilege it was to "pray for the peace of Jerusalem" right on Mt. Zion, God's holy hill, and to be able to look out the window and see the beautiful City of Peace. We sang one worship song after another and prayed for the Jewish people and their city.

Curtis and I were blessed to be friends and partners in ministry with Bessie and Percy. She had a serious illness in July of 2003 and "graduated" to the New Jerusalem above. Her memory lives on with me. I am grateful she was the one who instigated my regular prayer times for God's chosen people, praying that they may fulfill their destiny to be the ones to welcome Sar Shalom, the Prince of Peace, back to the City of Peace, Jerusalem! He is the only One who can bring peace to the Middle East.

God led me to form an Israel Prayer Group at Trinity Church, and we met weekly until Curtis felt God had called him to leave Trinity and plant a church in Tuscaloosa, Alabama. We were in Tuscaloosa only a year-and-a-half, but the biggest blessing I had during that time was God's gift of a new friend, Karen Thompson. Karen had a children's ministry in her church, as well as a prayer ministry, and she spoke regularly to groups to inspire them to pray. I first met her at a prayer meeting in preparation for the Franklin Graham Crusade in Tuscaloosa.

Karen and I developed a friendship after a home meeting in which I taught about the Jewish roots of the church. She was blessed by the teaching. At the time, she was writing a children's curriculum on Genesis and Exodus, and she asked me questions. I taught her more about our Jewish roots, and she incorporated this in her material. The curriculum was copyrighted and sold to other churches. Not only did the children learn about their Jewish roots, but the parents did, too. Karen even wrote a dedication to me on the inside page of the curriculum. I was so honored and blessed to know I was bearing fruit from the things God had planted in me.

In the year 2000, Curtis and I left Tuscaloosa and moved into his childhood home in Petrey, Alabama. I soon sought out a prayer group who prayed for Israel and found a Lydia Prayer Group in nearby Prattville. I attended several times, beginning on January 8, 2001, and then those ladies came to Petrey and helped me launch an Israel Prayer Group in my home on October 4, 2002. A few ladies from Luverne and Elba attended once a month, and occasionally we met in Elba at the home of Janice Bell, my Jewish ministry partner, or at my church, South Luverne Baptist. We brought the needs of Israel and the Jewish people, as well as personal needs, before the throne of God, and we saw many answered prayers.

It is not a suggestion, but a command to "Pray for the **peace** of Jerusalem." The verse continues, "May those prosper who love thee." Prosperity is God's reward. Remember that Jerusalem is the "city of the Great King" (Matt. 5:35), and it is the city King Yeshua

Israel Prayer Group at the home of Nancy & Curtis Petrey

will return to (Zech. 14:4). From there He will not only reign as the King of the Jews but as the King over all the earth! However,

He will not come back until the Jews are ready to welcome Him back. Yeshua said to the religious leaders, "For I tell you, you will not see me again until you say, 'Blessed is he who comes in the name of the Lord'" (Matt. 23:39). If we love His appearing we must pray for the peace of Jerusalem.

The Hebrew word for "peace" is *shalom*. This word has a very rich meaning. It means much more than we have ever thought. Strong's Concordance, #7965, amplifies it thus: "Completeness, wholeness, peace, health, welfare, safety, soundness, tranquility, prosperity, perfectness, fullness, rest, harmony; the absence of agitation or discord."[13]

In Isaiah 53:5, the chastisement necessary to bring us *shalom* was upon the suffering Messiah. When the Jewish people "look upon Him whom they have pierced" (Zech. 12:10), they will be saved! Only then will they say, "Blessed is He who comes in the name of the Lord" (Matt. 23:39) as they welcome back their Messiah.

Knowing this should motivate us to pray for the peace of Jerusalem. It will only hasten the coming of the Lord. In the final words of Scripture, Yeshua said, "Surely I am coming quickly." And we must respond "Amen. Even so, come Lord Jesus!" (Rev. 22:20)

5

You Thought Jesus Spoke Aramaic?

My intense attraction to the Hebrew language began after our return from Israel in February of 1994. My journal entry shows that I prayed, "I really want to learn Hebrew. Lord, please enable me to learn the language of your chosen people." In March of 1995, I started Hebrew lessons with Maria Flising, who taught two other ladies and me in our home. Maria had come to Columbus from Sweden to tutor Lars and Harriet Enarson's children. It was a delight to learn the Hebrew *alephbet* (alphabet), some vocabulary, and phrases, such as *Boker tov* (Good morning) and *Shabbat Shalom* (Have a peaceful Sabbath). To be able to print the name of our Lord *Yeshua* (ישוע) was a very satisfying experience. We also learned to spell our own names in Hebrew. My name Nancy looks like this: ננסי

Some of the Hebrew pronouns are very funny. The English *he* sounds like *who* in Hebrew! *She* is pronounced *he*! *Who* is *me*! Got that? Then there are no *J* sounds or vowels! Vowels are indicated by dots and marks over, under, or inside the letters. Some literature, including newspapers, do not even use vowel markings. Alas! How much more difficult can it get? But it does. In ancient or biblical Hebrew, there were no capital letters, often no spaces between the words and no punctuation. Hebrew is written right to left, and the books are opened from the back. "That's backwards!" we say, but maybe our English is backwards. It just depends on your viewpoint. Ha!

I was greatly blessed by a devotional book entitled, *Messiah and His Hebrew Alphabet* by Dick Mills and David Michael.[14] The authors show how the 22 letters in the alphabet paint a portrait of the Messiah. Hebrew is a picture language, and from the first letter, *aleph* - א, the sacrificial animal (ox), to the last letter, *tav* - ת, originally a cross,[15] it is easy to see the Messiah in each of the letters. [See Appendix A.] Michael points out that six of the letters are actual names of Jesus in Scripture. Six concern His ministry. Another six represent His physical features. Three letters have to do with His sacrificial death, and one letter, *nun*, has to do with His Resurrection. How neat that God has "hidden" Jesus in the Hebrew language.

A cross-shaped *tav* was used as the first **sign or mark** mentioned in Scripture. God placed this mark on Cain as His sign of protection (Gen. 4:15). The *tav* was also placed on the foreheads of the righteous men in Jerusalem in the days of Ezekiel to spare them from God's judgment by angel-warriors (Ezek. 9:4). Jesus died on a cross and *marked* us as His own, purchased by His blood, and protected from death. How fitting that the last letter of the Hebrew alphabet signifies our redemption, completing the portrait of the Messiah.

Almost 60 per cent of the Hebrew language is made up of three-letter words. Why the Hebrew triads? To Christians this is a reminder of the Trinity. Some Bible scholars say that Zephaniah 3:9 could refer to the Hebrew language. "In that day the peoples of earth will speak one common language." It stands to reason that when Jesus sets up His kingdom on earth, He will undo the confusion at the Tower of Babel and change the languages of the earth to one universal language, Hebrew! After all, God spoke the earth into being using Hebrew.

Besides the fact that Hebrew is earth's parent language, Hebrew is unlike any other language, because it is built around the peoples' worship. We worship the One who calls Himself "the Alpha and the Omega," the first and last letters of the Greek language, but the Hebrew equivalent is "I am *aleph*, and I am *tav*" (Isaiah 44:6). Jesus is the First and the Last for both Old and New Testament believers. He sums up His identity for Jew and Gentile in the final chapter of the Bible: "I am the Alpha and the Omega, the Beginning and the End, the First and the Last" (Rev. 22:13).

This devotional book, *The Messiah in His Hebrew Alphabet*, is now out of print. I found some copies and bought them all, because I treasure these marvelous insights into God's holy language. In the Epilogue by David Michael, he explains the significance of the little word, *et*, which is spelled with the first and last letters of the Hebrew alphabet, *aleph* and *tav*:

> It is a word that is not translatable into English. It simply shows that an active verb is about to receive its direct object. The word occurs many hundreds of times in the Bible. For example, it occurs two times in the first verse of Genesis: "In the beginning God created *[et]* the heaven and *[et]* the earth." Because this word appears to be merely a peculiarity of grammatical structure, it has received little attention. But in Zechariah 12:10 we read, "And they shall look upon Me *[et]* they have pierced...."

> In order for this scripture to make sense in the English language, the translators provided the pronoun "whom" in the place of the word *et*. In English it reads, "they shall look upon me whom they have pierced," which means the same as the concise Hebrew words "they shall look upon me they pierced."

> Who is this "whom" that was pierced? He is the *alpha-tav (et)* that fits directly between "Me" and "they": "and they shall look upon ME et THEY have pierced." *Here is the one intermediary between God and man – pierced to bring them together!*

> How do we know that *aleph-tav* is the name of Jesus? It is because He Himself said so! Revelation 1:11 in the Hebrew New Testament says, "I am the *Aleph* and the *Tav*," that is to say, the *sacrifice* of the cross, AND the pierced one of Zechariah 12:10!

> *Jesus is the Aleph and the Tav, the First and the Last, the A through Z of God's plan of Redemption!*[16]

If you didn't get that, go back and read it again! This revelation is a shining jewel worth digging for! Oh, the grandeur and the delicious **truths** to be found in the holy Hebrew language.

After Maria returned to Sweden, I continued studying on my own. I found a Berlitz book in the library and used it for awhile. Eventually, I ordered *Everyday Hebrew* by Eliezer Tirkel[17], which includes the book and cassette tapes. I've been all the way through it three or four times and can read the stories in Hebrew print (square letters) fairly well. The verb tenses are the most difficult thing. The questions of each lesson are in print, but the answers must be written in cursive script. The alphabet in cursive was given, but there were not any exercises in **reading** the cursive script, so I didn't develop that skill very well. Reading and writing print is easier for me. Thankfully, most of the signs in Israel are in Hebrew print.

One of my motives in learning modern Hebrew was to try to speak to Israelis in everyday life, hoping to witness for the Lord. I tried this several times on my visits, but when people answered me back, I would be at a loss to know what they were saying! My hearing disability coupled with the inability to understand conversational Hebrew made for quite a discouraging situation. Nevertheless, I didn't totally give up.

In 1998, I was on a bus full of Jews. What a joy! I began to speak Hebrew to the man next to me. He was carrying some eggs, and I remarked that I liked *baitzim* (eggs). I found out he was from Morocco, an immigrant. The young man across from us seemed to be amused at our "conversation." Speaking in English, he revealed to me that the Moroccan and I did not understand each other! Oh well, I tried.

This young man and I had a good conversation in English. He said I spoke Hebrew well. What a shock! He was going to the same place I was, so he helped me know when to get off the bus. I told him that God always sent someone to help me. He asked why I came and why I like Israel. I told him, "It's my homeland where my Savior Jesus lived, and He's coming back again here." He laughed and said, "In two years?" I guess he meant at the millennium year 2000. I replied, "Nobody knows." It felt good to be able to plant a few seeds in a young Jew's heart.

When Janice and I were on the plane going to Israel in 2003, I struck up a conversation with the man next to me. He got a big kick out of my efforts to converse in Hebrew. He told me my Hebrew was "cute!" I didn't know if that was a compliment or not. Janice thought it was funny, and she likes to tell others about my "cute" Hebrew to poke fun at me.

The most rewarding time I had speaking Hebrew was in September of 1996 in Jerusalem. My friend Esther and I did some volunteer work at the Christian Friends of Israel office, and then we walked to the Post Office. After buying stamps, we sat down to write our postcards and got into a conversation with a 25-year-old Jew, Uri, who asked all about our beliefs. He was so open and kind. We talked about two hours, and I even got to preaching. He needed more proof. Esther and I took turns explaining things. The Lord obviously set this up. Uri kept getting up and then coming back. We finally figured out that he was working there. He had a pistol strapped on, so we guessed he was a security officer.

Whenever I could tell he didn't understand me, I would substitute a Hebrew word, and he would get it. I was talking about Yeshua's disciples. Uri looked puzzled, so I said, "Yeshua's *talmidim*," and he understood. Ah, success at last!

Uri told us a lot about himself. He had been married six months, lived on a settlement, and had cried only twice in his life, once when his friend got killed and once when his grandmother told him about the Holocaust. She had told no one else, not even Uri's father. We said to Uri that we had been volunteering at Christian Friends of Israel and that we had brought blankets for the Holocaust survivors. Uri said he loved CFI. They had helped his grandmother.

Eventually, I had to go to the bathroom, so I told Esther we had to leave. We walked down the street quickly, and I said, "Let's go in here, Esther. I can't last much longer!" When we got inside, we could see it was a Christian bookstore. God had surely led us there. I was so glad they had a bathroom! As we looked at the books, we talked to the manager about our experience with Uri. He reached inside a cabinet and took out a book of Jewish testimonies in Hebrew. He had to keep these books hidden, he said, because he could be shut down for distributing such books. He **gave** us the book! We immediately returned to the post office, gave it to Uri, and left. We continued to pray for Uri's salvation long after the trip.

Esther and I were doing the very thing that had motivated me to learn Hebrew in the first place. My purpose was simply to get to know ordinary Israelis by at least trying to speak their language. Hopefully, this would show them my genuine interest in them and love for them. I didn't want to be viewed as only a tourist acting out of curiosity. Talking to Uri surely did "light my fire!" I am believing I will see him in heaven.

I continued to study Hebrew over the years, intensifying my study right before each trip to Israel, and I attempted to use it as often as I could. I never became fluent, but I acquired a deep appreciation for this sacred language. Curtis bought me a Hebrew Bible, and someone gave me a New Testament with side-by-side pages of English and Hebrew. I also have New Testament tapes in Hebrew.

I taught a course on Hebrew at Trinity Church in the 1990s and more recently at South Luverne Baptist Church in 2008. (See Chapter 23.) Since I have reams of paper filled with my study of Hebrew, it is the least I can do to share this valuable study with others.

I believe that Jesus spoke Hebrew in everyday life, not just in the synagogue. But you may say, "I thought Jesus spoke Aramaic." Most people believe that. Mel Gibson had the Jesus character in his movie, "The Passion of the Christ," speak Aramaic. However, David Bivin and Roy Blizzard, Jr. in their book, *Understanding the Difficult Words of Jesus*, assert, "Many scholars in Israel are now convinced that the spoken and written language of the Jews in the Land of Israel at the time of Jesus was indeed Hebrew; and that the Synoptic Gospels were derived from original Hebrew sources."[18] **They all agree the language of Jesus was Hebrew.** Furthermore, the writings of Josephus, the foremost Jewish historian of the first century, make it obvious that Hebrew was the spoken and written language of the first century.

Although no Hebrew copies of the New Testament have been found, only Greek, there is much evidence that Matthew wrote his gospel in Hebrew, which was later translated into Greek. The testimony of the <u>early</u> church fathers validates Hebrew as the primary spoken and written language among the Jews in Jesus' day. Papias, a mid second-century bishop, said, "Matthew put down the words of the Lord in the Hebrew language, and others have translated them, each as best he could" (Eusebius, *Ecclesiastical History* III 39, 16). There are many references in the writings of the <u>later</u> church fathers. Epiphanius writes concerning the Nazarene sect: "They have the entire Gospel of Matthew in Hebrew. It is carefully preserved by them as it was originally written, in Hebrew script" (*Refutation of All Heresies* 29,9,4). I was thrilled to learn this.

The sign Pilate had nailed to the cross, "This is the King of the Jews," was written in Greek, Latin, and Hebrew (Luke 23:38; John 19:20), not Aramaic as the New International Version indicates. Acts 26:14 quotes Jesus speaking Hebrew, and Acts 21:40-22:2 quotes Paul speaking Hebrew.

The Old Testament, which the Jews call the *Tanach*,[19] was written in Hebrew (with a very small part of Aramaic). All the New Testament books were translated into Greek, but the Synoptic Gospels of Matthew, Mark, and Luke, plus Acts 1:1-15:35 are highly Hebraic. Add the New Testament quotations of the Old Testament, and you see that possibly over 90 per cent of the Bible was originally composed in Hebrew!

Martin Luther encouraged the study of Hebrew, even though he became anti-Semitic later in life. He said, "For although the New Testament is written in Greek, it is full of Hebraisms and Hebrew expressions. It has therefore been aptly said that the Hebrews drink from the spring, the Greeks from the stream that flows from it, and the Latins from a downstream pool."[20]

Many problems in exegesis and doctrine arise in the Church because non-Jews have imposed a Greek/Western mindset onto the pages of the Jewish Scriptures. The key to understanding both Old and New Testaments, the peculiar Hebrew idioms, and especially some of the hard sayings of Jesus is knowledge of the Hebrew language! What greater motivation can there be for studying Hebrew?

6

Surely Martin Luther Didn't Say That!

The single event that most impacted my life as a Mizpah for Israel was a conference at Christ for the Nations Institute in Dallas, Texas, in July of 1995, named "Israel in Prophecy." At the time I was secretary of Trinity Church which my husband pastored. He was glad for me to attend the conference and also to visit our daughter Susan in Ft. Worth after it was over. I drove by myself from Columbus to Dallas and felt like quite an adventurer.

The first thing I did was to explore the campus and look for a couple that I knew, Bruno and Rhonda Essary, who were attending Christ for the Nations. I had a

Nancy – Mizpah for Israel and Trinity Church secretary

good visit with them. At the bookstore I bought a beautiful print of Yeshua at the Western Wall ("Wailing Wall") in Jerusalem. He looked very Jewish, wearing a tallit (see Appendix B) and a kippah (scull cap or yarmulke).   He was gazing down, lovingly, at three Jewish men in black, praying at the Wall. One man had on a long tallit. Another man with a black hat and prayer book in his hand seemed to be looking straight at Yeshua. The man in the middle was an old, white-bearded orthodox Jew with a cane, sitting on a little stool, and his head was bowed low in prayer. One hand of Yeshua held what appeared to be a miniature tablet of the Ten Commandments. The other hand was placed so tenderly on the back of the old Jewish man in the middle. Most arresting of all was the sight of tears running down Yeshua's cheeks!

The message of that poignant painting is that Yeshua is yearning for the Jewish people to look and see Him as Messiah. **It is He**, Jesus of Nazareth, and He is Jewish, just as they are. How many times have I and millions of other Christians prayed the prayer, "Oh, Lord, please remove the blindness of the Jews." What is so ironic, however, is that most of the Church is also blind. Blind to her Jewish roots. Blind to her history of anti-Semitism that turned the Jews away from learning the identity of their Messiah!

Here I was, about to have the blindness removed from my eyes at the Israel in Prophecy Conference. The ominous-sounding theme of the conference was "The Final Countdown." Many of the things I learned were shocking and hard to swallow. But I returned home, fueled with a desire to shout these fresh revelations to anyone who would listen! My life was forever changed.

So, "What in the world did you learn?" you may ask. The messages were so riveting that I could hardly write down the notes fast enough. Actually, I think I wrote down almost every word that was uttered. That had to be God! When I got back to Trinity Church, I copied my notes, stapled the pages together, and put a stack on a table at the back of the sanctuary. That table became known as "The Israel Table," and it soon was laden down with resources from every facet of Jewish ministry.

In my notes I summarized the conference in 38 powerful statements. To answer your question, I have to say that the statement about Martin Luther, the "Father of the Reformation," probably impacted me the most. Here it is: "Martin Luther wrote a booklet, <u>Concerning the Jews and Their Lies</u>, and it became official Nazi propaganda (published by Goebbels in 1936). Only in 1980 did the Lutheran Church disown this book." This is the same Martin Luther who wrote the hymn, "A Mighty Fortress is Our God," and the same man whose brave actions against the Catholic Church resulted in the protestant reformation. He grasped the scriptural principle, "The just shall live by faith," and the following renewal rocked the world! But Luther injected a dangerous virus into the emerging Protestant churches, a virus that had already been at work hundreds of years in the Roman Catholic Church.

Hear Luther's words: "What shall we do with this damned, rejected race of Jews? First, their synagogues should be set on fire. ... Secondly, their homes should likewise be broken down and destroyed. ...We ought to drive the rascally lazy bones out of our system. ... Therefore away with them. ... so that you and we may all be free of this insufferable devilish burden – the Jews."[21]

Another man, known as one of the most eloquent preachers of truth and love back in the fourth century, had his say about the Jews. He was St. John Chrysostom and was esteemed as one of the greatest of the "Church Fathers." He said, "The synagogue is worse than a brothel ... it is the Temple of demons ... and the cavern of devils ... a criminal assembly of Jews ... a place of meeting for the assassins of Christ. ... As for me, I hate the synagogue. ... I hate the Jews for the same reason."[22]

How could Martin Luther and St. John Chrysostom have been so vitriolic against the Jews, the people who gave birth to our Savior, who were trustees of the Scripture, and who formed the first church?

The answer to that question is the fact that the Church was cut off from its Jewish roots in the late second century, and this became official Church policy by the time of Emperor Constantine and his

Council of Nicea in A.D. 325. Jewish believers had to abandon their so-called "Jewish practices," which were really **biblical** practices, such as keeping Passover and not Easter (a pagan celebration), keeping the Sabbath (one of the Ten Commandments), etc., or else they were excommunicated from the Church. Pagans were coming into the Church by the droves, because it was "user-friendly" with their pagan culture.

The Church adopted "replacement theology" in those days which persists right down to the present time in many mainline denominations. This is the belief that "the Church" has replaced the Jews in God's covenants and promises, the Church now inherits the blessings of God and the Jews are left with the curses! Replacement theology, stemming from an allegorical interpretation of Scripture, regards almost every reference to "Israel" in the New Testament as a reference to "the Church." The Church has become the "New Israel" (a term not found in the Bible). This belief system disregarded Paul's clear admonition to the church not to "boast against the natural [Jewish] branches," to remember that the Jews "are beloved for the sake of the fathers," and that "the gifts and the calling of God [for His chosen people] are irrevocable," (Rom. 11:18, 28, 29).

The Jews are still God's **chosen people** (Deut. 7:6), and His covenant with them for the Land is everlasting. He reiterated it four times in these verses: "The covenant which He made with Abraham, and His oath to Isaac, and confirmed it to Jacob for a statute, to Israel as an **everlasting covenant**, saying, 'To you I will give the land of Canaan as the allotment of your inheritance'" (Psalm 105:9-11). Paul said that the Abrahamic covenant for the Land could not be annulled (Gal. 3:17).

The replacement theology of the Church led to awful atrocities against the Jews in the Crusades, the Inquisition, the pogroms, and the Holocaust. Not only that, but time and time again entire Jewish populations were expelled from many countries. It was new information for me to learn that all the Jews were expelled from Spain in 1492 by order of King Ferdinand and Queen Isabella.

The deadline for expulsion was the very day Columbus set sail for the New World, and he had on board many Jews, one of whom was the first to set foot on American soil![23] I also discovered that Columbus himself was most likely of Jewish background, a marano (secret Jew).

For years I have been the grateful recipient of many newsletters and other material that educated me on the sordid anti-Semitic history of the church, but none was more powerful than what I learned from Dr. Michael Brown, both as an author and in person as a guest preacher at our churches in Southaven and Columbus, Mississippi. I also heard him speak at a "Let the Thirsty Come" Conference for Jewish and Arab believers in Tel Aviv in 2002, which was sponsored by Lars Enarson's ministry.

Dr. Brown, a "completed" Jew (or a Messianic Jew) wrote a book on the tragic story of the Church and the Jewish people, entitled *Our Hands are Stained with Blood*.[24] This book, which is certainly a classic on the subject, should be read by every serious Christian and taken to heart. Witnessing to Jewish people is imperative and even a priority for us, because Paul said, "I am not ashamed of the gospel of Messiah, for it is the power of God to salvation for everyone who believes, **for the Jew first** and also for the Greek" (Rom. 1:16). We just have to remember to be humble and do our homework first. Christians should be armed with the knowledge of our anti-Semitic history and the harmful forced conversions foisted upon the Jews in the past. Then we should proceed prayerfully as the Holy Spirit leads. Nothing is more satisfying than winning one of Yeshua's natural brothers or sisters to Him, especially the "least of these" (Matt. 25:40).

Now back to the conference in Dallas that changed my life. All the speakers were fantastic. The first speaker, Dr. Duane Weis, had me sitting on the edge of my seat, and I couldn't take notes fast enough. His subject was "Why We Honor Israel and the Jewish People." Weis was a CFNI faculty member and former pastor. He said he went to Israel in 1975 and came back a Zionist. At that time he had led 23 CFNI outreaches to Israel. They ministered in Arab churches also.

Weis declared that we should honor Israel, because our blessings are directly related to how we treat Israel. Using Genesis 12:3 as his text, he proved this thesis historically, physically, and spiritually. After Bible examples he used the examples of modern nations. For instance, he showed how England's treatment of the Jews has resulted in their decline from a world empire to a weak, socialist nation. After the Balfour Declaration of 1917, providing a homeland for the Jews in Palestine, England divided the land and gave swamp land to the Jews and the best land to the Arabs. (However, the Jews planted eucalyptus trees that soaked up the water in their swamps and made the land an agricultural wonder!)

When Hitler rose to power, hundreds of thousands of Jews escaped from Europe and headed to Palestine. But, the British issued a "White Paper" policy severely limiting immigration in May of 1939. This policy stated that only 75,000 Jews could come into Palestine over the next five years (10,000 a year plus an additional 25,000). "But Hitler was killing 25,000 a day!" Weis said. Not only that, Britain turned back shiploads of Jews fleeing the Holocaust, sending them back into the clutches of Hitler.

When the historic Partition Plan, dividing Palestine into a Jewish state and an Arab state, came to a vote in the United Nations on November 29, 1947, Britain abstained from voting. The plan passed, and Britain gave guns and ammunition to the Arabs who did not accept the plan! The Arabs could have had their so-called "Palestinian state" right then without firing a shot. Unfortunately, they wanted all the land, not just a part of it.

On its small allotment of land Israel declared itself a nation on May 14, 1948. The next day five Arab nations, led by British and Nazi advisers left over from World War II, attacked the fledgling Jewish state! Weis said this is well documented and that due to the anti-Semitic administration of the British Mandate, England was judged by God and eventually became an economic disaster. He reiterated God's promise that those who bless Israel will be blessed, and those who curse Israel will be cursed (Gen. 12:3).

Many people know about the British betrayal of Israel, but the ways in which the United States has acted against the welfare of Israel are not widely known. I was shocked to hear Dr. Weis say that the quagmire in Vietnam was directly related to the refusal of our government to intervene and stop the atrocities at Hitler's concentration camps. Weis said that from 1933 to 1945 (12 years) the American government knew what was happening to Jews under Hitler and did nothing. This intelligence report was kept secret from the American people.

Weis strongly recommended the book, *While Six Million Died*,[25] which he said was a very powerful, accurate, documented story of how our government turned its head on what was happening to the Jewish people in Europe. Weis said, "Jewish soldiers in a rag-tag resistance army came to the American government and said, 'Give us the guns and ammunition, and give us the bombs, and we will do what we can. Give us some planes, and we'll bomb the concentration camps. Sure, it will kill some people, but it won't kill millions. It will save millions from being annihilated.' And America would not let them have the resources to try to stop the slaughter."[26]

In the Holocaust Museum in Israel, there are photographs taken in 1941 by American pilots, showing Jews marching to their deaths in the concentration camps! The U.S. Government knew but stood by and let six million Jews die. Weis said that the Vietnam War lasted twelve years, according to an official statement of the U.S. State Department. Why such a long and inconclusive war? World War II only lasted five years. This bothered Dr. Weis, and he sought to find out why.

It is his opinion that America was judged for our refusal to help the Jews during the 12 years of the Holocaust by having to endure 12 long years of war in Vietnam. This was a fulfillment of the negative part of God's promise to Abraham and his descendants - "<u>I will bless those who bless you, and I will curse him who curses</u>

you; and in you all the families of the earth shall be blessed" (Gen. 12:3). I was deeply impacted by this message that how we treat Israel and the Jewish people will determine if we are blessed or cursed.

Another outstanding speaker was Lance Lambert, an Israeli citizen since 1980 and a well-known speaker on the end times and the Middle East. He spoke about Jerusalem. He said it has been occupied by foreign forces 20 times and 20 times has been liberated. It has been obliterated 14 times and 14 times has been rebuilt! He reminded us of the Six Days War of June 1967, when Jerusalem came back into Israeli hands, that it was a fulfillment of Luke 21:24 - "And Jerusalem will be trampled by Gentiles until the times of the Gentiles are fulfilled." He lamented, "Why don't Christians know this?"

Lambert said that Joseph in the Genesis account appeared to be an Egyptian to his brothers. They did not recognize him. They did not know that he was their brother, just as the Jews do not know

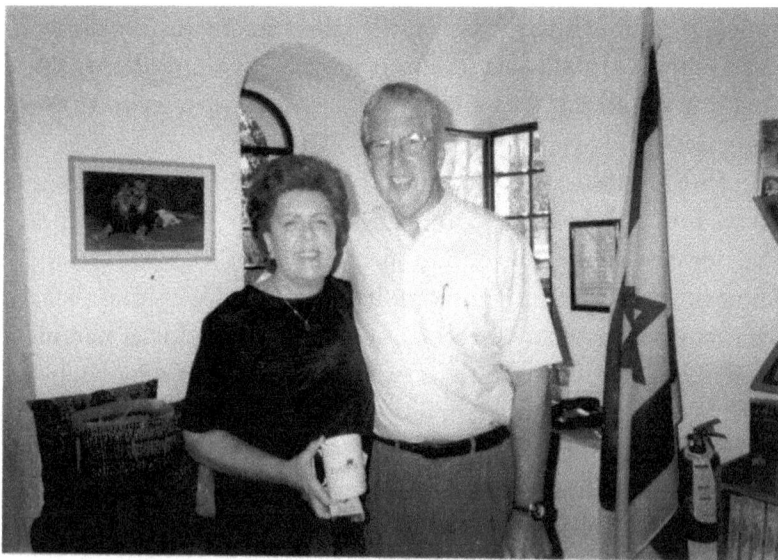

Sharon and Ray Sanders, founders of Christian Friends of Israel in Jerusalem

that Yeshua is one of them, their Messiah! He said that Benjamin was symbolic of the Messianic Jew. He is the "guarantee" that the rest of the Jews will come (Gen. 43:13-15; 44:12-18, 33-34; 45:1, 13-15; 46:26-27). Hallelujah, what a wonderful revelation!

Lambert had many more teachings on Scripture that filled my head with marvelous insights, but the speaker who touched my heart the most was Sharon Sanders. She and her husband Ray, ordained ministers through Christ for the Nations, were asked to establish the ministry of Christian Friends of Israel-Jerusalem in 1985. Their ministry is multi-faceted, reaching all segments of Israeli society with their humanitarian outreach and mercy ministry. They have branches throughout the world.

`Here are some of Sharon's quotes: "We are dealing with the wounded heart of a nation. The healing balm is God's love. Some Holocaust survivors say they haven't told their stories for 40 years. It is like Jesus massaging hearts as you minister to them. It takes a long time in working with them. If we don't have His love, we are as bland as French fries without salt. God's love helps us to undo the damage caused through historical Church wrong doing."

Sharon and Ray went to Belarus where there are hundreds of Holocaust survivors. She and her team experienced the smell of rats, garbage, heaviness, drunkards, darkness, and evil as they went into old apartment buildings. The KGB was watching them, and they were stopped, but God protected them. They saw spiritually as they had never seen before. They saw dark countenances change before their eyes! Here are some of the statements from survivors she wrote down: "How can I speak? I can't cry. Maybe I'm stone. I see how they stacked my people up like cords of wood." One of us began to cry, Sharon said. The lady said, "Your tears come to my heart. You believe in God, don't you?" The team did not give their names or say anything about God. The lady said, "You're from God. I can see it in your eyes." She asked for a Bible. The team watched her turn from a stone to a candle! She had worn black since the war. Sharon gave a party for them on their last day there. The survivor wore a lavender blouse. She said she would never wear black again!

Another Holocaust survivor named Joseph said, "Now I believe. He appeared to me in front of your faces." Another man said, "Now I believe He exists, because He sent you to us."

"They made us eat grass like cows. The hardest part was the ovens where they burned my people," Miera said. The team brought afghans made by blind Christians in England, and they gave Miera one. She held it and said, "Oh, for my suffering." (She had never been given reparations for her years of suffering in Auschwitz.)

Sharon said the team had such feelings of unworthiness in the presence of these suffering people. "God gave them beauty for ashes, these gentle, meek, mild, tender, precious jewels of God's kingdom." Sharon never heard one person speak against his or her persecutors. They had complete forgiveness with no bitterness. Miera even fed German soldiers after the war because they were hungry! Amazing! So like the Lord, yet she was not a believer.

Sharon talked to one of Schindler's survivors in Tel Aviv one time who asked, "What changed your heart toward us?" Sharon answered, "God. The Word came alive, and it was all about your people." She was asked by another Holocaust survivor, "Why didn't the Christians help us? They didn't have to love us, but they could have helped us." Sharon told her she did not have all of the answers, but she thought Christians had gotten so far away from their Jewish roots that they forgot Jesus was a Jew!

I could share so much more, but the last statement summed up what my mission would be – **to teach the Church her Jewish roots**. One creative way that Christ for the Nations accomplishes this is to have an **Honor Israel Day** every year and cancel all the classes. As soon as I returned home, I began to put plans in motion to have an Honor Israel Day at Trinity Church! I also planned to offer an **Israel Awareness Class** and to start an **Israel Prayer Group**! Holy Spirit, help me!" I prayed.

7

Messenger Girl

God gave me a song in June of 1995, named "Messenger Girl." I wrote the music and words down, and sang and played it. Right away I shared it at a prayer group led by Lars Enarson. The people there felt that it truly was from God. Lars was about to go to Israel with a small group for a prayer journey, and the song seemed to fit their mission. Our group prayed for this mission.

A lady from our church, Inez, was planning to go to Israel a little later to serve at Jerusalem House of Prayer for All Nations. I felt like she must be the "messenger girl for Messiah Yeshua," so I wanted to dedicate the song to her at church. As it turned out the next year, we had a group of six from our church going on a ten-day Mission to Jerusalem on September 4-15, 1996. This song described what we were doing, and I claimed it for us but especially for myself! Here is the first chorus:

> I am a messenger girl for Messiah Yeshua –
>   His name is Jesus!
> I'll take His Word to the world,
>   but first to the Jews, and where His Spirit leads me.
> I will be bold, and I will have no fear;
>   His Spirit is in me, and His call is clear.
> I'll spread His Word, and I'll sing and praise His name!

The second chorus changed to "**We** are the messengers sent by Messiah Yeshua ...." I tried to teach the song to the other five messengers. Oh, well, I tried.

I had another song I taught to our 1996 Jerusalem mission team, "My Only Hope is You." It would have been easy to learn, except that I translated the words into Hebrew! I think I was the only one who mastered it. The Jewish travel agent from Friendly Planet (funny name) helped me with the Hebrew words. As I talked to him on the phone, I was praying hard that the name Yeshua would be a Holy Spirit "bullet" in his heart!

What excitement I had planning for this mission trip to Jerusalem. I had been on a sight-seeing tour of Israel over two years before and vowed I would be back. Well, it was happening. There was intricate planning with the travel agent, the ministries we planned to volunteer for, and the host for our lodging. My file got thicker and thicker as I printed out e-mails and faxes back and forth to Jerusalem. Only ten days in the precious Holy City, and

Chain Gang displaying blankets for Holocaust survivors in Jerusalem

I wanted to make every hour count.

Back in May, I had joined a group of ladies, called the "Chain Gang," to crochet blankets and afghans for Holocaust survivors in Russia. (A chain is a crochet stitch.) At the send-off service for our mission team the 22 blankets were prayed over, and a large offering was taken to give the Christian Friends of Israel ministry. They would take the blankets to Russia as an expression of God's comforting love. We were trying to put into practice what Paul had instructed the Romans regarding his offering to the poor saints in Jerusalem, "... if the Gentiles have been partakers of their [Jews] spiritual things, their [Gentiles] duty is also to minister to them [Jews] in material things" (Rom. 15:25-27).

Our volunteer work in Jerusalem was with two similar ministries, Christian Friends of Israel and Bridges for Peace. The

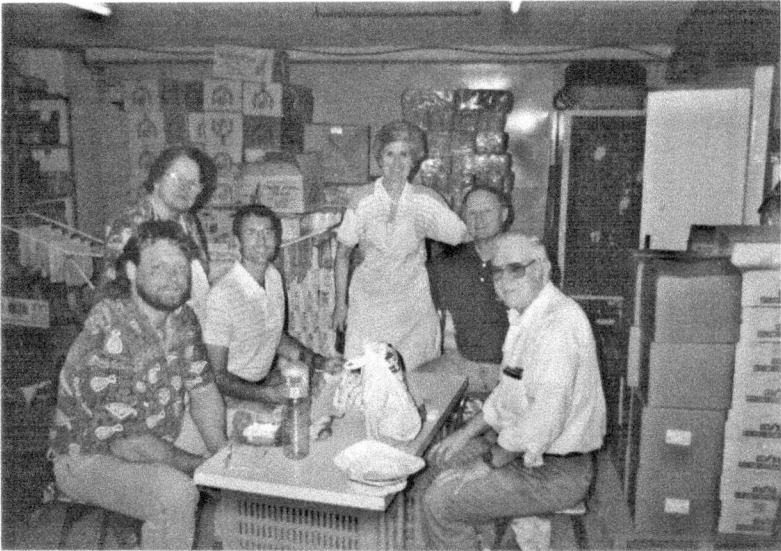

Louis, Esther, Randy, Nancy, Curtis, and Frank - taking a break at the Bridges for Peace Food Bank

latter had a food bank, and the four men on our team worked there, while Esther and I worked in the CFI office, doing clerical work. My work was with the Wall of Prayer ministry. At the food bank the men packaged food for the olim (immigrants). Some of the olim came in and got their packages of food, and to others the food was delivered by the volunteers. Esther and I joined the men to help out one day.

Frank & Esther Troskey presenting banner to Christian Friends of Israel Distribution Center in Jerusalem ("Trust in God" in Russian)

Another thing we did was to present a beautiful burgundy velvet banner with gold letters in Russian, "Trust in God," to the CFI Distribution Center, a different location from the CFI office. One of our church members, Ann Alley, who was very artistic and whose husband knew Russian, created it for us. This banner would be seen by the olim as they came in the Center to get much-needed clothing and other items to set up housekeeping in their new homes. Just as the blankets for the Holocaust survivors provided emotional comfort, the banner would signal spiritual encouragement for the impoverished olim. We also presented a used wedding dress to the CFI Bridal Salon ministry, which a member of our church had donated. This wedding ministry provides everything needed for a Jewish wedding, and CFI gets invited to the weddings to build relationships. (See Chapter 17.)

On my trip in 1998, I took six jackets from our church for CFI to distribute to Holocaust survivors. They were handmade by six ladies and each uniquely decorated. The words on the back were "Israel, My Beloved." When I delivered them to Sharon Sanders, the co-founder of CFI, she remarked that their upcoming Shavuot[27] conference would have as its theme that very same

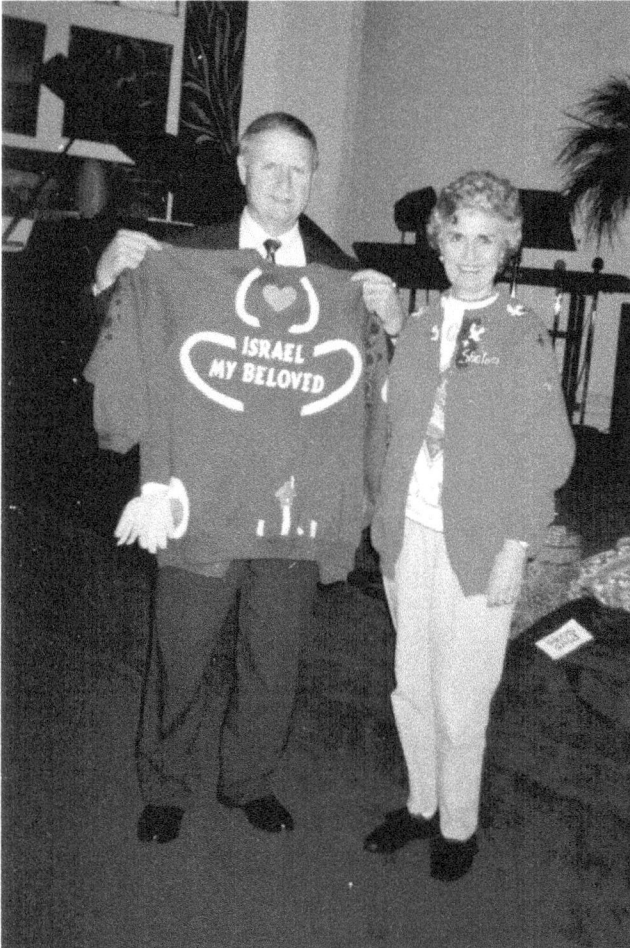

Trinity Church send-off service for Nancy's solo mission to Israel – Jackets for Holocaust Survivors

statement! One of our ladies had placed packets of sunflower seeds in her jacket's pockets. Imagine my surprise to find out that CFI had recently been giving out seeds with scriptures on them. The Holy Spirit surely had led us in preparing the jackets.

Other items were sent with me in 1998 for the ministry of CFI. I also took a large sum of money that had been donated by individuals in our church. The money was divided between CFI, the Kendalls for their School of Worship, and to the Enarsons for their prayer ministry. This messenger girl also gave out verbal encouragement to these precious ministers of His Word.

Our team of six in 1996 were truly "messengers sent for Messiah Yeshua" to Israel to minister in practical ways to His chosen people. We sought to do that in word and in deed. As Paul taught us, Christians are indebted to the Jewish people for all our spiritual blessings, and it is only right that we give back in material things. What a joy it was to do this. We had many adventures along the way, but the times of "close encounters" with the Lord that I had were the best of all experiences on my many trips to Israel.

8

Feeling His Presence in His Land

Before I went to Israel the first time in February of 1994, I got pointers from a friend at church who used to live in Israel with her husband, who was a Lieutenant Colonel in the Air Force, serving in a United Nations peacekeeping mission. Denise told me I would have a unique encounter with Jesus somewhere in the Holy Land.

Curtis and Nancy on the Sea of Galilee

She wanted me to let her know where it turned out to be. I kept this in mind as we walked the Land.

We had a worship service on a boat in the middle of the Sea of Galilee, and it was very moving, as the Scriptures were read about Jesus in that very place. But it wasn't there.

We sang "Standing on Holy Ground" as we viewed the exact spot where it is believed that Jesus was born in Bethlehem. We sang other songs of worship and felt it was indeed a holy place. But it wasn't there.

I kept "looking" for Him every place we went. Finally, it happened. In Nazareth I had that "close encounter." I had anticipated something special at Nazareth, and I was not disappointed. As I stood in the Church of the Annunciation and looked at the grotto where Mary conceived Jesus, suddenly I was overwhelmed with His Presence! I stood there crying and worshiping the Lord. It was amazing to think He would stoop down to such a humble place and person to become flesh and dwell among us. How awesome that God became a baby, and His mother was a simple, young peasant girl. What Mary said has certainly come true (especially among Catholics): "From now on all generations will call me blessed." Almost every site we visited was a Catholic church where Mary is honored.

The tour group began to move away from that spot, but my feet were glued to the floor. Time seemed to stand still for me. I wanted to stay and continue to feel His glory. Finally, someone gently persuaded me to move on.

Another Holy Spirit moment happened to me on the Mount of Beatitudes. After we crossed the Sea of Galilee we walked up the mount and went in a small church, where we were greeted by a very small nun. The church was octagonal (symbolizing the eight beatitudes) and was a place of prayer. Curtis said, "Let's pray here," and we knelt at the circular altar. The Spirit of the Lord swept over us as we prayed, and our hearts were moved with gratitude. Yes, this place had been saturated with prayer, and it was good

[5](5)

to be there. Outside we saw the green hillside. Its beauty was indescribable. Peace literally permeated the hillside and the church.

Before our trip, I was afraid that the holy sites would be so commercialized that the meaning of Christ's simple birth, life, death, and resurrection would be lost in all the formal, religious trappings. After we got there, I saw that indeed all of it was commercialized to the nth degree, and huge, ornate churches and shrines were built over every holy place. It seemed to be the exact opposite of what Jesus lived and taught. It looked as though man tried to improve on what God had done and produced a ridiculous caricature. But as we visited more and more churches, I began to see that we owe a great debt to the Catholic Church for preserving all these holy places. Also, the architecture and elaborate paintings are just expressions of devotion to God and not for us to judge the thoughts and intents of the heart. After all, it was in one of these churches that I had my special encounter with Jesus!

What a beautiful land is Israel. We saw fulfillment of Scripture – the desert blossoms like a rose. Crops of every kind cover the land. Israelis are an energetic, bustling, industrious people, God's chosen ones. God said, "... the Land is Mine" (Lev. 25:23), and His people are a treasure to Him. He said, "For you are a holy people to the Lord your God; the Lord your God has chosen you to be a people for Himself, a special treasure above all the peoples on the face of the earth" (Deut. 7:6). How can we not love the Jews, seeing as how much God loves them! He is watching over this Land and His people, and His Presence is evident.

Fast forward from 1994 to 1996 on our second trip to Israel. I felt a strong presence of the Holy Spirit when we visited King of Kings Assembly in downtown Jerusalem at the YMCA building at their Sunday evening worship service. The service had already begun as our group walked down to the front of the auditorium and filed in. The praise team was leading the congregation in singing the Shema in Hebrew, a capella: "Sh'ma Yisrael, Adonai Eloheinu, Adonai Echad. Baruch shem k'vod malchuto, le'olam, va'ed." (Hear, O Israel, the Lord our God, the Lord is One. Blessed be His glorious name Whose kingdom is forever and ever.) Oh, the glory of it! The natural voices were like a mighty pipe organ bursting forth with deep passion. Oh, how holy is our God! We were standing on holy ground. This Holy Spirit experience was the highlight of the whole mission trip for me.

Roy Kendall was on the stage as part of the praise team. His wife Mary and two children were in the drama presentation that night of the Binding of Isaac, which is the story always told on Rosh HaShanah.[28] We had just enjoyed a Shabbat meal in their home the Friday night before, so we felt right at home in that worship service among mostly Christian volunteers in the Land, people like us who loved Israel and the Jews.

Another experience of the strong Presence of the Holy Spirit was during a devotional time in the office of Christian Friends of Israel on that same trip. Esther and I were doing our office work there, when we were told to stop and get ready for the Wednesday afternoon devotional time for the staff. I don't know how it happened, but I got the **job** (really the **joy**) of playing the keyboard and leading the worship. It was a glorious time, and I did feel the presence of the Holy Spirit as we sang.

On my next trip to Israel in 1998, which also included volunteer work at CFI, they remembered that I had led the worship at the office devotional time in 1996, and they asked me to do it again. I'll never forget as we sang, "I Will Come and Bow Down at Your Feet, Lord Jesus," that sweet anointing of the Holy Spirit spread over me once again! What a blessing. And for it to happen in the Lord's own city was more than I could ever ask for.

Feeling the presence of the Holy Spirit in the **land**, in the realization of His **incarnation**, and in the **music** - all these experiences towered over the other experiences I had in Israel. The Psalmist says it best, "In Your presence is fullness of joy; at Your right hand are pleasures forevermore" (Psalm 16:11).

9

Aren't You Afraid to Go to Israel by Yourself?

By February of 1998, I felt like a veteran of international travel. I had been to the Philippines, Romania, and to Israel two times. I didn't think twice about planning my third trip to Israel. It was booked for February 3-22, and would be my longest trip, almost three weeks. I was making double good on my promise in 1994 to go back to the land! Actually, this mission was thoroughly prayed over, and my husband was not worried at all about my traveling alone. He told me to enjoy the trip.

It seemed to be a habit, going to Israel every other year. I'm sure people were questioning my sanity and saying, "Don't you want to see some other part of the world?" Others thought it was too dangerous to go to Israel, especially alone. They questioned, "Aren't you afraid to go to Israel by yourself?" However, backed up by prayer warriors and confirmation from the Lord through many of our church members, I was fearless!

It so happened that there were three couples, friends of ours living in Israel, who were more than glad to host me! We had visited in the home of the Simons in Jerusalem on our last trip. Before that, the Kendalls and the Enarsons had been in our home in Columbus. Does it get any better than that?

What a "God-incidence" we had in 1996 to meet a young woman who had lived in our city, Columbus, at one time! As if that weren't enough of a "co-incidence," her husband was the Jerusalem correspondent for American Family Radio out of Tupelo, Mississippi, and my husband Curtis was on their Board. Now I would say that qualifies as a bona fide **God**-incidence. There really aren't any **co**-incidences for us who have surrendered control of our lives to the Lord Jesus. God orchestrates our lives from then on.

This Jewish couple we met at the King of Kings Assembly worship service in Jerusalem, Mark and Michelle Simon, had only been married six months. They invited Curtis and me for breakfast on Shabbat at their apartment. What a blessing. After we got back to Columbus, I kept in touch with them by e-mail, and they insisted I come stay with them on my next trip. Now, two years later, I was accepting their offer.

The second couple, Roy and Mary Kendall, Jerusalem residents who have a School of Worship[29] ministry, and who hosted our team

Mark & Michelle Simon of Jerusalem hosting Nancy and Curtis for breakfast

for a Shabbat meal two years before, were eager for me to come stay with them also. Their secretary for the school was away for a time, and I was welcome to stay in her room, they insisted.

I had first met Roy, Mary, and their two children, Marianne and Chip, at a New Year's Eve church service in Columbus in December of 1995. The music they presented was beautiful, and their vision for the Lord's work in Israel was compelling. Mary's aunt, Betty Fancher, is a friend of mine, because we share a common love for the Word of God, especially as it pertains to current events in Israel and with the Jewish people. Because of her invitation, I was at that service and met the Kendalls. Two years later they visited us in Columbus and ministered at our church.

Roy, Mary, & Chip Kendall and Frank & Esther Troskey dining with the Petreys in Columbus, MS – Christmas 1997

Roy and Mary have the gift of hospitality. On each of five trips to Israel, they invited us to their home, and they usually fed us! They are spreading their music and their love all over the land of Israel through a multi-faceted ministry. They also minister in other countries, including the United States.

As well as being a part of the Praise Team at the King of Kings Assembly in Jerusalem, Roy is a worship leader for the International Christian Embassy Jerusalem (ICEJ) and also other organizations. The ICEJ sponsors the annual Feast of Tabernacles, an event that draws thousands of Christians from around the world. In 1980, the Israeli Parliament (Knesset) declared the city of Jerusalem to be the undivided, eternal capital of the State of Israel. Political protests followed, and 13 nations closed their embassies in Jerusalem! Christians living in Jerusalem sensed Israel's deep hurt and decided to open a Christian Embassy in God's Holy City. They called it the International Christian Embassy Jerusalem, and it represents Christians around the world speaking words of comfort and support to Israel. "Comfort, comfort My people. Speak comfortingly to Jerusalem" (Isa. 40:1). The ICEJ has additional ministries besides the Feast.

Roy is also a worship leader for the Knesset Christian Allies Caucus. This takes him into many countries, acting as a public relations agent for Israel with His music ministry. God has given Roy this place of influence with political leaders as **His** agent. He and Mary have also acted in Bible dramas which are presented all over the Land, and this is only a little of what they do in Israel! (See Chapter 25.)

The third couple, Lars and Harriet Enarson, moved from Columbus to Haifa in December of 1997 to pursue the vision the Lord gave them in 1974. Harriet told me about it, as she pointed out a place on the beach where she and Lars had an awesome experience with God. At that time they both instantly **knew** they would be married and some day do a work for God in Israel, although they did not share this revelation with each other until later. This happened in February, and it was in November that year that Lars proposed marriage (the second time) and Harriet accepted. Harriet chuckled as she told me it had taken time for God to show her specifically that Lars was to be her husband.

Their move to Israel was the next step in fulfilling the prayer ministry they were called to, and it was becoming a worldwide ministry. The house in Haifa was perfectly suited to their calling. When I arrived, workmen had just completed a large upper room on the third floor to be used for prayer. The only access to it at that time was by a precarious ladder, but it was worth the effort to climb. What a breathtaking room! The view toward Jerusalem in the east was heavenly. It was easy to imagine the prophet Daniel praying right there with the windows thrown open wide. You could also see the Carmel forest and the Mediterranean Sea over the mountains. Windows encircled the room. Later that first day I could hear Lars and his Arab pastor friend praying there.

The Enarsons' house was located just off Sweden Street, a clue to them that they had chosen the right house – they are from Sweden! Another clue was their proximity to Mount Carmel. They lived in the last residential area up the mountain, and next was the Carmel national forest.

Enarsons' house in Haifa

Lars calls his prayer partners The Elijah Prayer Army, and he never misses sending out a weekly prayer alert to them by e-mail.

How appropriate to live close to the actual spot where Elijah the prophet called down fire from heaven in a prayer contest with the prophets of Baal! That Bible story is a model for their Watchman International prayer ministry.

Now that I have introduced you to three outstanding couples in ministry in Israel who were my hosts in 1998, I will tell you some of my experiences on that solo journey. Being in Israel by myself was not frightening at all, but it certainly did have all the ingredients for fear.

Lars and Harriet had not yet received the shipment of their belongings when I arrived. Their house looked like a marble palace, but the entire furnishings consisted of mattresses on the floor, five plastic chairs, a camp-size refrigerator, an electric pot for hot water, a table, and stacked-up clothes. In the midst of this spartan existence they were hurriedly stocking the bomb shelter located in the center of their home! They could only afford supplies for two weeks, and that had to be the priority. Everyone was taking very seriously Saddam Hussein's threat to bomb Israel if the U.S. bombed Baghdad. A week before I left for Israel the news report was that Hussein had enough biological weapons to blow away Tel Aviv!

The government was making preparations, requiring everyone to have a safe room and handing out gas masks to the citizens. Tourists were the last on the list to receive gas masks, but it didn't worry me, although it was possible the bombing would happen before I flew out. When I was at the Simons', they were buying duct tape and making a safe room.

This reminded me of the time I was in the Philippines in 1990, and we were glued to the television set, watching Saddam Hussein attack Kuwait and threatening to attack Israel with scud missiles, which he later did. Here I was in Israel eight years later, and the same madman was making the same threat. In both instances I was constantly watching CNN, and I was in a foreign country. It was a déjà vu moment for sure!

Saddam Hussein didn't scare me. What scared me the most was what happened upon my arrival in Haifa to visit the Enarsons. Mark Simon had put me on the bus in Jerusalem. When I got off the bus in Haifa, I walked toward the terminal without getting my bags out of the bus! As the bus was pulling away, I remembered and panicked, waving my hand at the bus driver to stop! He kept going, and my heart sank. God provided help in the form of an old man who came up to me and told me not to worry. He took me over to the far end of the parking lot where the bus driver had parked. The driver was taking a break. He came toward me, knowing I had left my bags, and took me back to the bus. The young Jewish bus driver and I carried the two heavy bags to the curb behind the bus terminal. He was very sympathetic and clasped my hand warmly to reassure me. I gave him Harriet's number, and he made the call and handed his cell phone to me. I described to Harriet where I was standing, so Lars could come pick me up.

I waited and waited, anxiety threatening to overwhelm me. The cold wind was whipping around the corner, but I stood steadfastly beside my bags, unable to leave. I didn't want to miss Lars, and also the bags were too heavy to move. An old man from the Egged cooperative tried to help me. When he came by the second time, he gave me a piece of cake. Then he looked and looked in his billfold, slowly and shakily going through its contents to find his phone card for me. By this time I had been waiting 30 minutes, and my panic was rising. Suddenly, Lars walked up!

Praise the Lord! I was so relieved to see him. The handle on one of my bags broke, and the strap had pulled loose on the other heavier one. Lars had to carry the bags a very long way, going up steps, and finally coming to his car, which was parked in a no-parking zone. In all, it was an extremely stressful time. That was my most fearful time in Israel. Saddam Hussein's threats did not register on my radar!

On Shabbat we drove up Mt. Carmel to the very top to Kehilat (Assembly) Carmel which was meeting in an Anglican mission while the new Worship Center was under construction. Lars' prayer ministry would be housed there.

As we were going into the building, I met Ray and Sharon Sanders, the co-founders of Christian Friends of Israel-Jerusalem, and I introduced them to Lars and Harriet. Israel is such a small country that the Christian community is like a large family. Now the founders of two big ministries, one largely outreach and the other prayer, had met.

Ray touched my heart when he said he had tried to contact me before I left Jerusalem with news that the United States planned to bomb Iraq on February 26th at the new moon, the darkest time. Saddam Hussein warned the U.S. that the consequences would be the bombing of Israel. Ray was concerned for my safety, but I planned to fly out on the 22nd, so I wasn't shaken.

The dedication of the new building was planned to coincide with Israel's 50th birthday, her Jubilee Year. Dave Wilkerson had been invited to speak on May 15-16. The founders of the church, David and Karen Davis, came out of Wilkerson's Times Square Church in New York City. I enjoyed the service with Karen leading the singing – what a powerful voice – and David preaching an anointed sermon.

The congregation walked over to the unfinished building, and the altar call was given. I felt this was an historic occasion, and I was privileged to be a part of it. We offered ourselves to God as we held hands and sang, "Refiner's Fire." We wanted the fire to fall as it did when Elijah prayed. It was a holy moment, almost as awesome as the time at King of Kings Assembly in Jerusalem when we sang "Sh'ma Yisrael."

After this trip to Israel I made some comparisons of the three trips I had made thus far:

1. The last trip we observed the 3,000th birthday of Jerusalem. This trip I observed the 50th Jubilee Year of Israel's founding as a State.

2. This trip I was in three different homes for Shabbat. One was with a Jewish couple, Israeli citizens. All three homes had challah[30] bread and special blessings.
3. On the first trip we stayed in first-class hotels. On the second trip we stayed at a bed & breakfast. On the 3rd trip I stayed in three homes, the last of which was "camping out."
4. On the first trip we did sight-seeing all over the country for ten days. The second trip was ten days for missions and only in Jerusalem. The third trip was for missions in Jerusalem and Haifa for 19 days.
5. In three trips to Israel, I did not once eat a falafel, Israel's answer to the hamburger.[31]
6. The first two times six of us came. This time it was only me.

I didn't realize I had violated two directives from Jesus. He sent the apostles out two by two, and I came alone. He said to stay in the same place, and I stayed in three places. Nevertheless, I feel that God did send me alone for His own purpose, and He certainly blessed me greatly.

I was not afraid to go to Israel by myself, but after a tiring 26-hour flight home, I made a declaration that my next trip would be with my husband! How good it was to see his face and feel his embrace at the airport in Columbus. Other friends were there also. I couldn't wait to share with the church some of my escapades as a Mizpah!

I missed the experience of eating a falafel, but on my next trip in 2002, I would get to enjoy eating a falafel several times.

10

Prayers, Persecution, and Suicide Bombings

I vowed never to go back to Israel alone after I returned home in 1998, so when I felt the Lord's call to attend Lars Enarson's Passover Prayer Tour in 2002, I looked for traveling companions. I found two sisters from Huntsville, Alabama, who were receiving Lars' prayer alerts for The Elijah Prayer Army, and they soon made a decision to go on the tour. These ladies, Mary Jo Morgan and Phyllis Huie, became my friends over the phone and by e-mail.

When friends and family learned of my plans, the warnings began to roll in – "It's too dangerous over there right now. Please don't go!" Curtis and I prayed about it, talked about it, prayed about it, and talked about it. Curtis and I vacillated back and forth. Finally, the Lord led me to call Roy Kendall in Jerusalem, and his advice hit home. I had the answer. Roy said that any trip to Israel should be taken because God called, not for any other reason. He gave an example of a lady who planned to go to Israel but backed out at the last minute because of perceived danger in the land. She was in an accident and died right in the good ole USA. Roy said, "If you are in the center of God's will, that is the safest place to be."

Little did we know that the number of suicide bombings during our 15-day stay in Israel, March 19-April 3, would escalate greatly and result in Operation Defensive Shield, launched on March 29 by the Israeli Defense Force (IDF). The year of 2002 would see 56 suicide bombings in Israel by the Palestinian terrorists. Because of the success of the IDF, there would be a drop in half in the number of suicide bombings from February-March to April-May and a 70 per cent drop in executed attacks between the first half of 2002 and the last half of 2002. But alas! Our Passover Prayer Tour would take place at the **height** of the bombings and Operation Defensive Shield.

Curtis drove me to the airport in Atlanta where I met up with Mary Jo and Phyllis. We arrived in Israel several days before the prayer tour was to begin and checked into Christ Church Guesthouses in the Old City. The Old City is a .35 square mile walled area within the modern city of Jerusalem. Until the 1860s this was the entire city of Jerusalem. It is divided into the Christian Quarter, the Muslim Quarter, the Jewish Quarter, and the Armenian Quarter. Following the 1948 Israeli War of Independence, the Old City was occupied by Jordan.

During the Six Days War of 1967, Israel won back the Old City and the rest of East Jerusalem. Now the Jews would have control of Israel's holiest site, the Temple Mount, for the first time in 2,000 years! Here is the way it happened, taken from an original recording of the voices of the Israeli soldiers as they entered the Old City on June 7, 1967. I heard this recording when I attended the Israel in Prophecy Conference in Dallas in 1995:

> The Temple Mount is in our hands. The Temple Mount is in our hands. All forces stop firing! The time is 10:20, the 7th of June. At this moment we are passing through the Lion's Gate. I am at present under the shadow of the gate. And again we are going out to the sunny street. Lion's gate. We are in the Old City. We are in the Old City. The soldiers are standing very close to the walls. We are marching now on the Via Dolorosa. Do you understand this? The Old City, we are again within the Old City. Al Aksa Mosque. Under the ruling of the mandate we could not enter here. One moment. Straight ahead is the wailing wall. Hurrah! Hurrah! Hurrah! Hurrah! It is hard to express in words our feelings."[32]

> (General Rabbi Shlomo Goren, chief chaplain of the IDF, sounded the shofar at the Western Wall to signify its liberation. This caused a great celebration of the Jews all over the world!)

Wow! What an historic place we were in. Likewise, Christ Church is also quite an historic place. It is the oldest Protestant church in the Middle East, built to evangelize the Jewish people. It's founding bishop in 1842 was an Anglican Jew, Michael Solomon Alexander.

Once inside the church, the building has more similarity to a synagogue than to a church, with Jewish symbols and Hebrew script everywhere, including the Hebrew words of Jesus. It is the only church in the Old City that fully acknowledges in symbol and architecture the Jewish roots of Christianity. It came to be known as the "Jewish Protestant Church." To Bishop Alexander an Hebraic understanding of Jesus, the New Testament and Christianity's Jewish roots was vital for churches in the west. Today his vision is being carried out in the Shoresh Study Tours and Alexander College, which are both committed to teaching the Jewish roots of the church. He believed this can help bring the healing that our families and churches so desperately need.

My calling as a Mizpah for Israel gave me a kindred spirit with the late Bishop Alexander, and I felt right at home in this place that had such strong Jewish roots. This was the location of the Passover Prayer Convocation and Seder meal that we would participate in some days later.

We had a visitor at our guesthouse who was somewhat of a celebrity, and she is kin to me. It was Jennifer Griffin, the Fox News Correspondent for

Jennifer Griffin, Fox News reporter, and daughter Annalise with Nancy at Christ Church in the Old City

Jerusalem at that time! Actually, Jennifer is Curtis' great-niece. We had a good visit with her and her one-year-old daughter Annalise. Then Jennifer led us on a short tour of the Old City to the Western Wall. She had to report to work, so we prayed at the Wall and went on to see other sites. When we got back to the room, we heard sirens and wondered what happened.

Later that day Jennifer called us to see if we were okay. Her

Nancy, Mary Jo Morgan, and Phyllis Huie with Annalise Myre

voice was tense. A suicide bomber had detonated near the Ben Yehuda Walking Mall at the French Bakery on the corner of King George and Jaffa Streets. Jennifer's Filipino babysitter, Rose, lived right above the bakery. Her balcony was splattered with blood and glass! Rose threatened to go back to the Philippines. Jennifer said in anguish, "When is this going to stop?" We got the report later that three were killed and 57 wounded. That wasn't the last suicide bombing in Israel during our stay.

We had a few wonderful days on our own in Jerusalem, but then it was time to go to Ben Gurion Airport in Tel Aviv to meet the group for the Prayer Tour. What a joy to see Lars and Harriet again after so long a time. They had led several prayer tours in the Land since I last saw them, and many times I had expressed my desire to join them on one of these tours. We had a good hug, and Harriet said, "Well, you finally made it, Nancy!"

Our first night was at the Carmel Netanya Hotel. (Netanya would be making the headlines a few days hence.) The next day we began our prayer tour, stopping at Caesarea and then at Mount Carmel. How wonderful to be in the midst of serious prayer warriors on site in the beautiful land of Israel. When we got to the Galilee we checked in the Nof Ginosaur Kibbutz Hotel. Lars immediately called an emergency prayer meeting for our group.

We were beginning to experience the fierce persecution that dogged Jesus' steps when He was on earth, and it was the same spirit attacking us that had attacked Jesus through the Pharisees and religious leaders. This satanic spirit was working through the Yad L'Achim (Hand for Brothers), a group of ultra-orthodox Jews who oppose evangelism and Messianic church meetings. Lars was notified that the Yad L'Achim had lawyers and were planning to shut down the outreach conference we would have in Tel Aviv at the end of the tour. They charged it was an illegal missionary activity. Actually, proselytizing is legal in Israel unless a minor is targeted without parental consent. The Yad L'Achim had already distributed thousands of leaflets to mailboxes, defaming The Watchman International ministry. Our group had an intense time of warfare prayer and worship concerning this threat. We knew God heard our prayers, and we returned to our rooms with a confident trust in God for His protection and for the outreach conference to be held.

This threat by the Yad L'Achim reminded me of a similar situation back in 1996. One day as our group waited for the bus to leave the Old City, we had an encounter with some Jewish men who must have been part of the Yad L'Achim. One of our team, Louis, saw a beggar woman who was selling red threads. He told her the red threads represented the blood of Yeshua, and then he prayed for her.

Louis witnessing to a woman selling red threads (Louis explained "blood of Jesus")

The men were watching. One of them snarled at Louis, "There are no churches here!" We got on the bus, and so did these Jews. At a bus stop the Jews got off. Looking back at Louis, that same man pointed his finger with hate blazing in his eyes and barked, "We'll crucify you, too!" That gave us chills. Surely the same demon spirit that spoke through that man was the one almost 2,000 years before who had stirred the mob to cry out before Pilate, "Crucify him! Crucify him!"

Back to the prayer tour. We traveled to the north of Israel and prayed at the border with Lebanon, which is home to the terrorist group, Hezbollah ("party of Allah"). Modern suicide bombings began in Lebanon as a result of Israel's 1982 incursion in Operation

Peace for Galilee. The most famous attack was the suicide truck bombing against the U.S. Marine barracks in Beirut that killed 241 Marines in 1983. Our group prayed for Kiryat Shmona, the Israeli town that was taking the most rocket fire from the Hizbollah terrorists across the border. Lars and Harriet's son-in-law Ron grew up in Kiryat Shmona, and he was with us as we prayed.

We also prayed on the Golan Heights at the Syrian border for Israel's protection. The Golan Heights is Israel's buffer from hostile enemies, and it must not be given away! Then we visited the Enarsons' 27-bed House of Prayer in the Golan Heights town of Katzrin and prayed for the salvation of the Jewish people and revival in the Middle East. Lars and Harriet had moved from Haifa to the Golan a few years earlier and established this House of Prayer.

When we got to Jerusalem, we had the Prayer Convocation at Christ Church for three days, including a fabulous Passover Seder Meal, served by the people of the church. Lars had written a Messianic Haggadah[33] for the occasion. The annual Passover feast is

Nancy and Pastor Shmuel Suran at Passover Seder in Christ Church, Jerusalem

a mandate from God for His chosen people (Ex. 12). This Messianic Haggadah revealed the Lamb of God, Yeshua HaMashiach (Jesus the Messiah), in the ancient ritual throughout the celebration.

That night at the conclusion of the Seder, Lars stood and made a shocking announcement. Thirty people had just been killed and 170 wounded in an horrific suicide bombing at the Park Hotel in Netanya! (Our first night of the tour was spent in Netanya.) This attack became known as the Passover Massacre. It was the spark that gave rise to the IDF's Operation Defensive Shield, launched just two days later on March 29 with an incursion into Ramallah. Yasser Arafat was placed under siege in his Ramallah compound and confined to two rooms. Seven of his buildings were bulldozed. This was followed by the IDF going into the six largest cities in the West Bank to route out terrorists.

After the bombing in Netanya, our intercession on the prayer tour became even more intense. On March 29, our tour group left Jerusalem and went south to Timnah in the Negev desert close to Eilat, away from the violence.

In the afternoon our tour bus leader asked me to call Jennifer on her cell phone and find out what was going on in Jerusalem. I dialed Jennifer, and her first words were, "I'm covering a suicide bombing in a super market near Yad VaShem." We gasped! Another suicide bombing. She told us that her husband Greg, reporter for the New York Times, was staying overnight in Ramallah. She was worried about him, because the IDF was right then attacking Arafat's Ramallah headquarters! She also said that Sharon wants Arafat deported. We stopped and prayed for Jennifer and Greg.

The prayer tour took us next to the tall watchtower of Har El Brigades, a point close to Jerusalem where Israel was victorious over the invading Arabs in 1967. We climbed to the top and could see all the way to Ramallah. There we offered special prayers for the suicide bombers and the Palestinians. We also prayed for the Kabbalistic orthodox Jews who place the curse of death on people, such as the former Prime Minister Yitzhak Rabin who was assassinated in 1995 by an orthodox Jew.

The next day we drove to Ramat Gan, a suburb of Tel Aviv, where the outreach conference would be held at the Kfar Maccibeah Hotel. We had not had access to television for quite a while, so once we got checked in, we rushed to turn on the set. There was Arafat on CNN, being "quarantined" in his Ramallah headquarters. We made a mental note that we were in an historic time of war in the land of Israel, but it never got to our hearts. It was amazing that we had no fear at all. These terrible things were happening all around us, but we were not touched. Surely God had led us here to be a part of the solution with our prayers, and He was protecting us. We marveled at the goodness of God and were humbled that we could play a small part in His purposes in the Holy Land.

The purpose of the conference, titled "Let the Thirsty Come," was to encourage and bless the believers in the land, both Jew and Arab, by offering this event with lodging and food free of charge! Whole families were invited, and there were also activities for the children. These poor believers were facing hard economic times, increasing violence, and discrimination in employment, and this was to be a spiritual oasis for them. The expenses mounted to around $350,000, but the donations poured in. God rewarded this leap of faith with miracles.

The anti-missionaries, Yad L'Achim, came each night to harass the people. Once they even tried to slit the tires of the buses. The police and security guards took care of them. Lars employed the top security guy in Israel. The Yad L'Achim had threatened to remove the hotel's kosher license if they allowed the conference to take place. Angry rabbis from all over the country contacted the hotel. The largest newspaper in Israel carried the story. The hotel manager determined that everything about the conference was legal, and he refused to give in to the Yad L'Achim. We had already prayed on the first night of the tour, and God said to stand still and see the salvation of our God. Now we were seeing our prayers answered!

No wonder the enemy was upset. What a miracle during the present violence to have so many Jews and Arabs come together under the same roof! What a powerful testimony that only the Messiah of Israel has the answer to the conflict in the Middle East.

Our tour group of about 75 people from 20 nations was joined by more intercessors to carry out the work of the conference. Approximately 1,500 people registered, which included Jewish, Arab, Ethiopian, Lebanese, and Russian believers. There was translation with headphones for all of them. This was the largest gathering for believers in Yeshua ever held in Israel since the days of the Early Church! My assignments were greeter, helper with two and three year-olds, and prayer leader for a shift in the Secret Prayer Room.

The glorious climax of the conference was the "Tunnel of Blessing" formed by the staff's and speakers' hands raised and touching the others' hands opposite each other to make a tunnel for the participants with their families to come through. I was a

Enarson family and staff for "Let the Thirsty Come" outreach conference

part of the tunnel. We reached out and laid our hands on the "thirsty" as they came through the tunnel, and we blessed them. You can imagine who was blessed the most.

There were many testimonies. One person wrote, "I was crippled from a terrorist attack in 1997 and have taken 20 pain killers every day, but I was still in much pain. In the first meeting I felt the Spirit lift me, and the next morning when I woke up, I did not have any pain left at all. I am healed!" Another person said, "My husband and I cannot afford to take a vacation, and this is a gift from the Lord, not only hotel and food, but water from heaven for both us and our children. We are so blessed!"

What an exciting way to end my fourth trip to Israel! I had seen the worst and the best in the Land, engaged in high-level spiritual warfare prayer, seen prayers answered, and met many new friends. I also was able to leave a generous monetary blessing behind from the donations sent by churches and individuals. My present church, South Luverne Baptist in Luverne, Alabama, sent a good offering. Each of these donors would be rewarded according to the Word of God given to Abraham, "I will bless those who bless you ..." (Gen. 12:3).

11

Musical Mizpah

Until God called me to be a Mizpah for Israel, my primary ministry for Him outside my roles as wife, mother, and grandmother had been through music. My mother made sure I had piano lessons, starting at only five years old, and we had a grand piano in our home. Mother, or "Miss Nan," as her high school students called her, was adept in playing the piano for practically every musical activity in Luverne High School. Naturally, I grew up as a carbon copy of her, for I was frequently called on to play the piano at church and school.

Mother was determined that I get a college degree with a teacher's license. I chose the field of music education, majoring in piano with a minor in voice. My career began as a junior high choral teacher in Montgomery, Alabama, but that didn't last long. Four months after the school year ended, we moved to Corinth, Mississippi. Our daughter Susan was soon born, so I decided to stay home and not pursue a teaching job. Instead I taught piano lessons at home to our four children – Perry, Susan, Jim, and Bert – and then to others as the years went by. Eventually, I taught choral music again in two more Mississippi towns, Tupelo and Horn Lake.

My husband was called into full-time ministry in the United Methodist Church on January 1, 1976, and I felt called by God for this ministry the same day. My musical ability was put to good use in the churches Curtis pastored over 24 years. I formed and directed youth and adult choirs, accompanied the choirs, and played for the church services. Besides singing solos, at various times I also led the congregational singing and a praise team with instruments.

After my husband retired from pastoring, and we moved to Petrey, Alabama, to his childhood home, I continued my musical activities, but in a limited way.

Musical Mizpah and Minister of Music at South Luverne Baptist Church in Luverne, Alabama

When God called me to be a Mizpah for Israel, I asked Him if my work was to be a dual ministry, both music and Mizpah, and it seemed He answered that I was a "Musical Mizpah." For years I had already been learning Hebrew songs and teaching them to others in Hebrew and English. Entering into the Israeli culture certainly involved music, and what could be a better way to touch the hearts of Christians and connect them with the natural brothers and sisters of Jesus than teaching them vibrant Jewish-flavored songs? I reasoned that theology was not the only area in which the church needed teaching about her Jewish roots. Learning correct doctrine may change the mind, but learning Jewish songs and dances would change the heart! Jewish music could kindle a love in Christian hearts for their Jewish roots. So, God was equipping me on two fronts. I embraced my role as a Musical Mizpah.

On my first trip to Israel in 1994, I experienced the kindling of love in my own heart for the Jewish people and their music by attending a folk music program at the YMCA. Frank, Esther, and I went with our group to see the Tzabarim Folklore Ensemble. These were sabras,[34] young men and women born in Jerusalem, doing Israeli and Arab folk dances. I kept saying the whole evening, "I wish I could do those dances." At the end of the program, the young dancers came down in the audience to coax people to come up on stage and learn the dances. As one girl held out her hands to me, I pulled back and resisted. Esther reminded me of what I had been saying all evening. "This is your chance, Nancy. Go up there!" she urged. With some apprehension, I took the girl's hand and went onstage, joining others from the audience. We got in a big circle and began following instructions to learn the Israeli national dance, the Hora. It is the king of Israeli folk dances, a dynamic dance, full of the pioneering spirit which filled the hearts of the first Jews coming to Israel. The primary step we learned was the *mayim* (Hebrew for "water"), a sideways step, crossing our legs before and behind. It gives the appearance of waves of water, hence the name. What a thrill it was to be in Jerusalem, the cradle of our faith, with God's chosen people, dancing with wild abandon and joy. I was making the connection with my Jewish roots without even realizing what "Jewish roots" meant! And Frank got it all on video tape.

Another dancing experience I had in Jerusalem was in 1998 when Mary Kendall took me to worship at King of Kings Assembly in that same building, the YMCA. After the worship service, Mary had a surprise for me. We went to a room where people were learning the Jewish dances! The teacher of the class was Rebecca Brimmer. I recognized her as a writer for the Bridges for Peace[35] publications I had been receiving. She is now the International President and CEO of Bridges. We not only did Jewish dances but interpretive dance and even a line dance to the music of Dennis Jernigan.

At Trinity Church back home in Columbus, I participated briefly as a dancer on our Jewish Dance Team. The church was learning about its Jewish roots not only through me but through other members who were teaching the Jewish dances and sharing with other churches.

When teaching at DayStar Bible Institute in 2000-2001 (see Chapter 22), I began the sessions with Hebrew songs. It was a surprise to learn that one of the songs, "Hineh Ma Tov" ("Behold, How Good" from Psalm 133:1) was also the theme verse of the DayStar Assembly of God where we were meeting! The verse was on their church bulletins. God has many ways to confirm a ministry, doesn't He?

There were two more musical experiences God blessed me with in Israel. On our Israel tour in 1994, our friend, Frank Troskey, asked the group captain if I could sing a song. What could he say? No? "Of course," he said. We were standing on the pavement where Jesus was horribly mocked and beaten by the Roman soldiers who demanded that he carry His cross. The street is known as the Via Dolorosa, meaning "way of suffering." I stood there on the Via Dolorosa street and sang the song, "Via Dolorosa."[36] Wow! The song has a Spanish section in it. Afterward, a lady in the group told me my Spanish was just right. I was so glad I didn't know that anyone knew Spanish before I sang it. What a memorable experience and an honor to sing at that holy spot.

In 2002, on the Passover Prayer Tour, I had another satisfying music experience. After checking in the Mt. Zion Hotel in Jerusalem, I spotted a grand piano across the lobby. It didn't take me but a minute to get to it and begin playing Hebrew songs. The tour group danced all over the lobby, and we had a great time of rejoicing. A man from Paris, two little girls, and a little boy came over to the piano. They loved the music. The man danced. Then a pastor from Portugal came to the piano also. On another day at the hotel, two little girls came up to me, grinning. I wondered if they were the same ones that had gathered around the piano, and they probably were. They wanted to know my name, and they gave their names. I didn't understand much because of the language barrier and also my hearing loss. However, we clasped hands, and we liked each other! Truly, music is a unifying gift from the Father.

My hearing had begun to deteriorate 15 years before, and now it was getting harder and harder to distinguish the bass notes on my spinet piano. I thought to myself, "Here I am a music major, and I have been playing the piano since I was five years old. I only have this little spinet piano, and the quality is terrible. Plus, I can hardly distinguish the pitches I am playing! What I really need is a grand piano, so I can hear the bass notes. This is a need, not a luxury." I was playing and singing solos more at church and getting such positive feedback, that I realized God was not through with me in the area of music. I began to pray earnestly about my situation, and I thought God said it was a good idea for me to buy a grand piano. By July of 2002 I had become certain God wanted me to have a grand piano.

Curtis and I found a used Kawaii grand, not a baby grand, but a 5'10" gorgeous instrument, which had had only one owner. Though large, it would fit nicely in our high-ceiling living room. The condition of the piano was like new, and the price was excellent, just $6,800. The only problem was my husband said we couldn't afford it. I reminded him that he had just paid cash for a car which cost much more than the piano! This caused quite a lot of conflict, but I stood my ground – something unusual for me – insisting that the Lord wanted me to have the piano. Truly He did, because our friend, Esther Troskey, offered to lend us the money. The piano was delivered to our house on September 2, 2002, the day before mine and Curtis' 44th anniversary. I was "one happy camper." In a matter of months, our debt was paid, and I was enjoying playing the piano like never before!

Dedicating the piano to the Lord was the first order of business, so I planned a home concert for 20 people on November 3 that year. The opening number was a distinctly Jewish-sounding song by Paul Wilbur, "It is Good to Praise the Lord (Psalm 92)." I stood as I played and sang, inviting the guests to join me on the "lai-lai-lai" chorus. Great fun. Another song was "His Eye is on the Sparrow."

One day before the concert as I was practicing "His Eye is on the Sparrow," Curtis was sitting right outside on the front porch with his feet propped up, listening. A sparrow flew in the porch and lit on the chair in front of him. He thought, "I wish Nancy could see this." He watched it a good while, expecting the sparrow to fly off any minute. But the sparrow didn't move. Finally, Curtis' legs began to cramp, and he needed to stand up. He had not moved for a long time, because he knew the sparrow would fly off if he did. He stood up anyway, and the sparrow still didn't move. Then he eased over to the sparrow, reached out, and took it in his hand! Amazing!

Curtis walked in the living room, where I was still practicing, and held the sparrow up in front of my face. He said, "His eye is on the sparrow!" Ooh! I knew at that moment that God had sent his little "messenger" to both Curtis and me. God was saying to me, "I'm watching you. It is my will that you have the piano and that you have the concert. It's not egotistical." I chuckled as I thought, "God is also saying to Curtis, 'You see, your wife really did need this piano, and I wanted her to have it.'" What sweet vindication.

In case you think there's a natural explanation for this phenomenon of picking up a sparrow with your hand, take note of what happened next. Curtis immediately went back outside and released the sparrow. It was not sick. It was just an ordinary sparrow in the hands of an extraordinary God. The sparrow flew away. Mission accomplished. And, of course, God was watching and must have smiled!

Oh, what a gracious heavenly Father we have. He meets our needs, but He also gives us the desires of our hearts. As time has gone by, and my hearing has deteriorated more, I realize what a gift this grand piano is. Whereas I once had many varied pleasures in listening, directing choirs, playing and singing music, my sole musical pleasure now, outside of singing, is playing my Kawai grand piano. My heart overflows with gratitude to God.

Hearing loss or no hearing loss, God was far from finished with me in music. While I was on the Passover Prayer Tour in Israel in 2002, I was called on to lead singing from the keyboard at one of our night sessions in the historic Christ Church in Jerusalem. The group sang and danced to the lively Hebraic music. Earlier on the tour bus a lady named Mary Jernigan was very complimentary of my singing, and she wanted to learn the Hebrew songs I had been leading. Even after the tour was over she contacted me several times and insisted I make a recording.

The next year in February of 2003, I took the challenge. A friend of ours, Paul Davis, who had once been a radio engineer, brought his microphones and old-style reel-to-reel tape recorder to the house, and we did the recording of 16 songs almost straight through with hardly a glitch. I knew the Lord was empowering me, as I sat at the piano, sang and played. I wasn't trying to get a perfect recording, my purpose being to use it as a teaching tool for Christians to learn the Hebrew songs. It's a good thing I wasn't striving for perfection, because Paul's recorder began to malfunction before we finished the recording. I was really worried that all the grinding sounds from the reel-to-reel recorder would be on the tape.

With fear and trembling, I listened to the tape to see if the malfunction affected the recording, and if my voice and piano performance was acceptable. Curtis and I evaluated it and decided we might as well continue with the process of duplication, although I was not convinced it was good enough.

The name of my CD was *Hatikva (The Hope)*[37], the Israeli national anthem. I sent off the reel-to-reel tape to a company to duplicate 100 CDs and 50 cassette tapes to give away and sell. A man at the company amazed me with his ability to "fix" a sour note by talking to me over the phone. He simply found the same note on another verse and exchanged that note for the sour note. Voila! I helped him know which note to select and where the sour note was. All this was done with his equipment as we talked on the phone. Then he removed the air noise between songs. It turned out to be an excellent recording, almost as good as if it had been done in a studio. Paul really knew what he was doing. All my doubts were gone. Praise the Lord! I was a recording artist at last! Mary Jernigan was overjoyed to get her CD, and she ordered many more. Others genuinely enjoyed the recording. I sold the CDs and tapes at seminars and shared the music in other ways.

The most heart-warming compliments I received from *Hatikva*, however, were from my granddaughters, Taylor, who was 6, and Hannah, who was 4 at the time. Taylor started crying when she listened to it and told her daddy, Jim, that she missed "Mama Nancy." They called me and told me they loved the CD. I asked Taylor why she was crying, and she said through tears, "Because I love you!" Later Jim asked the girls, "Isn't Elvis Presley the best singer in the whole world?" Taylor said, "No! Mama Nancy is the best singer in the whole world!" Both girls listened to my CD every night before they went to bed. There aren't words to express how that blessed me. With fans like Taylor and Hannah, what more satisfaction could I find?

Through this recording, I believed that I was fulfilling my dual role as a Musical Mizpah. I planned to take some CDs and tapes with me the next time I went to Israel. My life thus far as a Mizpah for Israel had been tremendously blessed. The blessings included a new dimension of ministry in the form of a Jewish woman who lived only 30 miles away from me.

12

One New Man

A new chapter opened in my life as a Mizpah the day I met Janice Horowitz Bell from Elba, Alabama. A friend, Edna Ruth, invited me to attend a ladies' meeting at First Baptist Church in Luverne and hear a Jewish lady give her testimony. This happened only a few days after "9-11," the horrific terrorist attack on the World Trade Center in New York City, so I will always remember the date I met Janice. It was September 17, 2001.

I listened intently as Janice told of her life. She was born in New York, the middle child with two brothers and two sisters. When she was six months old, her parents moved the family to Miami Beach, Florida, along with all the other New York Jewish people relocating to South Florida. When Janice was 12, her family moved to West Hollywood, Florida, an area with mostly people from Alabama and Georgia (non-Jews). That is where she met her goy (Gentile) husband-to-be, Jack Bell, who was originally from Elba. She was only 15, and Jack was 21. Their love quickly flowered, and they eloped. Eventually, Mr. and Mrs. Jack Bell made their home in Elba, where there weren't any Jews.

Her family immediately disowned her, and for 34 years her oldest sister would not even speak to her! After being married about ten years, Jack and Janice's marriage was on shaky ground, not only because of her marrying at such a young age and marrying "outside the faith," but because neither one of them included faith in GOD as part of their marriage. Finally, the breach between Janice and her parents, brothers, and younger sister was healed, but then Janice did something else to anger her family. She became a believer in Yeshua! Doing this was a long, hard decision for her, because she feared the family alienation that would surely come again.

Janice's testimony has many extraordinary elements, but the first encounter she had with her Messiah was unmistakably supernatural. She had already begun to attend church with Jack, motivated by the fact that their oldest child insisted, "There is no God!" She had told Jack they either needed to take their children to temple or to church. Visiting churches, they found themselves "fair game" for every door-to-door visitation program in the area, which landed them in a Southern Baptist Church.

In the summer of 1976, during a revival meeting at the church, the pastor and evangelist called on them at their home. Jack gave his heart to the Lord that night, much to Janice's surprise. She thought he was already a Christian. She incorrectly reasoned that she was born a Jew, so Jack was born a Christian. She had been attending Sunday School, her purpose being to convince the class that Jesus was not the Messiah! That class attendance grew by leaps and bounds as Sunday after Sunday, Janice took the floor and threw out her theological challenge.

Jack's salvation experience now threw out a challenge to her, because she could see the changes in his behavior, and they were all good. Her heart and her head fought a war. One day working her job, running an insurance debit, she almost had a collision with another car, which had crossed the center line and was headed straight toward her. The car was so close, she could actually see the pupils of the driver's eyes! She prepared to die, but it didn't happen. At the moment of anticipated impact, she heard a distinct voice, **"I didn't promise you another day. Make a decision!"** She had no doubt Who was speaking and what He meant. She also knew her escape from death was a miracle. "The ball was in her court."

Revival services at her church were still going on. Janice no longer doubted that Jesus was the Messiah, but she wasn't ready to pay the price of losing her family again. She resisted the pull of the Holy Spirit at the altar call each night. Finally, after an encounter with the Lord in the middle of the night, she got on her knees and yielded, giving her life completely to Yeshua, her Messiah.

Janice and Jack's marriage would most likely have "crashed and burned" without Jesus as Savior and Lord, but at the time I met Janice, they had been married 40 years and had produced four children who married and gave them grandchildren.

I was so impressed with this bold, attractive Jewish woman when I heard her speak. I got her e-mail address and began to correspond with her. She had given her testimony in churches many times since becoming a believer in 1976, but she was discouraged that more Christians were not interested in their Jewish roots. It greatly encouraged her when our busy lives intersected. There were occasional times of joint ministry in the months ahead, but the next big step happened the very same day my Kawai grand piano was delivered to the house.

My e-mail name at that time was Mizpah Tikvah (watchtower of hope), and Janice thought it would be a good name for our joint ministry. Our purpose would be to help churches reconnect with their Jewish roots and to enlist individual Christians and churches to pray for the peace of Jerusalem, according to Psalm 122:6. We would offer special presentations of Shabbat and Passover as teaching tools, showing Jesus Christ as the Jewish Messiah.

It dawned on me that Janice and I were an example of the "one new man," a concept Paul taught to the Ephesian church. As a Gentile I was an "alien from the commonwealth of Israel and a stranger from the covenants of promise, having no hope and without God in the world. But now in Messiah Yeshua I, who was once far off, had been brought near by the blood of Messiah. For He Himself is our peace, who has made both one, and has broken down the middle wall of partition [to separate Gentiles and Jews in the Temple], ... so as to create in Himself ONE NEW MAN from the two, thus making peace, and that He might reconcile us both to God in one body through the cross, thereby putting to death the enmity .... For through Him we both have access by one Spirit to the Father" (Eph. 2:11-18, personalized).

It was perfect! I am a Gentile, and Janice is a Jew. Our ministry would model the **"one new man"** that Jesus prayed for in the Garden of Gethsemane before His arrest, "that they all may be one, as You, Father, are in Me, and I in You; that they also may be one in Us, that the world may believe that You sent Me" (John 17:21). The oneness of Jew and Gentile was Jesus' hearts desire.

Our first invitation was to New Ebenezer Baptist Church, six miles south of Elba, for the Women's Missionary Union meeting on Labor Day, September 2, 2002. Our husbands went with us, and Curtis led the reading for the Shabbat service, dressed in a tallit and kippah. Janice lit the Sabbath candles in the traditional Jewish way, saying a blessing, and welcoming the Sabbath as has been done in Jewish homes on Fridays at sundown for thousands of years. She then shared the traditional braided challah bread which she baked herself. The two loaves symbolized the double portion of manna collected by the Israelites in the wilderness before the Sabbath. As is customary in typical Jewish homes, our husbands pronounced tender blessings over us, their wives, and we did the same for our husbands.

Next on the program was my sharing about the unique connection Alabama has with Israel. In the midst of World War II in 1943, Alabama led the nation as the first state in America to officially call for the establishment of a Jewish homeland in Palestine. This official call was set forth in a unanimous Joint Resolution of the Alabama State Senate and the Alabama House of Representatives, approved and signed by the Governor on June 10, 1943, **five years prior** to the establishment of the modern State of Israel on May 14, 1948! A copy of the resolution was forwarded to the President of the United States, to the Senate Co-Chairmen of the American Palestine Committees, and to the British Embassy in Washington for transmission to the proper authorities in London. By making this resolution Alabama set the right example for future United Nations action in the Partition Plan of 1947.

After my Alabama history lesson Janice gave an overview of the history of the church in regard to the Jewish people and the instances of anti-Semitism that have resulted in Jewish resistance to the gospel. She shared some personal experiences with anti-Semitism. As a 12-year-old, the first day she attended school in their new town, a boy called her a "dirty Jew." Janice said, "When he called me that, I knocked out his two front teeth! That's exactly what my dad told me to do, if I was ever called a dirty Jew!"

Janice related another instance of anti-Semitism, which reared its head when she gave her testimony to a church in Enterprise, Alabama. After her speech, people came up to Janice to thank her for coming. She was feeling good about this warm reception, but then a lady said to her, "I always thought that all Jews had horns." "The lady was dead serious and really believed this to be true," Janice said. She explained to the lady the origin of that ridiculous rumor, but it amazed Janice that any intelligent or even an ignorant person could possibly believe such a lie!

At the very same meeting, another lady told her how much she enjoyed Janice's testimony and added, "If **all** Jews were like you, we could love them." Janice told me, "Now how do you respond to a comment like that? What the lady thought was a compliment was actually the opposite." These two instances of anti-Semitism happened in a church setting. That really wasn't surprising, however, in view of the anti-Semitic history of the Church. (See Chapter 6.)

Going back to our program at New Ebenezer Baptist Church, next came the handing out of prayer commitment cards. The people signed them, promising to pray for the peace (salvation) of Jerusalem. I closed the meeting by blowing the shofar, a ram's horn, sometimes called "trumpet" in Scripture. This distinctively Jewish instrument was an appropriate way to end. Afterward I had an assortment of books ready to sell as an additional way to educate the church on her Jewish roots.

On our way home I reported to Curtis that I had made $27 from the sale. Curtis exclaimed, "Just as you said that, we passed a 27 sign!" This was another one of those God-incidences. Both of us agreed the 27-27 was a funny little clue from the Lord, affirming our ministry that night.

Mizpah Tikvah Ministries was getting a solid foundation. Our husbands were supporting us, and now both Jack and Curtis were going to accompany us to an important conference the very next month.

13

"In Whose Heart are the Highways to Zion"

Jack and Janice and Curtis and I attended a conference in Point Harbor, North Carolina, presented by Ebenezer Emergency Fund-Operation Exodus on October 17-20, 2002. How interesting that our first place of ministry with Mizpah Tikvah was at New **Ebenezer** Baptist Church. Now we were going to attend a conference of the **Ebenezer** Emergency Fund. Two Ebenezers – again no coincidence, but another God-incidence.

What is this word "Ebenezer?" It means "stone of help." It was the memorial stone set up by Samuel to commemorate the divine assistance to Israel in their defeat of the Philistines at **Mizpah** in Benjamin (I Sam. 7:12). Ah! Here was another little clue from the Almighty that we were on the right track in our ministry. This site of Israel's military victory was at Mizpah, the place where their hope was renewed, and our ministry, Watchtower of **Hope** (Mizpah Tikvah), would also be a means of hope to God's people, both the Church and the Jews. When Samuel set up the stone to mark the spot of victory, he said, "Thus far the Lord has helped us." And we could say, "Thus far the Lord has helped **us**!" We could hardly wait to see what the Lord would do next in our ministry.

Yes, we were definitely on the right track. We were on a holy highway. It reminded me of God's Word, "Happy are those … in whose heart are the highways to Zion" (Ps. 84:5-7, NRSV). And the theme of the conference was "A Holy Highway Home." Elsa Scheller, the widow of the founder, Gustav Scheller, was one of the speakers. God called them to help the Jewish people return to Israel, or to *make aliyah*,[38] in fulfillment of Biblical prophecy. Beginning in 1991, Gustav and Elsa pioneered this work in the former Soviet Union. They poured their great wealth into the purchase of ships to bring the olim home to Israel. The Schellers saw this as a preparation for the coming of the Lord. Jesus foretold that the Jews must be back in their ancient homeland to welcome their Messiah (Matt. 23:39). Other ministries understand this and also are assisting the Jews to return home.

Gustav and Elsa Scheller, founders of Ebenezer Operation Exodus, at Trinity Church

Curtis and I had a history with Gustav and Elsa Scheller. Back in 1997, we invited them to Trinity Church to speak about their Ebenezer ministry. They came on August 3ʳᵈ, the date I set as "Honor Israel Day" in our church. After they got there, Gustav said that August 3ʳᵈ was also "Honor Israel Day" on the Moravian calendar! (The Moravians have their roots in the Czech reformer, John Hus, who preceded Martin Luther as a reformer 60 years before the protestant reformation.[39] John Wesley was impacted by the Moravian missionaries in the 18ᵗʰ century, which led to his conversion experience.) The significance of setting August 3ʳᵈ as our "Honor Israel Day" on the same day set by the revered Moravians was yet another confirming clue from God that I was right on track in my Mizpah ministry.

At the conference in North Carolina, Elsa spoke about hers and Gustav's initial call to the aliyah ministry. While attending a Bible college in the USA in 1982, the Lord revealed to them His plan for the return of His chosen people to the Promised Land, and that they would be involved in a practical way. They were arrested by the Word of God, "See, I will beckon to the Gentiles, I will lift up My banner to the people; they will bring your sons in their arms and carry your daughters on their shoulders" (Isa. 29:22). Elsa and Gustav responded to God's beckoning.

It was during an International Prayer Conference in Jerusalem in 1991, in the middle of the Gulf War, when 120 intercessors from many nations had gathered to pray for Israel, that the Lord spoke to Gustav and told him **now** was the time to bring home His people from the disintegrating Soviet Union.

Elsa reminisced that they were sitting in the basement of the hotel with gas masks on, as missiles were striking Jerusalem! She remarked how amazing it was that in the basement there was an atmosphere of peace and the presence of the Lord. Gustav shared the Lord's revelation with Johannes Facius, the spiritual head of the conference. Facius thought, "Who among the Jewish people would like to return to a nation being bombarded with Saddam Hussein's Scud missiles? And how on earth would we be able to transport

Jews right in the middle of the war?"[40]   To his astonishment, however, out of his mouth came a hearty agreement with Gustav. The next day an offering was received from the 120 intercessors for $30,000! (By 2011, Ebenezer had assisted 130,000 Jews to immigrate to Israel. The ministry has 13 bases and 47 regional representatives in the Former Soviet Union.)[41]

It is true that God scattered His people from Israel. Moses first warned the Israelites that they would be taken from their land because of their idolatry and disobedience. "Then the Lord will scatter you among all peoples, from one end of the earth to the other ..." (Deut. 28:64a). This happened in the Assyrian captivity in 722 B.C., the Babylonian captivity in 586 B.C., then again in A.D. 70 and A.D. 135 by the Romans. The Jews outside the land of Israel from those scatterings are considered to be living in the Diaspora (dispersion).

Moses also foretold the plan of God to regather His people back to the land when they turned their hearts toward Him. "... the Lord will bring you back from captivity, and have compassion on you, and gather you again from all the nations where the Lord your God has scattered you. .... Then the Lord your God will bring you to the land which your fathers possessed, and you shall possess it. He will prosper you and multiply you more than your fathers" (Deut. 30:3, 5). Moses went on to say that God would circumcise their hearts to love Him. That is also the pattern in the prophecy of Ezekiel 36:25-28, first the regathering to the land and then the regathering to God Himself. Jewish Rabbis say that Ezekiel 36 is the "I will" chapter, because God declares fifteen times in this chapter **He will** bring His people back!

At the Ebenezer conference we were inspired by the stories of the "fishermen" in the former Soviet Union. Their guiding Scripture was:

> "Therefore, behold, the days are coming," says the Lord, "that it shall no more be said, 'The Lord lives who brought up the children of Israel from the land of Egypt,' but, 'The Lord lives who brought up the children of Israel from **the land of the north** [former Soviet Union] and from all the lands where He had driven

them.' For I will bring them back into their land which I gave to their fathers. Behold, I will send for many **fishermen**," says the Lord, "and they shall fish them; and afterward I will send for many **hunters**, and they shall hunt them from every mountain and every hill, and out of the holes of the rock" (Jer. 16:14-16).

We learned that the fishermen are the ones who search out the Jews in hidden places, read to them what God says about their return to their ancient homeland, and assist them through the red tape and transportation, whether by ship, plane, or bus, in preparation for aliyah.

The "hunters" in the past have been Pharaoh, Haman, Hitler, Stalin, Hussein, and other anti-Semites up to the present day. They prey on those left behind. God allows the hunters to come as a last resort to drive His people home. It often takes this kind of pressure for families to pull up roots and obey God, Who graciously provides a way of escape for His chosen people from every corner of the earth through various aliyah ministries. (Christian Friends of Israel and Bridges for Peace mentioned in earlier chapters also provide this ministry.)

The Ebenezer fishing teams saw the warnings of the "hunters" written on the walls in the train stations as they traveled in the Moscow region. Some epithets they saw were: "All Jews will be shot in the head by the end of this year." "We have been slaves to the Jews since 1917." "Down with the Jews."

Some may interpret this passage in Jeremiah, referring to the "hunters," as the time of the Babylonian Exile. However, this "second Exodus" could not have been the Babylonian exile, because then the Israelites were led captive to only one nation, Babylon, and it was not in the north. This passage could only speak of the modern-day regathering of the Jews to Israel, which is increasing every year and is a fulfillment of hundreds of biblical prophecies. Every evangelical Christian sees this phenomenon as a portent of the Second Coming of the Lord!

At the conference the fishermen told us how they find the "hidden" Jews. They are sent out two by two, a volunteer and a local person to translate. First, they pray about what to do. They find Russian villages not on the map, going even to the far reaches of Siberia. The Jews, as well as other persecuted minorities in Russia, hid from Joseph Stalin, who killed over 46 million of them. Many are still hiding, and the fishermen go to find them. They may have to visit homes three times to convince the Jews to make aliyah. The people are touched that a person from the West would come such a long way to help them and want to know why. When the fishermen speak the Word of God and say "**Your** God," they change their minds and want to make aliyah.

The Ebenezer workers help them find papers which prove their Jewishness. They assist in obtaining passports and visas and getting the olim on buses. At Odessa, Ukraine, they stay in a camp four or five days. While there, the young fishermen teach them Scripture and the songs of Zion. Finally, comes the time to board the ship to take them to Israel!

The speakers showed how the aliyah ministry is a very holy work for the Lord, and that He is bringing His chosen ones home on a "holy highway." The prophets mentioned the "holy highway" many times. Isaiah paints a beautiful picture of the returning exiles:

A highway shall be there, and a road, and it shall be called the Highway of Holiness.

> The unclean shall not pass over it,
> but it shall be for others.
> ….But the redeemed shall walk there.
> And the ransomed of the Lord shall return
> And come to Zion with singing,
> with everlasting joy on their heads.
> They shall obtain joy and gladness,
> and sorrow and sighing
> shall flee away (Isa. 35:8-10).

The Lord started drawing His people in the Diaspora back to the Land in the late 1800s, when the Jews were fleeing pogroms (organized massacres) in Eastern Europe and Yemen. The second wave of aliyah was mostly from Russia because of pogroms. The third was after World War I. During World War II – 1939 to 1948 – approximately 480,000 Jews fled the Nazi Holocaust, both legally and illegally. The floodgates opened after Israel declared statehood in 1948. Out of the ashes of the Holocaust, Israel was reborn as a modern nation. By 1951, the immigrants – 687,000 – more than doubled the Jewish population of the country. And they continued to come. A great deliverer like Moses was not leading them, but it was the sovereign hand of God, fulfilling His word.

When Israel declared itself a nation on May 14, 1948, an invitation was extended to the Arabs living there to become equal citizens in the new state. Unfortunately, most of them fled the country, encouraged by Arab leaders to come out until the war was won, and then they could go back to their homes. Many stayed, however, and became Israeli citizens. According to the Israeli Central Bureau of Statistics, on the eve of 2012, Israel's population stood at 7,836,000 people. Some 5,901,000 (75.3%) are Jews, and 1,610,000 (20.5%) are Arabs. Israeli Arabs have fared well in the State of Israel.

The Arabs who left in 1948 were not welcomed into the surrounding Arab countries. They languished in refugee camps on the border and "were deliberately used as a political pawn by the Arabs at the United Nations. ... One day's oil revenue from the wealthy Middle East nations ... could have covered the cost of resettling all ... the dislocated Palestinians. But not one penny was forthcoming ..."[42]

"The number of Jews fleeing Arab countries for Israel in the years following Israel's independence was roughly equal to the number of Arabs leaving Palestine. Many Jews were allowed to take little more than the shirts on their backs. ... Of the 820,000 Jewish refugees, 586,000 were resettled in Israel at great expense and without any offer of compensation from the Arab governments who confiscated their possessions." They have never been compensated.[43]

One outstanding story of aliyah is Operation Magic Carpet. When the people of Yemen heard that Israel was now a nation in

1948, they began to make a mass movement to the city of Aden. One of the refugees tells the story: A letter came with the news, urging the people to go to Israel, because "without you Israel will not be redeemed." The people sold their houses and possessions and left their synagogues to the Gentiles. They prayed for forgiveness, because they believed that the Land of Israel would atone for all sins. They took the Scrolls of the Law with them, but if they could not take them, they buried them. The people camped on the way and prayed beneath the canopy of heaven. There came a day when they had no bread. They cried out to the Lord, and while they were still praying, Arabs came and brought them food. Many became sick on the way. Some women gave birth while riding on their donkeys. A messenger from Israel came and promised them that none of the Jews would be left in Yemen, and all their troubles would end in a little while.

The Jews of Yemen came to Aden, bruised and robbed and penniless, even most of the rich people. They camped on the desert sands in large numbers under the sky with mighty sandstorms raging about them. They prayed for aliyah, to fly "on eagles' wings" to their country.

The airlift was organized with converted bombers, containing only benches, enabling up to 130 people to be loaded into one plane. The people smiled and explained God's promise, "... they shall mount up with wings as eagles." Altogether, 48,000 Jews were flown to Israel from Yemen. By September 1950, Yemen was empty of Jews. The "Magic Carpet" could be rolled up and the eagles could rest. No Jews were left in Yemen. God had spoken and fulfilled His promise "I will say to the South, keep not back" (Isa. 43:6).[44]

Another exciting Exodus II story is Operation Solomon. This happened as recently as May 24, 1991. In just 36 hours 14,200 Ethiopians were airlifted from Addis Ababa to Israel. It took 41 flights, and seven babies were born in the air! One Boeing 747 carried a record number of people, over 1,000 on a single flight.

The entire Ethiopian community had been snatched from the threat of civil war and famine and arrived safely in Israel. What a miracle!

At the Ebenezer conference we learned, according to the Israeli Absorption Ministry, that 98 per cent of the olim are employed by six months' time. Within two years' time 80 per cent of families have bought a home. And there are enough world-class musicians in Jerusalem to staff 50 orchestras! The tiny little miracle nation of Israel has absorbed well over one million olim since 1991, bringing the Jewish population to nearly six million Jews today.

The end result of this aliyah ministry is described by Isaiah in his famous evangelistic passage: "How beautiful upon the mountains are the feet of him who brings good news.... Your watchmen lift up their voices. ... When the Lord brings back Zion. ... the Lord has comforted His people, He has redeemed Jerusalem. The Lord has made bare His holy arm in the eyes of all the nations, and all the ends of the earth shall see the salvation of our God" (Isa. 52:7-10). Yes, God is glorified in bringing His people home in the sight of all nations. First, home to the Land, and then home to their God!

We eagerly await the national salvation of Israel that the Apostle Paul foretold, "And so all Israel shall be saved" (Rom. 11:26). We want to obey God's admonition to provoke the Jews to jealousy (Rom. 11:11) and not be conceited (Rom. 11:18), so they will want our and **their** Messiah! This reinforces our motivation to assist ministries like Ebenezer in getting the Jews home to Israel.

It is sad that most people, even Christians, do not realize that the steadily increasing aliyah going on today is a fulfillment of Bible prophecy and is one of the most exciting indicators of the soon return of our Lord to planet earth! Jack, Janice, Curtis, and I were greatly inspired by the conference and learned so much about God's activity in the earth today. We were admonished to take three things home with us from the conference:

First, there is no question about God's agenda, and what is at the top of the list. We would take this new knowledge home with us. God is making a Holy Highway to bring the Jews home. In his book, *Let My People Go!*[45] Tom Hess lists 700 verses from Scripture

where God promises the land of Canaan to His chosen people and
commands or encourages them to return to the land of Israel which
He gave to them as an everlasting possession. The sheer number
of the verses, possibly more verses on this subject than any other
subject in the Bible, tells you what is closest to God's heart. It
should be close to **our** hearts.

Secondly, all of us should be watchmen (Isa. 62: 6-7). "I have
set watchmen on your walls, O Jerusalem; they shall never hold
their peace day or night. You who make mention of the Lord,
do not keep silent, and give Him no rest till He establishes and
till He makes Jerusalem a praise in the earth [the future national
salvation of Israel]" (Isa. 62: 6-7). This involves prayer, watching
world events and God's hand in them, teaching the church our
responsibility toward the Jews, and warning the Jews to escape
while there is still time to come home to Israel.

Thirdly, we cannot carry out His call without the power of the
Holy Spirit. The four of us left Point Harbor, knowing we had
been entrusted with a message close to the heart of God. With
the guidance and strength of the Holy Spirit, we planned to share
it, because "Happy are those … in whose heart are the highways
to Zion."

14

Mizpah Tikvah Ministry Takes Off

At the Ebenezer conference I had been asked to play the piano. I played "Shaalu Shalom Yerushalayim (Pray for the Peace of Jerusalem)" and "Chariots of Fire." Someone created words to this beautiful tune. The chorus ended with, "Ignite me and make me a chariot of fire!" This was my prayer. Janice and I could see the answer in the Holy Spirit's guidance of our Mizpah Tikvah Ministry. We began to get numerous speaking engagements in the weeks and months ahead. Our "chariots" were about to take off!

Both of us had many speaking engagements before we met, but now that our ministries were merged, we saw the Lord using us in a greater way. We spoke at Ino Baptist, Janice's church. This huge church out in the middle of nowhere, close to Elba, was fertile ground to plant in because the pastor had a practice of leading a group to Israel every year. I led in singing the Jewish songs and gave a Bible lesson on our Jewish Roots. Janice told about the Miracle Nation of Israel and gave a Shabbat presentation. At the conclusion Janice taught the congregation to dance the Hora, as I accompanied on the piano with "Hava Nagila (Let's Rejoice)." It was a good meeting and stirred up a lot of interest. Even the pastor was getting an education in the Jewish roots of the church. We spoke there again and gave a Passover Seder presentation.

Probably the biggest meeting we had was a two-day seminar at Good News Church in Tupelo, Mississippi, in April, 2003. Our friends, Ruth and Bill Kitchens, who for years hosted our church cell group after Curtis and I gave our hearts to Jesus in 1968, sponsored us. There was a big promotion preceding the seminar. Janice gave her testimony at the church in February, and we both were interviewed at the local television station two times in March. I even got to sing some songs from my recording, *Hatikva!*

Before the seminar we compiled folders that covered every aspect of our ministry – a brochure with our testimonies, etc., song sheet to the *Hatikva* CD, "Guide to Traditional Shabbat Service," Challah recipe, and sheets entitled "Why Should Christians Know About Their Jewish Roots?" "Christianity is Jewish," "Let Us Learn Hebrew," "How Did Our Jewish Roots Get Cut Off?" "Prayer for Israel," "Feasts of the Lord," "The Truth about the Arab-Jew Conflict in the Middle East," "The Error of Replacement Theology" by BFP, "Sources of Information," and "Suggested Reading List." What an education one could receive just reading these materials!

But how in the world would we cover all these subjects? Very fast, that's how! People were fascinated. Our sale materials were grabbed up. I sold books and CDs, and Janice stocked the table with Judaica – mini-Torah[46] scroll, tallits, Hannukah menorahs,[47] Star of David jewelry, and mezuzahs.[48] We were not out to make a profit, because we kept re-investing in more sale items for future seminars.

The seminar was a great success, ending with a full-blown Passover Seder. About 70 people attended. Our husbands were there, supporting us at the head table.

More meetings followed in Opp, Alabama, and Chipley, Florida. At the second meeting in Opp at First Baptist Church, we spoke to the seniors group, and my subject was "Church, Be a Ruth." This small book in the Bible of only four chapters is a beautiful picture of how the Church should relate to the Jewish people, their "parents" in the faith, so to speak. It is historically true, of course, but it can also be seen as an allegory of the Church and Israel. Naomi represents Israel, Ruth represents the Church, and Boaz represents the Messiah, our Kinsman-Redeemer.

Naomi and her husband Elimelech left Bethlehem ("House of Bread") because of the famine and traveled to Moab, a pagan country, to settle down. This journey represents the Jewish people in the Diaspora, away from Israel. Naomi's husband and two sons died. She was bitter. Then she heard there was food in Bethlehem again, so she decided to leave Moab and go there. Her two daughters-in-law, Ruth and Orpah, started to go with her, but Naomi told them to go back to their families and their gods. Orpah did that, but Ruth would not turn back, insisting, "Entreat me not to leave you ... for wherever you go I will go; and wherever you lodge, I will lodge. Your people shall be my people, and your God, my God" (Ruth 1:16). This is a beautiful picture of the Church helping the Jewish people to return to their ancient land, comforting them, and identifying with them in their suffering. That is exactly what Corrie ten Boom and Lydia Prince did. (See Chapter 2.) In a literal sense, this is exactly what ministries like Ebenezer Operation Exodus do. And this is what I myself wanted to do, as Isaiah prophesied:

"Comfort, yes, comfort My people!" says your God.
"Speak comfort to Jerusalem, and cry out to her,
That her warfare is ended, that her iniquity is pardoned;
For she has received from the Lord's hand double for all her sins" (Isa. 40:1-2).

To continue the story – Ruth and Naomi had nothing when they returned to Bethlehem, but Ruth went out to glean in the fields of Naomi's close relative, Boaz. Ruth, through Boaz's generosity, provided for the impoverished Naomi. Is the Church doing that for the ones to whom we are indebted today, the Jewish people? The allegory unfolds to reveal Ruth's salvation. (Because Israel rejected their Messiah, the message of salvation was taken to the Gentiles.) The Gentile Ruth and the Jewish Boaz marry, showing the Bride of Christ and her Kinsman-Redeemer. However, this union would not have come about without Naomi's kinship with Boaz. The Church would not have known the Savior without the Jewish nation, who was the trustee of the Scriptures and the one through whom the Messiah, the Apostles, and the Church came! Also, Ruth needed Naomi's instruction in how to approach Boaz in a marriage proposal. And today, the Church needs the Jewish people to show them many treasures in the Scriptures that they so revere.

Ruth was saved, but someone else was saved also! The salvation of Naomi is implied in the final chapter of Ruth. When Ruth bore Boaz a **son**, the neighbor women came to Naomi and said, "Blessed be the Lord, who has not left you this day without a "close" relative [kinsman **redeemer** or **Savior**]; and may his name [the Child] be famous in Israel! And may he be to you a **restorer of life** and a nourisher of your old age, for your daughter-in-law who loves you, who is better to you than seven sons, has borne him" (Ruth 4:14-15).

The allegorical meaning shows that Israel will be restored (or saved) because of the Child! "For unto us a Child is born, unto us a Son is given. ..." (Isa. 9:6). The women further exclaimed, "There is a **son born to Naomi**" (vs. 17). Naomi was not the mother, but the grandmother, so why did the neighbor women say this? For one thing, Naomi became the baby Obed's wet-nurse! Amazing, but true (vs. 16). Obed was the grandfather of King David (vss. 17-22). Through his lineage came Yeshua of Nazareth, and He was called the Son of David. His name is the most famous name in Israel. We see through the allegory that because of the kindness of the Church, Israel will be brought to her Kinsman-Redeemer, Yeshua, and be saved! In our day, it is only fitting that the gospel that went out from Jerusalem should go full circle back to Jerusalem. The Jews brought the gospel to the Gentiles, and the Gentiles should take it back to the Jews!

I emphasized to the seniors' group at Opp that the Church can have two responses in our relationship with the Jews. Either we act like Ruth or like Orpah. Orpah went back to her people and her gods. It is sad to say, but since the Church was cut off from her Jewish roots, it adopted many pagan practices, and some continue today. Janice and I are trying to help the Church to follow the example of Ruth, not Orpah.

My friend, Diane McNeil, from Memphis, has written a verse-by-verse account of Ruth, as the Lord showed it to her over ten years.

I was privileged to read the manuscript before it was published and was amazed at the revelation she had. The book is entitled *Ruth 3,000 Years of Sleeping Prophecy Awakened.*[49] Her 12 chapters coincide with 12 segments entitled, "Did you Know?" which is a Christian primer of Jewish life and customs. This bonus section is of special value to the Christian who really wants to seek common ground with God's chosen people. Diane had already been doing special projects for the Jewish people, both in Memphis and in Israel, and she continues her work today. Our church had the opportunity to get in on one of her projects to buy an ambulance for Israel back in the 1990s. If there ever was a "Ruth" Christian, Diane is a perfect example. I marvel that God gave me the blessing and privilege of knowing her and reading that early manuscript. I heartily recommend Diane's book.

Ruth means "friend." We Gentile Christians, like Ruth, have been adopted into the Jewish covenant family. We should get to know the family and stand by them in their time of trouble. We should help them get back to the Land and learn from them. Finally, as the "Son was born to Naomi," we should let the Messiah be "born" to the Jews through us!

Janice is a Messianic Jew, and I strive to be a "Ruth" Christian. Janice and I started thinking about more ways we could help the Jewish people and the State of Israel. Going back to the Land looked so appealing. Janice had never been to Israel. "This should not be!" I thought. By now I had been to Israel four times, and I greatly desired that Janice should experience her Jewish roots in the Jewish land. In our hearts were the "highways to Zion." It was only a matter of time until the Lord made it possible for us to take a "chariot" to the Land of Israel!

15

Jerusalem, Here We Come!

It was my early morning devotional time that day on September 9, 2003. I was seriously seeking the Lord for direction for my life, and he spoke to me through several Bible verses. In my journal I wrote, "Matt. 12:46-50 – I am Jesus' sister if I do His will." The next entry was **"Deut. 31:7-8 – I am to go with Jesus (Joshua = Yeshua) to Israel, and God will be with me and not forsake me. I should call Helena* and see if Janice and I can go with her."** Following this I wrote, "Gal. 3:7-9 – I'm related to Abraham by my faith, so I should obey and go to Israel!" Then I wrote, "Jer. 12:7 – The Jews are 'the dearly beloved of My soul,' but He has allowed hard times for them from their enemies. I need to go to their aid." My final verse was Malachi 3:1 - "Behold, I will send My messenger ... even the messenger of the covenant." In the margin I had written, "Messenger Girl."

"Wow!" I thought. "All these verses seem to indicate the Lord's desire for me to go to Israel again! And this time I can take Janice, and the Lord will provide."

I did call Helena, thinking that she may have a trip to Israel planned, and possibly Janice and I could go with her. She knew the ropes, and I thought she could get us the best price and help us arrange it. Surprisingly, she gave me the dates on her calendar that were cleared for a trip to Israel right away, September 29 – October 10. Goodness! That was only 20 days away. I checked my calendar and checked with Janice. Everyone was good to go. The next words out of my friend's mouth floored me. She told me

---

*   Name changed

her husband wanted to pay our way! Oh, what a miracle-working God we serve!

The saga continued. I met Helena at a restaurant on September 11, and she gave me a check, made out to the church, for $3,333.33! She mailed a check in the same amount to Janice's church for her, and she also mailed a check of that amount to another lady who was going with us. Amazing - $10,000.00! That was besides her own airfare. She said, " Six weeks ago a prophetess told me that I will help three women. Well, this is it."

I was on cloud nine. However, the next night Helena called and said that maybe we should not go. She saw Yasser Arafat on T.V., calling for a million martyrs to march to Jerusalem!

Then came a second warning. Jennifer Griffin called me and told me it was the worst it had been in Israel. A suicide bombing had just occurred at the German Colony shops only a few blocks from her house! She said she could feel the explosion. An outstanding doctor was killed in the attack at the Café Hillel, Dr. David Applebaum. He had taken his daughter out for coffee and a father-daughter talk on the eve of her wedding! (A very heart-rending and graphic account of this tragedy is given in Jennifer's book.[50]) Jennifer talked with the devastated family afterward. Dr. Applebaum had the reputation of being the first man at the scene of suicide bombings, and now he had become a victim himself.

Should we heed Jennifer's warning? Janice, Jack, Curtis, and I prayed and waited to hear from God. We decided to make a decision by 3:00 o'clock the next afternoon. We had our answer at 10:00 in the morning. I turned to Isaiah 33 and read the passage from verses 17-22. "Your eyes will see the king in His beauty ... Look upon Zion, the city of our appointed feasts. (We would be there during a feast.) **Your eyes will see Jerusalem, a quiet home** ... For the Lord is our Judge, the Lord is our Lawgiver, the Lord is our King; **He will save us.**" The answer to the question, "Should we go to Israel?" was a resounding "Yes!"

We had God's green light, but for some reason Janice didn't seem to be very excited about the trip. Here is her story: "I was taking my friend Geneva back to Birmingham to the airport to fly back to Kentucky. Nina Brown rode with me to keep me company. On the way back home we stopped at the IHOP in Montgomery. I had been given the **desire of my heart**, yet I was unable to get excited about the trip to Israel. I think I just couldn't wrap my head around the fact that it would actually happen.

"When we pulled into the parking lot of the IHOP, all of a sudden I heard the music to 'Hava Nagila.' I couldn't tell where it was coming from, because I'm deaf in my right ear and cannot tell the direction of sounds. I asked Nina where the music was coming from. She said it was from the cell phone. At the time I had been using a loaner cell phone while mine was being repaired. I said to Nina, 'No way.' She said it was indeed my cell phone. I picked it up and just looked at it, finally answering the phone.

"I don't remember who called, because I was so perplexed that it had rung with that tune. I sat there looking at the phone. I thought I remembered the meaning of the words, 'Hava Nagila,' but I wasn't sure. I called Nancy Petrey and asked her. She responded, **'Let us rejoice!'** When Nancy said the words, it was like the Lord smacked me on the side of my head and said, **'For heaven's sake, I have given you the desire of your heart! The least you can do is get excited!'**"

I was thrilled to hear Janice say that. At last! Janice and I, the "one new man," were of one accord.

On September 23-24, Janice and I spoke at the North Mississippi Worship Center in Amory, Mississippi. Our hosts were Bill and Charleen Watkins, former members of Trinity Church. Other friends came, including some from Trinity. We had a fantastic time, and the church gave us a wonderful "send-off" to Israel with a hefty offering for our ministry there.

The dates for the trip were September 29 – October 13, two whole weeks. As it turned out, only Janice and I could make the trip. Something came up, and Helena and the other lady could not go. Confirming scriptures continued to come. I turned to Isaiah 48:16-17, "... And now the Lord God and His Spirit have sent Me [meaning Jesus, but we were His representatives]. Thus says the Lord, your Redeemer, the Holy One of Israel: 'I am the Lord your God ... **Who leads you by the way you should go.**'" Yes, we trusted the Lord to orchestrate our steps.

The day we boarded the plane in Atlanta I was dressed in all black with a long skirt, long sleeves, and white cuffs and collar. We were hoping to visit in the Orthodox community in Jerusalem, and this was appropriate attire. Their dress code required dresses with high necks, sleeves covering the elbows and long skirts. Unfortunately, this gave me the appearance of a missionary, and that raised red flags with the security people at El Al Airlines in New York.

The security man asked the purpose of our trip. I innocently said, "To bless Israel." Janice had the presence of mind to say "We're going as tourists." I bumbled again when asked why I was learning Hebrew. I said, "To be able to communicate with the man on the street." Janice rolled her eyes. "Oy!" She whispered, "You look like a dreaded missionary." Janice was questioned about what holidays she observed. After answering, "The Jewish ones," he asked, "And other holidays?" She replied, "My husband is not Jewish." She figured out the man was trying to prove we were Christians going to Israel to proselytize, which is technically legal, but definitely a "hot potato" in the culture. She had wisdom from above in her answers. However, we still didn't pass the test, evidently.

They must have looked upon us as a threat, because they meticulously went through all our luggage twice, and we were grilled in great detail. We were getting nervous. Departure was imminent. Finally, a 23-year-old sabra man escorted us to the plane for boarding, with only 15 to 30 minutes to spare. Ah, we made it through security just in time. Jerusalem, here we come!

After we landed at the Ben Gurion Airport in Tel Aviv, we again faced a security check. This time we made it through like we had an angel escort. An airport official said to me, "Are you alone?" When I said yes, she said "Follow me," and she led us straight through without a customs check! We went out the "group" door

Janice at Ben Gurion airport – She finally made it to Israel!

to the sherut (shared taxi), got in, and waited for a full load. Later we found out there was a strike at the airport. It didn't even affect us. We were thankful that God was orchestrating our steps.

The sherut driver let us off at the Eldan Hotel in Jerusalem, right across the street from the YMCA. A rental car came with the room, and we only had to pay the insurance, which was a mere $17 a day. What a deal. I used my debit card and rented the car for eleven days. Due to my poor hearing, I didn't realize I signed a contract for an upgraded car. (This "little mistake" caused quite a hassle a month later when we got our bank statement, because Curtis wasn't willing to ignore the overcharge.) On my part, however, ignorance was bliss, at least for a while. I was impressed with the sleek, dark gray, automatic 2004 Ford Focus car. The blissful feeling diminished, however, when I had to maneuver the car down a steep, narrow, walled driveway and take a sharp left into the garage under the hotel. Some men had to guide me. This was quite a challenging experience, not to mention embarrassing. I hadn't bargained for that. It took nerves of steel to get in and out of that garage. A few days later Janice and I regretted renting the car, because we got lost almost every time we drove it! It would have been so much easier to simply go by taxi and bus everywhere. That "good deal" was not all it was cracked up to be, we learned. However, the redeeming value of the car would be shown later near the end of our stay in Jerusalem.

The important thing was that at last we were in the Holy City, my Jewish friend and I. Ah! How good God was to us. It was during the celebration of the Jewish New Year (Rosh HaShanah). The very first night we arrived we met our Messianic Jewish tour guide, Pamela Suran. I had met her when she guided us on Lars Enarson's prayer tour in 2002. She agreed to guide Janice and me privately in Jerusalem for three days. We were going to have a licensed Israeli tour guide all to ourselves, taking us around Jerusalem in her vehicle on a custom tour of the highest quality. God was pulling out all the stops!

Pamela and her pastor husband met and married in Israel. Shmuel made aliyah from New York City after the Yom Kippur War in 1973, and Pamela came in 1980. She was fluent in Hebrew by 1989 but more so after going to Hebrew University in 1995. They have a ministry named Chazon Yerushalayim (Jerusalem Vision).[51] The Surans have spoken in churches, conferences, Bible schools, and colleges throughout the United States, Germany, Switzerland, Great Britain, Finland, and Indonesia. Pamela is a renowned prophetic artist with a ministry called "Pamela Suran, Biblical Artist,"[52] which she founded in 1986 .

One day Pamela took us to their ministry house, and she gave us coffee. Her marvelous paintings and banners were all over the walls. She said the building is owned by Christ for the Nations. Christ for the Nations! The significance of that statement by Pamela was not lost on me. That was the Bible school in Dallas where I attended the Israel in Prophecy Conference back in 1995, the place where God gave me a heart for the Jews and Israel. (See Chapter 6.)

The first night we met Pamela she took us on a brief walking tour in the oldest part of the city, Yemen Moshe. We walked a short distance from the hotel, going by Montefiore's Windmill and then by Lance Lambert's house. Lance Lambert! He was one of the speakers at the life-changing conference I attended at Christ for the Nations. Then Pamela said, "In the 80s Shmuel and I went to his house for a prayer meeting. Derek and Ruth Prince were there."

"Oh, she just mentioned two of my heroes right together, Lance Lambert and Derek Prince!" I thought. Lydia Prince was Derek's first wife who had passed away. She greatly impacted my life. (See Chapter 2.) All these connections in a short space of time were astounding. But God was directing our steps, so why should I be surprised? The Lord gave us the desires of our hearts. Here we were together, Janice and I – the "one new man" – right here in Jerusalem!

16

Looking at Our Real Estate

The next day we were stressed to the max. Using the map Pamela gave us the night before, Janice and I set out in our rental car to find Hadassah Hospital in Ein Kerem, the neighborhood of John the Baptist. We had brought several items in two suitcases to distribute to the children and new mothers. The drive that should have taken less than an hour took us two hours! We got lost several times. When we finally reached the hospital, we parked in a lower level parking lot and had to pull our suitcases a long way up the hill to the entrance. Oh, how my feet were hurting from ill-fitting shoes. Why didn't we take a taxi and get dropped off at the front door? But, no, we had this **free** rental car. Oh well, at least we saw a lot of our real estate on the prolonged drive. As a seed of Abraham through Yeshua, my Jewish Messiah, I was adopted into God's family and was the heir (Gal. 3:28) of all this beautiful Holy Land! Janice, on the other hand, was a "biological" seed of Abraham. She didn't need to be adopted. She came by her inheritance naturally. Either way, it was our inheritance, bought and paid for by the blood of Yeshua!

The lady who showed us around was from Holland. She had met Corrie ten Boom and had read *The Hiding Place*. The Lord really knew how to set things up! She first showed us the famous Chagall Windows in the synagogue. Each window was for a son of Jacob. The only bright one was the Judah window, which was lit up by the sun shining through on a hand! That spoke volumes to us. Yeshua was from the tribe of Judah. He is the Son shining on His people. God was saying to us that His hand is on His people and on **us**. We extended our hands to the sick children and their mothers as we distributed the items we had brought with us.

Janice and Nancy at Hadassah Hospital

On the way back to the hotel, we got lost again! We finally made it to our room in the Eldan Hotel and fell into bed, exhausted. My feet were hurting, and Janice's feet were swollen. It was comforting to remember Isaiah's words, "How beautiful upon the mountains are the feet of him who brings good news, who proclaims peace, who brings glad tidings of good things, who proclaims salvation, who says to Zion, 'Your God reigns!'" (Isa. 52:7). We had beautiful feet, and we had been Yeshua's messenger girls. He had ordered our steps, even if they were painful. I also felt good about being able to communicate a little in Hebrew, including asking for directions when we got lost.

After a nap, I called Jennifer Griffin. Jennifer is one of the most gracious people I have ever known, and I am blessed to be kin to her. She picked us up and took us to her house for a short visit. She had just come back from a meeting in Tel Aviv and gave us the latest news. "The Road Map is no more," she said. "Bush has pulled back." That was good news to us. The Israelis did not need to give away any more of their biblical inheritance. After all, it was **my** inheritance, too. Unfortunately, in months to come we found out the demands of the Road Map were ongoing.

Pamela Suran picked us up the second day. She was not feeling well, but she faithfully kept her appointment to guide us. This day we would be in the Old City and meet many Messianic Jews, as well as Christian Arabs, with the Lord directing our steps. Right away we met John Savage, who played keyboard at the Passover Convocation I attended the last year. He was from Georgia, a southerner, just like us.

John took us to what he called his "upper room" in the Jewish Quarter, where he led worship two nights a week. Besides being a musician, John was an artist and had some awesome paintings displayed there. He said he wanted to buy the apartment for $500,000, but it was worth millions. Oh, we were so privileged to have our personal guide to take us to a place like that. Our visit was in God's perfect timing. Pamela badly needed a place to lie down and be refreshed, so she could finish the tour with us. I suggested that John play the keyboard and lead us in worship, and he agreed. As Pamela lay quietly on the sofa, we were brought into the presence of God by John's playing and worship. In that atmosphere we prayed for Pamela's healing. After this Pamela was able to resume the tour. God had ordered our steps to the "upper room."

Pamela took us back to the Old City early the next day to see some places not usually seen in the average tour. We parked at Zion Gate and walked a path hugging the southern wall of the City. There was no one around. She showed us the unearthed houses next to the wall where the believers of Acts 2:46 were going from house to house. How interesting. We walked through the Pedestrian Gate on the recently unearthed street where Yeshua walked. After going through the Ophel Archaeological Park, we continued walking around the southern wall to the southern stairs of the Temple, leading up to the double Hulda Gates. Some scholars believe this is where Peter preached on the Day of Pentecost.[53] I wasn't sure I agreed.

Back in July of 1992, our family visited the Biblical Arts Center in Dallas and saw the magnificent life-size "Miracle at Pentecost" painting, measuring 124 feet wide by 20 feet tall, featuring more than 200 biblical characters. The artist, Torger Thompson, related in his book, *Creation of a Masterpiece*,[54] that he was trying to paint the scene in the upper room and then realized that 120 people could not assemble in a room. Finally, he consulted a Rabbi who assured him he knew the New Testament as well as the Old Testament. The Rabbi said Pentecost was a Jewish festival, having been celebrated over 1,000 years prior to the coming of the Spirit. He believed the Pentecost of Acts 2 happened in Solomon's Portico in the Temple, a place where a huge crowd could gather. He went on, "If you fellows would read it the way us fellows wrote it, you wouldn't have so many problems with it. Your 'New Testament' is a Jewish book, and it relates in Acts 2:2, 'And suddenly there came a sound from heaven as of a mighty rushing wind, and it filled all *the house* where they were sitting.' Well, when we Jews use the expression 'the house' we invariably mean our Temple. That's *the house!*'" Torger decided to draw the miracle at the Temple, not the upper room.

Trying to harmonize the three possible locations of the miracle at Pentecost – the upper room, Solomon's Porch, and the southern stairs of the Temple, I pondered the evidence. According to Acts 1:12-14, after Yeshua ascended back to heaven, the disciples, including Mary, the women, and Yeshua's brothers, assembled in an upper room in a prayer meeting. I reasoned that at some point they must have moved to an area in the Temple courtyard where Yeshua used to teach the crowds. Perhaps it was Solomon's Portico, as that rabbi believed, where they awaited the coming of the Holy Spirit that Yeshua had promised.

When the Holy Spirit came and baptized them, tongues of fire were on their heads! This fire on their heads must have set them on fire inside, because their tongues began to speak "the wonderful works of God" (Acts 2:11). As if that wasn't enough of a miracle, their speaking was in languages they had not learned! The Jews who had come from far and wide to celebrate Shavuot, their Feast of Weeks (or Pentecost, a Greek name), were attracted by this phenomenon of fire on the heads of people who were speaking languages that matched their own, no matter what country they had come from. This amazing thing drew them to Solomon's Portico.

The crowd continued to grow, but where could this huge crowd be accommodated? Trying to visualize this astounding event on the Day of Pentecost, I reasoned that perhaps Peter and the 120 people, followed by the huge crowd, took the southern Hulda exit gate, and Peter preached on the southern stairs, right where Pamela had taken us. This scenario of the Day of Pentecost is speculation, but at least I am convinced of the location of the mass baptisms that day.

We know from the Bible that after Peter's sermon, 3,000 were baptized (Acts 2:41). They were immersed in water, not sprinkled, so where could that many people be baptized? Pamela

Nancy & Janice on the Southern Steps of the Temple

showed us the large and numerous mikvaot (baptismal pools) right there below the southern steps. What a convenient place for the mass baptisms. In the days following, Peter, the other Apostles, and the new believers who had received the baptism of the Holy Spirit would continue to go to the earthly Temple and pray, but now the Spirit-filled believers had themselves become the **living and eternal** Temple of God!

Then Pamela showed us something wonderful. At the base of the southern stairs a fig tree and a vine were growing up out of a mikveh (baptism pool) through the iron grating on top. The Lord revealed to her that this green growth represented the growth of the Messianic Jews. The vine represented Yeshua (John 15:1), and the

Pamela Suran shows Nancy a vine and a fig tree grow-ing out of a mikveh (baptismal pool)

fig tree represented Israel and the Jewish people (Matt. 24:32, 34). Yeshua promised that this "generation" or "race" [of Jews] would not pass away until He returns. That means that Jews are virtually indestructible, because Yeshua is preserving them for His Second Coming. It is exciting to see the increase of Messianic Jewish believers, because that is a sign of His imminent return!

We saw the unearthed street by the Western Wall with a pile of stones that came down when the Romans used a battering ram (A.D. 70). The corner piece of the wall was on the ground. The inscription on this piece said "place of blowing." This corner on the wall had been the pinnacle of the Temple, where a priest would stand and blow the shofar each week to announce the beginning of the Sabbath. This also was most likely the place where the devil tempted Jesus to throw Himself down. And it could have been the place from where Jesus' brother James, the Bishop of the Church, was thrown down and beaten to death by a fuller's club in A.D. 62. Early church historian Eusebius contended that the catastrophes that later struck Jerusalem (the two Jewish Revolts against the Romans in A.D. 70 and A.D. 135 that resulted in the destruction of the Temple and Jerusalem) were a punishment for their treatment of one "who was the most righteous of men."[55] We were awed by the rich history that was presented to us by our excellent guide.

To complete our tour of the entire Western Wall we went through the Western Wall Tunnels. We saw the place on the wall that was closest to where the Holy of Holies in the Temple had been. This part of the "wailing wall" was actually "weeping!" We observed a group of Jewish school boys praying at that place. It made Janice cry, to think that they did not even understand Who God really is. She has such a burden for her people to know their Messiah, and she also has a burden for the Church to know their Jewish roots and to support the Messianic Jews in Israel.

On our last day with Pamela it was Shabbat. We took a tour all over Jerusalem, going by the Knesset, outlying villages, and two campuses of Hebrew University. We stopped at an overlook on

Mt. Scopus, then ate lunch at a Lebanese restaurant at the entrance of Abu Ghosh, which is about eight miles west of Jerusalem, just north of the Tel Aviv-Jerusalem highway. This restaurant is popular with Israelis on Shabbat (Jewish restaurants are closed). The Arab village of Abu Ghosh has remained neutral in the Arab-Jew conflict since 1948.

We visited the location of the biblical town of Kiryat Yearim, where the Ark of the Covenant resided for 20 years before King David brought it back to Jerusalem (I Sam. 7:2; II Sam. 6:2). It was on the grounds of St. Marie Alliance church and convent close by that we saw the spot where the Ark rested.

Nancy & Janice in the watchtower (mizpah) at Yad HaShmonah outside Jerusalem

Next was an even more fantastic experience, visiting Yad
Hashmona Moshav in the Jerusalem hills. They have guesthouses
now, but the moshav began as a cooperative settlement, founded
by eight Christian volunteers who arrived from Finland in 1971 to
help the Jews establish themselves in their old-new homeland. Yad
HaShmona ("Memorial for the Eight") is named after eight Jewish
refugees who were handed over to the Nazis by Finland in 1942.
Seven of them died at Auschwitz. In their fascinating Biblical
Garden we saw a wine press, a watchtower, and a synagogue under
construction. Janice and I had our picture made in the watchtower
or "mizpah."

In the synagogue sat some people Pamela knew, Ariel and
Dvorah Berkowitz, teachers of Torah. Janice and I recognized
them. We had heard them speak in Weoka, Alabama, of all places!
Weoka was close to Petrey. Happening upon them was another
God-incidence.

While there we were told of a suicide bombing in Haifa with
19 killed and 50 injured by a woman bomber. It happened at
a Christian Arab-Jewish owned restaurant, the Maxim Café, in
business for 40 years. The terrorist who carried out the attack was
evidently making a statement, "Arabs and Jews will not live together
in peace." Just to think, a little while earlier we had lunch in Abu
Ghosh, and the restaurant was filled with Israelis. The fact that the
Arabs of Abu Ghosh are friendly with Israelis could have aroused
the resentment of terrorists and made this restaurant a terrorist
target. There we were, enjoying our lunch in peace, not realizing
the potential danger we were in! However, why worry when the
Lord was orchestrating our steps? We could rest in Him and trust
Him to keep us safe as we continued to look at our real estate in
the Holy Land.

The next morning I called Jennifer. We had been planning to
have brunch at her house, but she couldn't do it, because she had
been at Ramallah all night. She told me more about the suicide
bombing at Haifa and said it was so evil.

On our last day in Jerusalem we finally had our second visit in Jennifer's home. She was ever the gracious hostess, serving us

Janice and Nancy visiting with Jennifer Griffin and family in her home in Jerusalem

pomegranates, sand tarts, and walnuts. This time we met her husband, Greg Myre, and their two children, Annalise, 2, and Amelia, 10 months.

Jennifer told us she had been to Jenin to interview the mother of the female suicide bomber. She learned that the bomber was a 27-year-old law student in Haifa. Jennifer sat with the mother in the rubble of her house that the Israelis had bulldozed. Jennifer said the mother had a hard face, saying she was glad her daughter was a martyr. I thought, "Oh, how deceived the followers of Islam are."

Then Jennifer contrasted the visit with this Muslim mother to her visit with a Jewish woman in Haifa, the wife of a man who had been killed at the hands of the Muslim mother's daughter. Also, the Jewish couple's child had been critically injured in the same blast at

Greg & Jennifer Griffin Myre with Amelia

the café. As this Jewish woman talked, Jennifer and the Fox News camera man, not an emotional person, began to cry. It was **that** heart-breaking. These horrible things were happening on our real estate. We needed to pray.

On a happier note, the next year, 2004, Jennifer was given an assignment by Fox News to work up a documentary on the life of Jesus to be aired from Jerusalem during the Easter season. She e-mailed me and asked for my suggestions. I felt so privileged that she asked me. I had two ideas. First, show Jesus as Jewish and the Last Supper as a Passover meal. Second, contact Pamela Suran for help. She took both my suggestions. Jennifer said it was a fabulous experience for her. She did hours of interviews with Pamela in the Old City, the choice part of our real estate, the place where Yeshua will sit on His throne in the new Temple one day.

Jennifer wrote me that it was the best experience of her life, and now she really sees Jerusalem in a brand new way. Pamela wrote that she fasted and prayed in order to be able to answer

Jennifer's questions and also to make a good witness before the Israelis helping Jennifer.

The special, entitled, "Who is Jesus?" aired on Palm Sunday. It was really great, and we were thrilled to hear that it was the most-watched program Fox News had ever done! It got 1.4 on the Nielson ratings. They showed it again on Good Friday and Easter Sunday. Janice and I got the word out to all our family and friends, and everyone was greatly blessed to see the Jewish Jesus being lifted up in the "City of the Great King."

On camera Pamela emphasized the Jewishness of Jesus, which thrilled my little Mizpah heart. What a blessing it was to me on my Jewish roots journey to connect these two wonderful people, Jennifer and Pamela, both residents of Jerusalem, Gentile and Jew, like Janice and me. They were privileged to actually live there, while Janice and I looked longingly at our inheritance, eagerly anticipating the day we could move in!

17

Paying on Our Debt

With the exception of the initial sightseeing tour in 1994, I always took gifts for the Lord's work on my trips to Israel. Paul's teaching to the Romans was my motivation, especially chapters nine through eleven, which is the centerpiece of his theology. These chapters show the relationship of the Gentile church with Israel, a vitally important subject to understand, in view of the sordid anti-Semitic history of the church.

Paul was willing even to be accursed from Christ for the sake of his Jewish brothers (Rom. 9:3). What a huge debt we owe to the Jewish people. Paul listed their credentials from which have sprung the Church's greatest blessings. "... who are Israelites, to whom pertain the adoption, the glory, the covenants, the giving of the law, the service of God, and the promises; of whom are the fathers and from whom, according to the flesh, Christ came, who is over all, the eternally blessed God. Amen" (Rom. 9:4-5). Yes, besides all the other reasons, we definitely owe a debt of gratitude to the Jewish people who produced our Messiah. Why can't most Christians realize this?

Janice and I determined to pay on our debt (Rom. 15:25-27). We took up offerings before we went to Jerusalem, and it was a great joy to distribute what the churches had so freely given us. Our donors knew there would be a reward in giving to the Chosen People. It can't be repeated enough what God promised Abraham, "I will bless those who bless you ..." (Gen. 12:3). Another promise is "He who tends to the fig tree [Israel] will eat its fruit" (Prov. 27:18). The blessings would come. You can't outgive God.

At our first place of ministry, Hadassah Hospital, we were taken to an area with Muslim mothers and their sick children. We handed out Rosh Hashanah Scripture cards, crocheted bookmarks, coloring books, crayons, balls, and teddy bears. Then we were guided around to the obstetrics ward. We visited the new mothers and gave them writing tablets and pens. One of the mothers of a sick little girl was the daughter of the Jerusalem mayor. We got lots of smiles and expressions of thanks. I practiced my Hebrew and sometimes really "hit the mark!" So, in spite of getting lost in going there and being two hours late, we had a fulfilling time giving to the Jewish and Arab people.

The first stop on the three-day tour of Jerusalem with Pamela Suran was Christian Friends of Israel. The co-founders of CFI-Jerusalem, Ray and Sharon Sanders, greeted us. Janice and I gave money from the churches' offerings to the "First Fruits Ministry" (the poor and needy believers in Jerusalem and Israel, the same ones Paul gave to) and for the Ethiopian Jews' children's school supplies.

Janice and I not only gave money to ministries, we gave our love, our prayers, and our Christian witness. While Pamela was guiding us, we stopped at the Mt. Scopus Overlook and sat on the benches. Sensing that Pamela was fatigued, we laid hands on her and prayed for hers and Shmuel's ministry. We can see the results from our intercession as Chazon Yerushalayim continues to bear fruit for God's kingdom.

Our next place to give an offering was at Ner Yaakov (Light of Jacob), a home for Holocaust survivors established by a German lady, Inge Buhs, to be a candle of hope for the last living witnesses of the Holocaust. On the 1996 mercy mission trip to Jerusalem, Esther and I had met Inge at CFI, and we fell in love with her. Inge felt shame and guilt, because she was a German, and her people had committed such awful atrocities against the Jewish people. Recently, Inge wrote me, "This was a process, and today I would like to say that I am not doing it 'out of guilt and shame,' but it is **my blessing**!"

Inge received a call from God to do all she could to alleviate the suffering of the Holocaust survivors in Jerusalem. Inspired by Ruth 1:16, she came to Israel in 1983. In Germany she had taken a course in senior care, so she got a job in a nursing home in Haifa. Later she worked for a German doctor. Inge grew close to one of the doctor's patients, Mrs. Steiner, a Holocaust survivor of Auschwitz, and they became good friends. Ner Yaakov is named for Mrs. Steiner's grandfather Jacob, or Yaakov. Inge learned more about the Holocaust from her Jewish friend and wanted to work in reconciling Jews and Christians. After her hospital experience, she continued to help survivors in their homes with cleaning, shopping, and nursing care.

Esther and I went with Inge to the nice, new home of Maria and Eli, Russian immigrants, where some survivors were gathered. Inge loved on them and distributed checks from CFI for their needs. The survivors spoke Yiddish. This language was similar to German, so it was easy for Inge to communicate with them. Eli could speak some Hebrew, so I talked with him in Hebrew a little bit. He had been an officer in the Russian army, and he was a poet. He showed me some books of poetry he had written. I told him I wrote songs. Can you believe I could say all this in Hebrew? We sang several Hebrew songs together – "Hevenu Shalom Aleichem," "Hatikva," and "Hineh Ma Tov." Then I sang a solo for him in Hebrew! How satisfying. All those hours of learning Hebrew songs and vocabulary was finally paying off.

Eli was excited about going to the Feast of Tabernacles put on by the International Christian Embassy. He was invited the year before to the Annual Israeli Guest Night, which included Russian immigrants, and he loved it. He said, "The Christians sing from their hearts, and it made me cry." He loved the way the Christians gave them up-front seats and showered affection on them. He boasted of having 50 tickets to give out to the Russian immigrants for the Feast coming up. I savored hearing this, because that generosity of heart is the ideal posture of Christians toward not-yet "completed" Jews. After all, these are the "natural branches" of the Jewish olive tree that were broken off through unbelief, but it is easy for God to graft the natural branches back into "their own olive tree" (Rom. 11: 17-24).

Inge's dream was to establish a special home for the Holocaust survivors. Esther and I prayed with her about it. And I continued to pray. That was in 1996. Now in 2003, Inge took Janice and me to see the answer to that prayer – Ner Yaakov! We had a wonderful visit with four survivors and one of the German volunteers. I saw a piano and went over to play it, intending to bring some joy, but I was surprised to get the opposite reaction! S., a survivor, was upset.

Inge Buhs, founder of Ner Yaacov for Holocaust survivors, with Nancy at Eldan Hotel in Jerusalem

He said the last time a lady came and played the piano, she wanted to get money from Inge. Inge comforted S. and assured him I was not trying to get money out of her. All the time she exuded "liquid love" to the survivors and attended to their every need. They had been so emotionally damaged, that they required much tender care.

Nancy & Janice visiting with Inge and Holocaust survivors at Ner Yaacov

We wound up around the table with hot tea and sweets, and everyone was smiling. I couldn't understand a word they were saying, but I could smile. Michael, a survivor, wanted to marry me! Janice knew a little Yiddish, so she could join in the conversation better.

We gave a monetary gift to Inge for her work. It was put to good use, because in a recent newsletter, I learned that Ner Yaakov is a veritable beehive of activity today. They have many projects and are constantly hosting visitors. One of the German visitors testified:

> Finally a dream came true and I could visit Israel. ...The most important meeting for me was one afternoon at Ner Yaakov with Holocaust victims. Inwardly distressed, we listened to their stories. It is truly different to read about the incomprehensible atrocities of the Nazis and see documentaries, than to hear them from survivors who suffered them on their own bodies. Still today I have to keep my tears away when I think of a survivor telling his story. Unimaginable this suffering, these

horrors he had to endure. And then, at the end a statement which almost knocked me out. He said, "But I forgive! We should forgive, we are taught to forgive!" All that was left in me was to cry! No sermon about forgiveness could have hit more in the middle of my heart. Since we were able to leave East Germany – a very unjust State 20 years ago – a deep hate against the Communist dictators stayed anchored in my heart. Totally blocked! And now, so many years later I hear from a man who went through incomprehensible sufferings.... I so much wish to be able to visit Ner Yaakov again soon. I want to say thank you and share what this testimony did in my life. Truly my inner thoughts were put right on this afternoon. Thank you![56]

Janice and I left there and drove our rental car to the Distribution Center (D.C.) of CFI. I kept making wrong turns, but I finally made it and parked right in front of the D.C. Surely the Lord had put that empty parking space there just for me. However, when I returned to the car, it had a parking ticket on it! Oh well, I guess the Lord has a sense of humor. I made a reluctant "contribution" to the Jerusalem Police Department of around $60!

The Distribution Center houses multiple outreach ministries, assisting the very poor, Ethiopian immigrants, Israeli soldiers, Household of Faith, Holocaust survivors, brides and grooms, immigrants, terror victims, and communities under attack. Janice and I spoke to each department head, as we made our way to the Bridal Salon, my favorite place in the D.C. Pam Bird greeted us. She showed us gorgeous wedding dresses, most of them brand new. A Jewish businessman in New York had donated designer gowns that would have been shredded had not an employee "rescued" them for Israel. We took a picture of a $10,000 dress!!

Pam told us that any Israeli can rent a wedding gown with a small deposit (the rate at that time) of around $150 U.S. or 600 NIS (New Israeli Shekels). If the person brings the gown back after being cleaned at the dry cleaners, she gets her money back. Also, male members of the wedding parties can rent suits. Pam gives each couple a book of Psalms and prays for them in the name of Yeshua. She was delighted to attend many of the weddings.

Pam is a widow, and the Lord sent her to Israel after her husband died some years ago. The Lord gave her a teaching on

Pam Bird showing Janice a $10,000 wedding dress in the Bridal Salon at CFI

the Jewish wedding, which she has since published in a book, *The Jewish Wedding & the Lord's Return.*[57] Through her work at CFI, attending the weddings, and reading God's Word, she could more fully appreciate the significance of the Jewish wedding. She began to understand from the teachings of the Jewish Jesus how the ancient Jewish wedding traditions were relevant in these last days. Her goal in writing the book was to give Christians fresh insight and excitement as we await the Bridegroom's soon return! The beauty of the Jewish wedding customs inspires Christians to want to know more about their Jewish roots.

We left CFI, and this time Janice got behind the wheel. This Jewish girl was an excellent driver in the city of Jerusalem. At last we found the perfect arrangement – Janice driving as I navigated! We were soon approaching veteran status!

A very nice Armenian Christian, Stephen Gejekoushian, taxied us around the Old City the day before we packed to return to the U.S. We met Stephen at the Yerevan (capital of Armenia) gift shop. He was one of three Christian brothers who operated the shop that specializes in Armenian ceramic pottery. We had gone back there to finish our shopping for gifts to take home. Stephen drove us to the bank, Emmanuel Messianic Book Store, and then to the hotel. He put in a lot of miles. We gave him money, even though he didn't charge us anything, because gasoline was extremely expensive in Israel. He was a delight to talk to.

I found out that Stephen helped John Savage with the music at Lars Enarson's Passover Seder, playing the drums. I didn't know either one of them at the time, but I had been there – another connection! Stephen told me that his grandfather escaped the genocide of the Armenian Christians and came to Israel. He was five years old and escaped with only his violin. All of his family were musically talented, Stephen said. I was shocked to learn that there was more than one holocaust.

The Armenian Genocide in what is now Turkey was carried out by the "Young Turk" government of the Ottoman Empire in 1915-1916 (with subsidiaries to 1923). One-and-a half million

Armenian Christians were murdered, out of a total of two million Armenians in the Ottoman Empire! Henry Morgenthau, Sr., US Ambassador to the Ottoman Empire, said, "I am confident that the whole history of the human race contains no such horrible episode as this. The great massacres and persecutions of the past seem almost insignificant when compared to the sufferings of the Armenian race in 1915."[58] Morgenthau could not have imagined that a future holocaust of the Jews would be even worse.

I had not heard of the Armenian Genocide until I went to Israel. There are several posters in the Armenian Quarter of the Old City giving information about it. In 2002, Mary Jo, Phyllis, and I happened upon the Convent of St. James, which takes up two-thirds of the Armenian Quarter, the Quarter itself taking up one-sixth of the Old City. I learned later that many of the residents of the convent compound are descendants of survivors of the genocide who sought refuge in Jerusalem.

As we entered the courtyard, a priest in a black robe met us. He asked if we would like to observe the service in progress. Going inside the chapel where people were gathered, we saw what appeared to be an ordination service for young priests, who were dressed in bright red robes. How handsome these young men were, and their faces were glowing with faith! Possibly they had just graduated from the seminary there. Since there were no pews, we stood at the back of the chapel and watched. I felt like we were observing something quite historic, and we had just stumbled upon it. Or had we? The Lord was always directing our steps. What an education I was getting in the Holy Land.

The Armenian Genocide preceded the Jewish holocaust, which took place in Europe from 1938 to 1945. Out of nine million Jews in Europe, approximately two-thirds were exterminated by the Nazis, which included over one million Jewish children, two million Jewish women and three million Jewish men (approximately six million in all). Almost the same number of non-Jewish civilians were murdered at that time also. Comparing the two holocausts, I could see a common denominator. Satan was behind the scenes, leading the attempted annihilation of God's people, both Christians and Jews. Thankfully, Stephen's family had escaped the Armenian Genocide, and Stephen was worshiping the God of Israel freely in Jerusalem, using his musical gift.

Back to the 2003 trip – Janice was about to meet two more special people, friends I first met in 1996, who had musical gifts and were using them in a School of Worship in Jerusalem, Roy and Mary Kendall. No visit to Israel would be complete without seeing Roy and Mary. Once again, they exercised their gift of hospitality. Roy picked us up to go to their daughter's apartment for Shabbat dinner. This evening was made more special, because there were other guests there, Jonathan and Sharon Settel. I was honored to be able to meet Jonathan, a well-known Israeli singer, who had just come from a recording session in Tel Aviv. I had some of his music on tape and was already a great admirer of his beautiful voice.

We were treated to Jonathan and Sharon's testimony. Sharon said the Lord pointed out Jonathan to her, saying, "There is your husband." She took the Lord at His word and married him four years before he was saved. She wanted her children to be born Jewish, so she converted to Judaism before the wedding. Sadly, Jonathan would not allow her to go to church.

God was at work, however, through Jonathan's band members at Disney World who were believers. Because of his respect for them, he went to their Bible studies. One night he went out on his balcony, and **he saw Jesus! Jesus was crying.** Jonathan said **he saw himself (not a reflection) inside the tears of Jesus!** He was born again that night. Then he found out that Sharon's mother was praying for him all the time. What a testimony! Here we were, Janice and I, in the home of professional ministers of music in Jerusalem, the city which was destined to be the global center of the worship of Almighty God! And we had just heard first hand the testimony of a renowned Christian recording artist. Talk about privilege and blessing.

Maribel Nez, the Kendalls' Mexican worker for their School of Worship, drove us back to the hotel. She had recently discovered

Jonathan and Sharon Settel at Kendalls' Shabbat dinner in Jerusalem

that she was Jewish and was planning to make aliyah. Interestingly, Roy had told us that night that he also recently discovered that his grandfather may have been Jewish. If so, that would make Roy Jewish, but he still wouldn't meet the eligibility requirements for Israeli citizenship. Janice and I gave money to both the Kendalls and to Maribel. We would soon meet another Messianic Jew and give money to her also. It was such a joy to pay on our debt to the Jewish people as we toured our real estate. We could tell the Lord was orchestrating our steps, especially in the way we would meet Judy, another Messianic Jew.

18

Celebrating Our Feasts

Janice and I were in Israel during the High Holy Days, the most solemn and important holy days for the Jewish people, the fall feasts.

God told Moses at Mt. Sinai that His people were to observe not only the weekly feast, the Sabbath, but they were to observe seven yearly feasts (Lev. 23). Three of them are in the spring – Passover, Unleavened Bread, and Firstfruits. Fifty days after Passover is the Feast of Weeks (Shavuot or Pentecost). Then come the three fall feasts – Feast of Trumpets, Day of Atonement (Yom Kippur), and Feast of Tabernacles (Sukkot). These three times of the year were required encounters with God. Sacrifices were to be offered in the place of God's choosing, which later became Jerusalem.

The first of the fall feasts is popularly known as Rosh Hashana, meaning "head of the year," or New Year's Day (Tishri 1 on the Jewish civil calendar). The biblical name is Feast of Trumpets. It is a special holiday for Jewish people. They eat apples and honey and say, "Hashana tovah," or "Have a good year." Of the six trips I have made to Israel I have been there twice during Rosh HaShanah. On this trip we just missed it by two days. Now we were in the "Days of Awe," the ten days between Rosh HaShanah and Yom Kippur. For religious Jews, this is a time of deep introspection and repentance. Indeed, the entire month of Elul, preceding the month of Tishri for the new year is a time of repentance.

On Yom Kippur (Day of Atonement) in the days of the Temple the high priest would make atonement for the people by going into the Holy of Holies with the blood of a bull (for his own sins) and the blood of a goat (for the nation's sins) to sprinkle on the mercy seat of the Ark of the Covenant in the Holy of Holies. He would also place his hands on the head of another goat, confess the nation's sins over that goat, and this "scapegoat" would be led into the wilderness to "take away" the sins of the people. The atonement was effective when the goat was pushed off a cliff (Leviticus 16).

Five days after Yom Kippur comes Sukkot, and we were in Jerusalem for the beginning of that seven-day feast. Of the three fall feasts only one is not an actual celebration, and that is Yom Kippur. It is a mandatory fast day (Lev. 23:27), the only one in the Bible. This is a day faithfully observed by all Jews throughout the world, whether religious or not. The enemies of Israel attacked them on this, their holiest day, in 1973. The war that ensued, the Yom Kippur War, was almost lost by Israel, because the soldiers were in their synagogues, fasting and praying, and they were caught by surprise. That is why the mobilization took too long, and the casualties were great.

Janice and I had some great experiences on the eve and the day of Yom Kippur, even though we both fasted and had no food or water for 25 hours! Janice had always observed the marathon services in a synagogue, but even more so since she gave her life to Yeshua. From our hotel we had a fairly short walk to the nearest conservative synagogue, Moreshet Yisrael, arriving a bit past 5:00 p.m. We were late and did not realize that reserved seats were required. The sweet lady greeter told us to go find seats, but it was possible we would lose them, if the people who reserved the seats showed up.

I sat next to a nice lady who helped me follow along, reading the Hebrew. The cantor who led did almost all the service by himself, and it was in Hebrew. He used a few words in English. Even though I knew the importance of the Day of Atonement in Scripture, this service had no meaning for me. However, meeting the lady I sat by and her husband afterward was a very meaningful encounter. She introduced herself, her husband, and three daughters to us. One of the daughters, Michelle Samuels, did public relations for the International Christian Embassy Feast of Tabernacles, and she knew Roy Kendall! That was a God-incidence! And here came another one. The lady's husband, Dr. Shimon Samuels, was and is the Director for International Relations for the Simon Wiesenthal Center,[59] a global Jewish human rights organization that confronts anti-Semitism, stands with Israel, and teaches the lessons of the Holocaust. I had already been receiving their e-mails and acting on them to petition various world leaders to act against anti-Semitism. That was my "connection" with Dr. Samuels.

He told us that at the United Nations Conference on Racism in Durban, South Africa, two years before, the participants called for the expulsion of Israel, accusing them of racism. They equated Zionism with racism. Samuels said the conference was horribly anti-Semitic, but 6,000 Christians came and stood with Israel! Then Dr. Samuels made a statement that blessed my heart. He said, **"Evangelical Christians are the best friends Israel has."** I sensed that he knew I was a Christian, and, hopefully, he understood that Janice was a Messianic Jew. I told him we got their e-mails and signed their petitions. He was surprised and happy about that, and I think both of us made a hit with him!

This was a God-encounter, and we would have another one the next day of Yom Kippur. That morning we walked back to the synagogue and arrived at 8:20 a.m. The service had already started at 8:00. It seemed we just could not get there on time, but God blessed us anyway. We got seats on the second row, right in the middle. I have to admit it was the most boring service I ever sat through. The Lord soon provided a little excitement for me, though.

An elderly man came up quietly behind me and tapped me on the shoulder. I jumped! He began to speak to me in Hebrew, which I did not understand. I hastened to answer him in my limited Hebrew, "I speak Hebrew a little." He walked away. Then I realized he must have been asking me to come up on the stage and participate in reading the Torah! I noticed there were several female readers. This was an honor, but I didn't dare expose my ignorance any further. Later, I reflected on that lost opportunity.

Maybe I should have gone to the stage and boldly proclaimed, "The Spirit of the Lord is upon me, for He has anointed me to preach the good news!" The left foot of fellowship would surely have been applied, but what a way to go. At least there was no cliff in Jerusalem to throw me off, as they attempted to do to Yeshua in Nazareth (Luke 4: 16-30)!

The service droned on, and I couldn't understand anything. Then something happened that Janice had prepared me for. Two men brought Torah scrolls down opposite aisles. Everyone eagerly reached out to kiss the scrolls. I, too, got to kiss the Torah, and I kissed it twice. This relieved the boredom somewhat. Then I saw a man behind us who looked like Yeshua! "If only He were here," I thought. That inspired me to pray for the fulfillment of Zechariah's prophecy, "And I will pour on the house of David and on the inhabitants of Jerusalem the Spirit of grace and supplication; then **they will look on Me whom they pierced**. Yes, they will mourn for Him as one mourns for his only son, and grieve for Him as one grieves for a firstborn" (12:3). Oh, that the Jews around me would have the veil from their eyes removed, and they would have a vision of Yeshua right then and there!

That stirred up my memory about the time that **Janice had actually seen Yeshua** in the synagogue on Yom Kippur one year. She said as the men stepped down off the bema (stage) to bring the Torah scrolls down the aisles, **one of the scrolls turned into Yeshua!** Hearing her tell it made my heart leap. She watched Him as he "worked the crowd," putting His hand of blessing on the people as they reached out to Him. Then, suddenly, He was standing right in front of her, putting His hands on her shoulders. He looked her directly in the eyes and said, **"I know you, and I love you!"**

Janice was overwhelmed with His love and thought, "Of course! Yeshua <u>is</u> the Torah. He is the Living Word of God!" Then she watched Yeshua turn back into the Torah, as the man stepped up on the bema to return the scroll to the Ark (cabinet). Janice knew more than ever that Yeshua was present with His people, whether they believed in Him or not. He unconditionally loved them. She set herself anew to praying for her non-believing family with that fresh revelation in mind.

Back to the Yom Kippur service in Jerusalem. As I said before, Yom Kippur services are a marathon, and Janice always completes the marathon. It would be different this time. It was 11:40 a.m., and we had been sitting there for over three hours with no end in sight. Besides being very hungry and thirsty, I was also extremely bored and felt like I could not last another few minutes. At that point I summoned my courage and leaned over to Janice, whispering, "Can we leave now?" I disappointed her greatly by acting like a wimp. However, she reluctantly agreed, and we slipped out. When we got outside and looked around, it occurred to us to try another route back to the hotel, a back route, so to speak. In my state of boredom I was grateful for the adventure.

My spirit picked up as we walked along the road which was more like a wide path. Someone was coming toward us. As she came into view we both got the impression that she could possibly be a believer. She was smiling. We struck up a conversation and soon found out she was indeed a Messianic Jew! She must have had us pegged right from the start, or else she would not have revealed herself to us.

Her name was Frances*. She had made aliyah from Virginia four years before. We invited her to come to our hotel room and tell us all about herself. And what an earful we got! She told us fantastic stories about supernatural experiences she had in Jerusalem. She saw Yeshua! She saw angels. She witnessed to religious Jews, the hardest ones to win over. We found out she was working undercover as she attended synagogue services. She was a "secret agent" for God in the Holy City. It was funny how she maintained her secrecy, using passwords among believers when referring to Yeshua. She called Him "our mutual friend" or "J.C.," or "Junior." Frances only had $300 a month after the rent was paid, but the Lord always provided her needs. We knew we should give

---

* Name changed

her some money, so we did. It was exciting to think that God was using her in orthodox circles to turn Sauls into Pauls. Our money would be well spent.

By this time, Janice and I were starving. After a nap we broke our fast, just shy of the required 25 hours, by drinking a little water. It was a miracle that I survived. Going without food was one thing, but going without water was really hard. We had a nice meal in the hotel dining room. Things looked rosier.

Yom Kippur ended on Monday night. Five days later, on Saturday, was Sukkot (booths or tabernacles), the time to remember the temporary dwellings that the Israelites lived in during their wilderness wanderings (Lev. 23: 33-44). This is the biggest holiday in Israel, but it isn't one day. It lasts for seven days, and people live in sukkot (booths) during this time. The religious Jews move into their sukkot, but most Jews just have their meals and spend a little time each day in them. Everyone decorates the booths in the way that we decorate Christmas trees. They invite guests over. Gifts are given and received. The day after Yom Kippur the decorating begins.

The Eldan Hotel where we were staying built a beautiful and wonderfully decorated sukkah attached to the front of the building. It was so festive and welcoming. It actually made you smile to see it. Janice and I invited Pamela to come join us under the hotel sukkah for a special Sukkot lunch. We had a wonderful time of conversation and relaxing with Pamela.

She said she was connecting with Arab Christians and attending their churches. Also, their Chazon Yerushalayim ministry had just started making up nice gift baskets to take to the Arabs whose houses in Beit Jalah had been destroyed by the IDF, when the Palestinian terrorists fired on the Jerusalem subdivision of Gilo from within these houses. Pamela shared about how Shmuel and she have invested in many believers to equip them to be effective servants of the Lord in Israel, and that some of these believers went on to establish important ministries. What jewels the Surans were, and we were privileged and blessed to be friends with them.

Pamela Suran, our guide, and Janice under the hotel sukkah for the Feast of Tabernacles

Janice showed Pamela the materials she wanted to give to our hotel clerk, Adi, a vivacious young Jewish girl that we had become friends with. One day Adi related her story of losing her purse on the bus and the way it was given back to her. It was easy to see that the freakish way her purse was returned to her had made an impact. From our viewpoint, this was a miracle that God orchestrated, but Adi said she did not pray. How could we get through to this admittedly non-religious Jew?

I had already given Adi one of my *Hatikva* tapes. Pamela looked over the free books Janice got from the Emmanuel Messianic Book Store and said *The Messiah in the Old Testament* by Riso Santolo, a Messianic Jewish scholar, was perfect. Janice wrote in this book, as well as a Brit Hadasha (New Testament), that they were gifts from us.

We had already been praying a lot for Adi to see Yeshua as her Messiah. Once I asked her if she had listened to my tape yet. She said, "Do you think I will become religious just overnight?" I replied that I wanted her to check out my Hebrew pronunciation on the songs. She had already been helping me with the language. Maybe one day in heaven we will know if our witnessing, the books, and the music was used to bring her salvation. We continued to pray for Adi.

I had another experience, witnessing about the Messiah to the hotel bellman, Daniel. He was Russian and was interested in history. I was surprised that he wanted to talk about the original split between the "regular" Jews and the Messianic Jews in the second century. He was easy to talk to, and I shared with him what I knew about the subject. Janice and I both talked to him. He had almost agreed to accept a book from me, *More Than A Carpenter*,[60] by Josh McDowell, but I bumbled it. Later, ace saleslady Janice explained to me the right way to "close the sale." Oh, well. At least I planted some good seed in Daniel. I watered it with a prayer that someone else would come along and lead Daniel to salvation in Yeshua.

It was a blessing to be in Jerusalem during the fall feasts. These feasts are not Jewish feasts only. They are called "the feasts of the Lord" (Lev. 23:2). Janice faithfully keeps Passover in her home and attends the synagogue or temple on Yom Kippur. You may say, "Well, yes, she is Jewish." However, we Gentiles have a Jewish Messiah and read a Jewish Bible. As for keeping the feasts, it is not a matter of "you **got** to," but "you **get** to." Yeshua kept all the feasts, even Hanukkah, the Feast of Dedication (John 10:22), which is not one of the seven required annual feasts of the Lord. Yeshua is coming back to Jerusalem, the capital of the Jewish State. Besides all that, we "wild branches" have been grafted into the Jewish olive tree and adopted into the family, the "commonwealth of Israel" (Eph. 2:12).

Gentile Christians are at liberty to celebrate the Lord's feasts out of love for our fellow Jewish believers and the natural kinfolks of Yeshua, but we are not obligated to. All of them are prophetic of the Messiah. What an exciting thing it is to see Him "hidden" in the rituals of the feasts. (See Chapter 23.) We should look upon them as a delight, not a duty.

19

Driving to the Golan Heights

The adventure of all adventures began on our ninth day in Israel. Finally, our rental car would be put to good use. It had been sitting in the garage under the hotel for most of our stay, but now we would drive all the way to the Golan Heights, doing some sightseeing along the way. We drove westward toward Tel Aviv, bypassed the city, and headed north, stopping at Caesarea to see the Roman Theater and the gorgeous Mediterranean Sea.

We had a private tour of the amphitheater at Caesarea, just the two of us. Chairs were set up in front of the stage, so it was obviously in use, not just "ruins" for tourists to view. The acoustics in the ancient theater were marvelous. Janice went up high in the tiered seats to serve as my audience, and I sang "Via Dolorosa" on the stage. Then we switched places, and Janice gave Mark Anthony's oration in "Julius Caesar." We envisioned 4,000 spectators present, and we bowed to the applause. Great fun! Then we went down to Herod's promontory palace and swimming pool to look at the Mediterranean Sea. We looked at the columns for Herod's amphitheater which had seated 10,000 people.

Our journey took an eastward turn, and we were careful to stay on course. Straying into Muslim territory in the "West Bank" would be very dangerous. Our next stop was at Tel Megiddo National Park southeast of Haifa and the scene of mighty biblical battles. We stood on the observation platform to view the magnificent expanse of land where the last war of the world will take place.

One day Yeshua will fight on this battlefield. "I am coming as a thief ... And they gathered them together to the place called in Hebrew, Armageddon, or Mount Megiddo" (Rev. 16:15-16). The description of the battle scene is breathtaking. Yeshua will come on a white horse with the armies of heaven following. "King of kings and Lord of lords" will be written on His robe, and the wicked will be killed with a sword out of His mouth (Rev.19:11-21)!

It was a tough climb over rocks to get to the Armageddon observation point, but it was worth it. Janice took much longer to climb up, and it looked like she wouldn't make it. Finally, she did. It was only after we got back to the USA, and a few days later when I read her account of the trip, that I realized it was a huge miracle of God that Janice survived the many steps, inclines, and rocky paths throughout our tour.

She had been through numerous heart procedures, including open heart surgery, and was still experiencing a lot of angina. She kept her nitroglycerin with her at all times. After surgery for a broken kneecap in 1994, Janice had not been able to use her knee properly. Added to all those infirmities, she is a diabetic and at that time was overweight.

Her feet and legs were terribly swollen from the flight to Tel Aviv. And little did I realize that walking the ramparts (top of the wall) in the Old City, going up and down many steps, would be a painful exercise for Janice. She was slow, but she made it eventually. It was truly a miracle that she could do everything anyone else did on the entire trip. In fact she rarely had to use her nitroglycerin. To God be the glory! As the saying goes, "Where God guides, He provides."

Our next stop after Megiddo was quite a contrast. We visited Nazareth Village, a recreation of Yeshua's childhood home. The Lord surely orchestrated our steps, because had we arrived a minute later, we would have missed the tour. Janice and I joined five people from Singapore. One of the men was a pastor in Israel. Our guide was also a pastor in Nazareth Ilit (upper Nazareth). Janice was especially happy to meet him, because he was a Messianic Jew, a Russian who made aliyah from the United States. His co-workers at Nazareth Village were Arab Christians, including some Bedouins.

The village had donkeys. One of the donkeys seemed to like me. Before I knew what was happening, another donkey joined my admirer, and the two of them pushed me up against an olive tree! A bedouin, dressed in first century garb, offered a donkey ride. A mother and baby from our group got on, and we were reminded of Mary and baby Jesus. To be more Hebraically correct, you should call them Miriam and baby Yeshua.

The Bedouin men and women acted out first century life – sitting at the cistern, laughing and singing, driving donkeys around a grinding stone to pulverize olives, and operating the olive press to get virgin olive oil dripping into baskets. They demonstrated how they smoothed wood, drilled in the carpentry shop, spun wool into yarn, and wove the yarn on a loom to make cloth. Finally, they served us pita bread and olives inside a first-century stone house. Then the guide took us inside a replica of a first century synagogue and read from the scroll of Scripture just as Yeshua would have done.

Nazareth Village was a very authentic reproduction of the Galilean village that Yeshua grew up in, and it could have been on the actual land that his parents lived. When the eight acres of land were being cleared for the Nazareth Village project in the early 2000s, archaeologists discovered an ancient wine press. They were thrilled, and this gave them confidence they would find more artifacts. Soon they excavated the base of a watchtower.[61] What treasures they had found! The watchtower was reconstructed and dedicated in February of 2006. When Janice and I returned to Nazareth Village with our husbands in 2007, we had our photograph made in the watchtower, or "mizpah." Now we could be seen as authentic watchmen in a watchtower. And to think, Yeshua could possibly have climbed up the watchtower right on this spot!

The timing on our trip across Israel was perfect, even though it didn't appear so at first. We arrived at the Mount of Beatitudes right as the man was closing the gate, but we prevailed on him to give us five minutes. Oh, what a breathtaking ten minutes we took! I had built up this site to Janice, and we were not disappointed.

We went in the beautiful chapel and briefly knelt to pray. Then we stood on the balcony and looked down at the scintillating Sea of Galilee. It was the perfect conclusion to our day of sightseeing, as we beheld the golden sun in the west slip down below the Galilee hills. Thinking of the **sun**, I mused, "Soon He, the **Son** of righteousness, will **rise** with healing in His wings" (Mal. 4:2). What timing, Lord!

On the final leg of our journey to Katzrin on the Golan Heights a gorgeous full moon was our companion in the night sky. The trip was exactly 12 hours. We left Jerusalem at 6:30 a.m. and arrived in Katzrin at 6:30 p.m., just in time for dinner at the Enarsons' Golan House of Prayer.

This wonderful house was a new, three-story building which would accommodate 30 people, dormitory-style. It was the place that God sent Lars and Harriet Enarson to mobilize prayer for the salvation of Israel, especially in the north. Lars believes that there is a spiritual link between Golan and Jerusalem. Like the Jordan River that supplies most of Israel with water has its beginnings on the Golan, God wants to release His river of living water from this area. The ministry of the Golan House was a continual intercession, 24 hours a day, for God's protection over Israel from military attacks, as well as for the promised end time outpouring of the Holy Spirit upon Israel.

Our hosts from the U.S. were Dawn, Stephen, their daughter Meagan, and Lois. Dawn and Lois prepared us a wonderful meal. The Enarsons' family – Johanna, John, Brad and Josefin and their three children – came in for a short visit. We visited Brad and Josefin later in their home close by. It was disappointing that Lars and Harriet were in Sweden at the time.

The next morning after prayer in the prayer room on the top floor, Janice and I joined our hosts for breakfast. Aterward I played my *Hatikva* CD, and we had a time of worshiping the Lord, which was a real blessing. Stephen said he was hoping we would have a word from the Lord for them. They were nervous about their proximity to Syria, especially since the IDF had just bombed a

terrorist camp inside Syria. The Lord led me to read Isaiah 17 about the destruction of Damascus. Stephen said that may have been the word they needed.

Dawn and Lois drove us to the Syrian border at Har Ben Tal, a place of army bunkers, to pray. The scenery on the way was gorgeous. As we drove up to the parking lot of the volcanic mountain, there were busloads of people arriving. Our intention was to pray on the border, but all these tourists would hinder our prayer time, I thought.

At the top of the mountain were signposts indicating distances to major cities in the world. We noticed that it was only 36 miles to Damascus, capital of Syria. The Israeli government wants people to come to this site to see how close Israel is to Syria and to know how important it is for Israel to keep the Golan Heights as a buffer zone. We heartily agreed that it must not be given away in a "peace" deal. We went down inside the underground army bunkers, praying for the soldiers of the IDF as we did so. Janice and I posed for a picture with the binoculars as watchmen at the lookout post.

Nancy & Janice being "watchmen" in an army bunker on Har Ben Tal on the Golan Heights at the border with Syria

When we came out to the overlook, it was empty of people. What a miracle all the tourists were gone from the observation point, and we could pray over the border in privacy. Good timing, Lord! We could see the road to Damascus clearly, and we thought of the Apostle Paul when he encountered Yeshua. Also, we could see the Kunetra Valley, the "Valley of Tears" region, which was the site of one of the Yom Kippur war's bloodiest battles in 1973. To the far left we saw the tip of Mount Hermon, Israel's tallest mountain. How beautiful and deceivingly peaceful the view was.

We were about to experience another God-incidence as we walked back to the concession building. I heard Janice exclaim to a man approaching us, "Avi! Avi!" Wreathed in smiles, they eagerly embraced! I marveled. "Obviously, she knows him," I thought. "But who is he?"

Janice meets Avi on Har Ben Tal – a miraculous encounter!

Janice explained that Avi was the Israeli tour guide for the group from her church, Ino Baptist, that came to Israel every year. Avi had even spoken in the pulpit at Ino. Janice was supposed to call him, but she had left his telephone number back in Elba, and she couldn't find out how to make contact. God knew all that and graciously arranged a meeting. Avi told us he had not been guiding groups for a year, and this was his first day back on the job. Again, God's perfect timing. Now beyond the shadow of a doubt, we knew that God had orchestrated not only our day, but our entire trip!

On the way back to the Golan House we passed by Nimrod's Fortress. Talk about ancient! (Read Genesis 10:8-10; 11:2.) Then we visited the waterfall at Banias. This was at Caesarea Philippi where Jesus asked the disciples, "Who do men say that I am?" We had to walk down 127 steps leading to the waterfall. This was at the headwaters of the Jordan River, coming from the melting snow flowing down Mount Hermon. As we stood on the observation deck at the waterfall, it reminded me of Isaiah's prophecy: "For as the rain comes down and the snow from heaven ... so shall My Word be ... It shall not return to me void ..." (Isa. 55:10-11).

We prayed there, "Send Your Spirit, Lord, as rivers of Living Water." It seemed that God answered, "Ho! Everyone who thirsts, come to the water; ... come buy and eat ... without money and without price" (Isa. 55:1). That powerful waterfall emitted a powerful promise.

We spent our second night at the Golan House. The next morning, I arose at 4:30 a.m. to go to the prayer room. It was a precious, holy time. Walking out on the balcony as the sun was about to come up, I felt refreshed by the cool air. After a good breakfast, we said goodbye to Dawn and Lois and headed south, via the Jordan Valley. Janice had driven all the way to the Golan, so now it was my time to get us back "home."

The scenery was magnificent all along the way, and we didn't even get stopped at the checkpoints. We arrived in Jerusalem at 11:00 a.m., gassed up the car, and turned it in. Mission accomplished.

The Feast of Tabernacles (Sukkot) began that night, but we would be leaving for the USA the next day. Janice and I felt tremendously privileged to have shared the burdens of the Messianic and Christian ministries in the Land. We got an overall view of the Body of Messiah and felt the Lord was saying to them, "Come out of the closet, stand together, and actively witness with boldness that Yeshua is the Jewish Messiah, telling others, 'You need Him.'"

We had visited the Temple Institute in the Old City and

Janice and Nancy leave the Golan House of Prayer at Katzrin on the Golan Heights

marveled at the preparations being made by religious Jews for the Third Temple. However, God impressed on us that the best way to build the Temple of the Lord in preparation for Yeshua's return was to build His living temple, the Messianic Jews and other believers in the land.

The Lord affirmed us many times as His messenger girls in the Holy Land to the people of the covenant. We praised the Lord for sending us and for Helena and her husband who made it financially possible for us to go. It was a miracle journey from beginning to end. On that trip in 2003, we looked at our real estate as a seed of Abraham, paid on our debt to the Jewish people, celebrated the feasts, and prayed over the land on the Golan Heights.

Here are some Israel-friendly words for Woody Guthrie's song written in 1940, and this sums up what Christians should feel about the Land of Israel:

> This land is your land,
> This land is my land,
> From the Mount of Olives
> To the Golan Highlands,
> From the Dead Sea Waters
> To the hill Golgotha,
> This land was made for you and me.

The Lord said, "The land is Mine" (Lev. 25:23) and "All the earth is Mine" (Ex. 19:5). It belongs to God who made it, and He can give it to whomever He chooses. Scripture verifies that He chose to give the Land of Israel to the descendants of Abraham through Isaac and Jacob.

God said to Jacob, whose name He changed to Israel, "The land which I gave Abraham and Isaac I give to you; and to your descendants after you I give this land" (Gen. 35:12). It just so happens that Yeshua is a descendant of Jacob's son, Judah, from whom we get the name "Jew." Since Yeshua became my Savior, Lord, and Bridegroom in 1968, I have also become an heir of that beautiful land of Israel. Praise the Lord!

20

Student of Jewish Roots

Looking back, I see that my Jewish roots journey up to June of 1998 had steadily filled my heart with a desire to teach. I wanted to share with a wider audience all the things the Lord had been teaching me about the Jewish roots of the Church. When Rhonda Essary told me about the Arkansas Institute of Holy Land Studies (AIHLS)[62] offering a correspondence course for a Master's degree in Middle East History, I felt the Lord's leading to begin a formal study and obtain that degree. Perhaps this degree, I thought, would enable me to teach in a college setting. That way I could reach more people, especially the unchurched. Was this not what a Mizpah for Israel was supposed to do?

My study with AIHLS began on June 1, 1998, with five introductory courses, which I completed, tests included, by March, 1999 – Jewish Roots, Understanding Hebrew Thought, Jewish Culture I, The Jewishness of Jesus, and Messianic Concepts During the 1st Century.

In the meantime, my husband and I had moved from Columbus to Northport, Alabama, in January, 1999, to start a new church in Tuscaloosa. Renting a small apartment, we now had a "down-sized" life with fewer responsibilities. It was an ideal setup for me to concentrate on my AIHLS courses. After purchasing a new computer, I was on my way to becoming a Mizpah in the college setting.

In addition to the five introductory courses to receive my master's degree, I was required to take ten more courses and write a ten-page research paper on each. The instruction for all fifteen courses was on videos with fill-in-the-blanks workbooks. Dr. Ron

Moseley, PhD, was my primary instructor. I enthusiastically dived into the writing of my first research paper on The History of Jerusalem and completed it on May 4, 1999. It was entitled "Jerusalem, the Jewish Capital."

How fitting that my first paper was all about the most important place on earth – the place where the Jewish Messiah was crucified, died, was buried, rose again, ascended into heaven, and will come back! My writing proved that the historical record, as well as the prophetic record of the Scriptures, completely validate the Jewish origin and rights to Jerusalem as the undivided capital city of the Jews in the land of Israel. In our day when the Palestinians deny even the presence of the Jewish temples in history and want to have the Old City as the capital of a Palestinian state, the proofs I cited are invaluable. Writing this paper, I was doing my job as a Mizpah for Israel, and I felt good about it.

Biblical Feasts and Holidays was my second course. In a little over a month I mailed in my paper, "Passover, Israel's Past and Future Deliverance." This was another very important topic, because "Passover is the oldest, continuously observed feast in existence today, celebrated for some 3,500 years."[63] I attempted to prove that the past deliverance of the Israelites from slavery in Egypt by the blood of the Passover Lamb was a prophetic picture of the future national deliverance of the Jewish people from the slavery of sin by their Messiah, the Lamb of God who takes away the sin of the world. It was a great compliment to me when Lars Enarson read my paper and said he would use it when he spoke at the World Prayer Center in Colorado that year.

In less than a month's time, by July 16, 1999, I mailed in my third research paper on the course, Bedouins and Major Cultures of the Middle East. It was entitled, "The Bedouin – Hostility to Hospitality." By definition a Bedouin is an Arab of any of the nomadic tribes of the Arabian, Syrian, Nubian, or Sahara deserts.

The Bedouin is a study in contrasts. He displays gracious hospitality on the one hand but also guerrilla hostility on the other. His present lifestyle dates from the days of the Bible and affords the

Bible student a look at the world of Abraham, Ishmael, Isaac, Jacob, Moses, and other dwellers in the desert of the Middle East. The descendants of Abraham through his two sons, Isaac and Ishmael, have been at enmity with each other throughout history. However, Bible prophecies point to a future time of reconciliation when hostility will give way to hospitality, and all the world will "see the face of God" (Gen. 33:10).

This study was totally new ground for me. I learned so much and developed an appreciation for the Arab culture. Ishmael, the first son of Abraham by his wife's Egyptian maidservant, Hagar, is the father of the Ishmaelites, a nomadic nation which lived in northern Arabia. Muhammad claimed Ishmael as his ancestor, as do most Arabs.

Esau is another ancestor of the Bedouin. Esau's brother Jacob stole his birthright and his blessing and fled to another country, because Esau threatened to kill him. Twenty years later, Jacob took his wives and possessions to return to Canaan, but he dreaded facing Esau, his offended brother. Sending his wives and possessions ahead of him, Jacob stayed behind at the River Jabbok. There he wrestled with a Man, whom he would not let go until the Man gave him a blessing. It turned out that this Man was the pre-incarnate Son of God, Yeshua, because Jacob said, "I have seen **God** face to face, and my life is preserved" (Gen. 32:30). At that time the Man changed his name from Jacob ("deceiver") to Israel ("prince with God"), because he had struggled with God and man and had prevailed.

Now Jacob would have the courage to face his brother Esau. As Jacob came near, Esau "ran to meet him and embraced him, and fell on his neck and kissed him, and they wept" (Gen. 33:4). Jacob said, "I have seen your face as though I had seen the face of God, and you were pleased with me" (Gen. 33:10). Evidently, because Jacob came face-to-face with God and made peace with Him, God let Jacob see His pleasure in the face of Esau! After this meeting, Esau offered hospitality to Jacob (Gen. 33:12).

I ended my paper with these words: "Arabs and Jews are family. Abraham is their father. God scattered the Jews, but He is gathering them now, and they are coming home to face their offended relatives. In the life of the Bedouin we can see the promise of hospitality even in the face of hostility. The Arab will receive honor and respect. The Jew will receive acceptance and forgiveness. Reconciliation will come, and the whole world will 'see the face of God'!"

I was clipping right along with my courses – three down and seven more to go – when I realized that a trip to the Arkansas Institute was in order. Was this the institution I wanted to graduate from? My husband agreed that I could fly to Little Rock, Arkansas, rent a car and drive to AIHLS in Sherwood for their annual Jerusalem Conference on August 12-14, 1999.

The conference took place in Dr. Moseley's Sherwood Bible Church which was a humble structure. Years later in 2007, it would be transformed into the American Institute building, a large and beautiful facility. I knew when I enrolled at AIHLS that the school was a work in progress, and it did progress as planned. In fact, Jewish Roots studies as a whole was an emerging movement that I was blessed to enter into at the initial stages. Our speakers, including Dr. Moseley, President of AIHLS, were pioneers in this movement – Dwight Pryor, President of the Center for Judaic Christian Studies in Dayton, Ohio; Dr. Marvin Wilson, a translator of the N.I.V. Bible, author of *Our Father Abraham*,[64] and professor at Gordon College; and Dr. Brad Young, president of the faculty at Oral Roberts University (ORU) who received his doctorate at the Hebrew University of Jerusalem.

It was a memorable and mind-expanding experience for me, and I was glad to finally meet my professors in person and talk to them. I believed that the Lord would have me continue studying at AIHLS, so I selected my next course, The Role of Women in the Biblical Text. I didn't start this course until October that year, because our activities in the new church had increased, and we were also holding Sunday evening meetings back in Columbus, not to mention all the time needed for our growing family. Whereas the first three of the ten required courses had been completed quickly, this next one took a while longer.

Back in January when we had moved to Northport, we moved what wouldn't fit in our small apartment to Petrey Apartments in Luverne. At the end of the year we took some time to go to Petrey, 10 miles from Luverne, and start working on the restoration of Curtis' old home place. It was a good place to be in preparation for Y2K, we figured. But by January 3, 2000, we realized all the stocking of food and water was for naught. We had survived Y2K intact!

When we returned to Northport, I got back to work on my fourth research paper, "The Power of a Woman's Influence," and finally mailed it in on February 1, 2000. Beginning with Eve, I traced the lives of women in the Bible and also in modern times whose influence for good or evil was very powerful and history-changing. I showed how a woman's power of influence is a balance to man's role as head of the home and society, according to God's design. Although a woman's leadership in church and society may be a controversial subject, truth on this issue can be found in God's Holy Word, and women can enjoy this special influence God has given them in His kingdom.

So far my courses were not hard, and the tests were easy. The research papers were a joy to write. The grades were either pass or fail, and I was passed on each one. Confidently, I began my fifth course, Paul, the Jewish Theologian, on February 23, 2000, and completed it, including the research paper, in April. To my chagrin, the paper came back with red marks and instructions to rewrite it. My first title was "Unpopular Doctrines of the Apostle Paul." By this time Curtis and I had moved to Petrey on June 28, and our lives changed radically. Curtis was now a retired pastor, and renovations on his childhood home took up a lot of our time. I finally got around to rewriting the paper, giving it a new title, "Important Doctrines of Paul Ignored." I sent it in on August 15, 2000. This was my most difficult research paper to date.

While I was waiting for the results on my second Paul paper, I completed two more courses and research papers. The sixth one was The Bible and the West Bank, which was largely based on the book, *The Mountains of Israel* by Norma Parrish Archbold.[65] My research paper, "Power Struggle for the Mountain of the Lord (Temple Mount)," was mailed in on November 18, 2000. Less than two months before, on September 28, Israeli Prime Minister Ariel Sharon had visited the Temple Mount, and the second intifada (uprising) by the Palestinians ensued. I began the course on October 24. How timely to be studying about the mountain of the Lord and writing a research paper right after the intifada broke out in that location! Surely I was on assignment from God!

Archbold's book was very revealing about the West Bank, more appropriately called Judea (including Jerusalem) and Samaria. I gave a copy of the book to Jennifer Griffin in Jerusalem. Most of the world has believed the Palestinian propaganda, and I felt it was important that Jennifer, a Fox News reporter, and her husband Greg Myre, journalist for the New York Times, read the true history of this coveted piece of land, so well told by Archbold.

In the prophecies of Ezekiel we see the curtain pulled back to reveal the evil root of the power struggle over the Temple Mount – Satan. Before his fall Satan was named Lucifer, "the anointed cherub" on "the holy mountain of God" (Ezek. 28: 14, 16). When he rebelled, he was kicked out of heaven (Rev. 12:9). He is still trying to ascend to the holy mountain of God through the Muslim presence there today.

However, Jerusalem is the City of the great King, and God said, "Yet I have set my King on My holy hill of Zion" (Psalm 2:6). Who is this foreordained King? Yeshua is "King of the Jews," so stated at His birth and at His death, with Pilate having His title nailed to the cross for all the world to see. Since Satan hates God, he most especially hates His chosen people, the Jews. That is the root cause of the power struggle for the Temple Mount, which eventually will be the "throne of the Lord" (Jer. 3:17) when Yeshua returns there and sets up His earthly kingdom.

My thesis was that whoever controls the Temple Mount in Jerusalem will eventually control all of Israel and, ultimately, the world! The power struggle will end when God fulfills the prophecy of Ezekiel: "I will make them [the Jews] one nation in the land, on the **mountains of Israel**, and one king [Yeshua] shall be king over them all....Moreover I will make a covenant of peace with them, and it shall be an everlasting covenant with them;....indeed I will be their God, and they shall be My people. The nations also will know that I, the Lord, sanctify Israel, when My sanctuary is in their midst [on the Temple Mount] forevermore (37:22, 26-28)."

My seventh graduate course was Josephus, and it was one of the most interesting of all ten courses. Josephus was a historian and contemporary of the Apostles. He authored what have become for Christianity perhaps the most significant extra-biblical writings of the first century, particularly New Testament times. He wrote *The Wars of the Jews*, the principal source for the history of the Jews from the time of the Maccabees to the Great War with Rome, ending with the fall of Masada in A.D. 73. He also wrote *The Antiquities of the Jews* for the non-Jewish world. This account covered the biblical creation narrative up to Josephus' own time.

My research paper was entitled, "Josephus, A Prophetic Voice." Quoting from his writings, including his autobiography, *The Life of Flavius Josephus*, I provided evidence of his divine calling, his godly character, and that he was indeed a prophetic voice to his people at the time of the Great War with Rome.

Josephus was a spiritual man, the son of a priest, and a disciple of Banus, who was possibly a follower of John the Baptist. The strongest evidence that he believed in Jesus Christ was his following statement in *The Antiquities of the Jews*:

> Now, there was about this time Jesus, a wise man, if it be lawful to call him a man, for he was a doer of wonderful works – a teacher of such men as receive the truth with pleasure. He drew over to him both many of the Jews, and many of the Gentiles. He was the Christ; and when Pilate, at the suggestion of the principal men amongst us, had condemned him to the

cross, those that loved him at the first did not forsake him, for he appeared to them alive again the third day, as the divine prophets had foretold these and ten thousand other wonderful things concerning him; and the tribe of Christians, so named from him, are not extinct at this day.[66]

Although many critics disparaged the veracity of some of Josephus' writings, illustrious writers, such as Eusebius, St. Jerome, Ambrose, and William Whiston who translated the works of Josephus into English in 1736, vouched for their authenticity. Whiston commented that Josephus was one of the Ebionite Christians (also called Nazarenes, the original followers of Jesus).[67]

The godly character of Josephus was shown in his refusal to take bribes, his honesty, lack of vengeance, avoidance of bloodshed, forgiveness to enemies, trust in God, and his crediting God with his many miraculous escapes from danger.

He had prophetic dreams in which God showed him the future calamities of the Jews and events concerning the Roman emperors. He had great favor with his people and was serving as a general for the Jews in Galilee when Vespasian, the Roman general, offered him freedom from punishment if he would surrender. The Jews in hiding with him threatened to kill him if he surrendered. They planned to commit suicide rather than surrender. When Josephus warned them that God would punish them for such a crime, they called him a coward and ran at him with swords. Their swords were ineffective because of God's protection.

Josephus, seeing he could not dissuade them from suicide, offered them a method of drawing lots to determine the order of their deaths. In the providence of God, Josephus and another man were the last ones. Josephus persuaded the man that they should remain alive!

Josephus went over to the Romans, and Vespasian said they would send him to Nero. Alarmed, Josephus immediately began prophesying that Vespasian would soon be Emperor and his son after him also. This was outside the normal succession of Emperors and seemed unlikely. At first Vespasian did not believe the prophecy and thought it was a cunning trick by Josephus to preserve his life, but he soon learned otherwise. In less than a year Nero committed suicide, and Vespasian was named Emperor by his legions! He freed Josephus and gave him the family name of Vespasian, Flavius.

Josephus became a reporter, interpreter, and go-between for the Romans in the Great War. General Titus, the son of Vespasian, besieged Jerusalem and sent Josephus to speak to the Jews in their own language to persuade them to surrender the city which was almost taken and thereby save themselves. Josephus went round about the wall, found a place out of reach of their darts, and began to exhort his countrymen to surrender. He reminded them of the Romans' reverence for the Jews' sacred rites and places, having kept their hands off until now. Famine was a second war the Jews were fighting and all the more reason to surrender.

The Jews threw darts at Josephus. He reasoned with them in a prophetic voice from their own history. Abraham did not free Sarah from the Pharoah by his army but by prayer. The Hebrew slaves did not fight the Egyptians, but they cried out to God, and He sent plagues. King Hezekiah prayed to God to save the people from Sennacherib, and an angel of God destroyed the Assyrian army in one night. On the contrary, King Zedikiah fought against the king of Babylon, ignoring the predictions of Jeremiah, and he was taken prisoner. The city and the Temple were demolished. Josephus concluded that the Jewish nation could not expect to use natural means for their deliverance like other nations did, but as the covenant people of God they were dependent upon Him and not their own strength.

These Zealot Jews had offended God with their thefts, plots, rapes, and murders, and they had polluted their own Temple, while the Romans had reverenced the Temple and accommodated the Jewish law. Dead bodies were everywhere, either from famine or from murder. If anyone was about to desert to the Romans, his throat was cut immediately. Josephus warned that the oracle of the ancient prophets foretold that "this city should then be taken when somebody shall begin the slaughter of his own countrymen! And are not both the city and the entire temple now full of the dead bodies of your countrymen? It is God therefore, it is God himself who is bringing on this fire, to purge that city and temple by means of the Romans, and is going to pluck up this city, which is full of your pollutions."[68]

Josephus even offered his own life and the lives of his mother and wife if the Zealots would repent and throw down their arms. Speaking with groans and tears in his eyes, Josephus continued to make his pleas amid the clamor and reproaches of the people, but he was not heard. In A.D. 70 Jerusalem and the Temple were destroyed by the Romans.

Titus gave Josephus permission to take whatever he wanted from the ruins. Spurning silver and gold, he received the liberty of his family, the lives of his brother and fifty friends, and about 190 captive women and children he knew, and he restored them to their former fortunes. With tears in his eyes, he went to Titus to ask for the release of three captives being crucified.

Vespasian took Josephus back to Rome, made him a Roman citizen, and gave him housing and an annual pension as well as tax-free land in Judea. This is reminiscent of Jeremiah whom God preserved when Nebuchadnezzar destroyed Jerusalem and the first Temple (Jer. 39-40). Likewise, God provided for his prophet, Josephus, after the war.

God preserved Josephus not only to exhort his people but to write down a most important account of the war. Titus ordered that his books be published. King Agrippa wrote 62 letters to Josephus, attesting to the truth of what Josephus had written. The critics of Josephus have been numerous and their words scathing, but these same critics still rely on his eyewitness accounts of the Great War with Rome.

I ended my paper with these words, "The reader of *The Works of Josephus* can draw his own conclusions, but therein is ample evidence that Josephus was the spokesman of God during the Great War with Rome. He was a prophetic voice to his people."

I began the course on Josephus on January 31, 2001 and mailed in my research paper on March 19, 2001. Learning about Josephus and his writings was a great blessing in my role as a student of Jewish roots.

21

Thesis and Graduation

Going lickety-split down the road toward my master's degree, I hit a bump and went sprawling! After waiting almost eight months to hear whether I passed or failed on my second writing of the research paper on Paul, the Jewish Theologian, I received the corrected copy in the mail in April of 2001. It had red pencil marks all over it! It was literally bleeding, and my heart was, too. The corrections were numerous and very detailed. No one had told me about the new and more stringent guidelines for writing research papers nor about the grading being handed over to South Central Graduate College. To say I was disheartened was an understatement.

Now I began to wonder about the last two research papers I had mailed in. I assumed that these two would also have to be rewritten, adhering strictly to the new grading criteria. I corresponded by phone and letter to Gina, the secretary and grading assistant, and to Dr. Moseley. I told them I would have to drop out, even though I was only three courses and a thesis away from a Master's Degree. I did not have time to re-write the papers. They patiently heard my complaints, then replied that I would not be required to rewrite papers for the last three courses – Paul, the Jewish Theologian, The Bible and the West Bank, and Josephus – since I was unaware of the new guidelines. Whew! What sweet relief. God was still showing me favor, and I praised him. I did not want to lose the credits for the volume of work I had already done.

Gina encouraged me to continue on, but I wrote her that I would not be able to take any additional courses in 2001, because I had been hired by DayStar Bible Institute in Northport to teach two ORU courses in the fall. This would require a three-hour commute one-way each week plus a lot of lesson preparation. I would not have the time to devote to any more courses at AIHLS.

By the summer of 2001, Arkansas Institute was a distant memory. My life got busier and busier as a Mizpah, speaking in various places, but more so after meeting Janice Bell and later forming our ministry (Chapters 12-14). I went to Israel for Lars Enarson's prayer tour and Passover convocation (Chapter 10), formed a monthly Israel prayer group, made a recording of Hebrew songs (Chapter 11), and Janice and I went to Israel (Chapters 15 through 19). How would I have had time to concentrate on three more courses and write a 70-page thesis? I didn't consider it at all.

Time passed. Then it was January 4, 2004. God began stirring my heart one Sunday morning in church. From beginning to end everything about the worship service seemed heavy with meaning. I felt that God was calling me, but I could hardly say the words, "to preach." How presumptuous of me, I thought. Besides I was a woman, and so much controversy surrounded women preachers. What would Curtis think? What would everybody else think? Besides, was I myself fully convinced it was biblical for a woman to preach?

After church that day, I was talking to a lady, and she told me something amazing, in light of the fact I had just been pondering that maybe God was calling me to preach. She said that at Thanksgiving time she asked her little grandson what he was thankful for. He replied, "The preacher and the preacher lady who sings and plays the piano." That was me! In the service that very day I had played and sung "The Holy City," and I played and sang a solo almost every Sunday, preceded by an introduction, apparently perceived by the little boy as "preaching." So, he thought of me as a "preacher lady!" Could it be, Lord?

I didn't know where it would lead, but later I contacted Covenant Bible Institute in Georgia by e-mail to see about a correspondence course. Two weeks later I got a call from the president. When I told him about my work at AIHLS, he said that I could probably get my Master's Degree at Covenant Bible Institute as early as the coming spring or summer! They would accept my courses, and I would only need three more. He said it was "doable." I called Gina at AIHLS, and she said she would send my transcript to Covenant Bible Institute.

I did a lot of praying and consulting with Curtis. He was concerned about the high cost of the thesis at CBI and that some of the work would have to be done on campus, a good little drive to Portal, Georgia. He suggested I call Gina at AIHLS and ask about the thesis cost there. I called right away and found out the graduation fee, including the thesis, was minimal. Not only that, but they would "grandfather me in," she said, at the same requirements I had when I started the ten courses with ten-page research papers and only a pass/fail grading system. Their new requirements of twelve courses and stricter guidelines would not apply to me. What a gracious offer! It was evident that God had again given me favor with AIHLS, and he was leading me to finish my degree there, after a three-year absence.

So, it was settled. My old zeal returned, and on February 9, I began my eighth course with AIHLS, Heresies in the Early Church. It took me three weeks to complete the course. I mailed my paper in on March 1, "Desert Fathers – Heretics or Heroes?" What an eye-opener. I had no idea how close Satan came to sabotaging the early church with an arsenal of heresies.

One of the prevalent heresies was extreme asceticism and celibacy as practiced by the desert fathers. The first of them was Antony, an illiterate Coptic Christian, who became the "father of monasticism." There were both heretical and heroic elements in his life. For 20 years he did not see the face of a man, and food was thrown to him over the wall. When he finally came forth, a crowd awaited him. He consoled the sorrowful and exhorted them to choose the love of Christ over all worldly pleasures. The Lord used him to bring healing to many and to cast out evil spirits. He organized a large body of monks. The last 45 years of his life he lived in seclusion but received many visitors. Before Antony died at the age of 105, he asked two disciples to bury him in secret, so that his body should not become an object of reverence.

Athanasius, Bishop of Alexandria from 328 to 373, championed Antony and wrote the story of his life. Considering the greatness of Athanasius, his endorsement of St. Antony carried a lot of weight, because God used him to end the long debate over which books should be included in the New Testament. In his annual letter to the Church, Athanasius listed the books inspired of God, which was the first time a church leader identified the books now called the New Testament. Athanasius was an arch foe of church heresies. In his battles against popular heresies he suffered exile time and time again. He did not consider St. Antony to be a heretic but came to his defense and desired that others should emulate him.

Marvin Wilson, in his book, *Our Father Abraham*, sheds some light on the source of the teachings of celibacy and asceticism, contrasting them with the biblical understanding from Hebrew thought.[69] The early church and those who withdrew from it were influenced by the Gnostic idea of Platonic dualism, the belief that the body is evil and not to be enjoyed in this world, that salvation comes by mental enlightenment. On the other hand, the Hebrews did not believe in the ascetic denial of physical pleasures, but rather that they should be stewards of these gifts and dedicate them to God in appreciation. Genesis 1:28 gives humanity a mandate to establish civilization, not to escape from it. The Bible further states, that "Marriage should be honored by all ..." and warns against "doctrines of demons ... forbidding to marry ..." (Heb. 13:4 NIV; I Tim. 4:3-4). Reconnecting to our Jewish roots helps us to discover a "more excellent way" than the ascetic, solitary life.

Nevertheless, my research brought me to the conclusion that the "desert fathers," despite the influence of heretical Gnosticism in their lives, were heroes of the faith. I could not deny that they stood in sharp contrast to the worldliness and decadence that would later take over the church. I ended my paper with these words: "Their voice and their accomplishments still endure as beacons, glorifying the Lord Jesus Christ, the One for whom they sacrificed everything. The desert fathers were indeed true heroes of the faith."

The same day I sent in my paper on the desert fathers, I started the ninth course, New Testament Apocrypha and Pseudepigrapha, and finished it in only a few days! This course included a long listing of books outside the New Testament canon of Scripture. This was all brand new information to me and turned out to be quite valuable. It gave me a deep appreciation for the sovereign guidance of God in the whole process of establishing the biblical canon. *Canon* comes from a Greek word meaning "reed" or "rule." It is the list of books considered to be authoritative as Scripture.

The word *apocrypha* means "hidden" or "secret." I had never heard of the word, *pseudepigrapha*. It refers to spurious writings that are falsely attributed to biblical characters or times, a type of forgery. Many of these books are dangerous, but a few were almost included in the canon of Scripture. For instance, *The Didache* (teaching), or *The Teaching of the Twelve Apostles*, is most likely the oldest surviving extant piece of non-canonical literature in existence. It is claimed that the teachings are derived directly from Yeshua Messiah through the work of the first Apostolic Council, ca. 50-60 (Acts 15:28). Scholars say it circulated in the early church. I read *The Didache*, and it holds great value, is very interesting, and is even funny in places.

Bishop Athanasius recommended *The Didache* and also *The Shepherd of Hermas* as instruction books for new converts. *The Shepherd of Hermas* has been called the *Pilgrim's Progress* of the second-century church. Both these books were considered Scripture at one time, but neither made it into the New Testament canon.

Other apocryphal books are dangerous. One of these is *The Sophia of Jesus Christ*, which was a Gnostic text unearthed at Nag Hammadi in northern Egypt in 1945. Some modern-day religious feminists have seized upon the warped theology of this book and have made an effort to incorporate it into mainstream Christianity. Sophia, this "goddess" of wisdom, was introduced at a large women's gathering of several main-line church denominations in 1993, and prayer was offered to her![70]

I found in this study that *The New Testament Apocrypha* and *Pseudepigrapha* represent a spiritual minefield of strange legends and blasphemous heresies, but *The Didache, The Shepherd of Hermas,* and a few others are worth the effort of discovery among this grouping of diverse writings.

The title of my paper was "Books for the Times, Not for All Times." I ended the paper with these words: "The truth is that the best of these books are only books for the times. The Holy Bible is the book of God's Word to all people for all times." I had begun the course on March 1, and I mailed in the research paper on March 10. I was back up to speed, on a roll, and enjoying it all the way.

My tenth and final course was Apocalyptic Literature of the 1st Century. The word *apocalypse* is a Greek word meaning "uncovering" or "disclosure," usually through the method of divine revelation in a dream, vision, or a trance. There were several books in Jesus' time warning the Jewish people with the same apocalyptic message as the Book of Revelation. This warning was usually directed against the Romans. These apocalyptic books included the Old Testament Apocrypha, the New Testament, the Dead Sea Scrolls, the Testaments of the Twelve Patriarchs, the Book of Enoch, the Apocalypse of Abraham, the Apocalypse of Ezra, and the Sibylline Oracles. I chose to write my paper on the Book of Revelation and entitled it "Relevance of Revelation."

Theologians through the years have attempted to establish the relevance of Revelation to their generation. Unfortunately, few have considered the interlocking destinies of the Church and Israel and have thereby failed to adequately prepare Christians for the coming of their Jewish Messiah, the most relevant event described in John's Apocalypse.

I concluded my paper with these words: "There is some relevance in most interpretations of Revelation, but two crucial elements of understanding to insure adequate preparation for believers in the last days are the unity of the Church with Israel and the willingness to face tribulation. The heroes of the faith listed in Hebrews 11 did not all receive deliverance. Moses chose to suffer affliction with the people of God rather than to enjoy the passing pleasures of sin (vs. 25). '... Others were tortured, not accepting deliverance, that they might obtain a better resurrection' (vs. 35). Jesus set the bar high for being His disciple and urged His followers to count the cost. Regardless of the details, the most obvious and relevant truth of Revelation is that Jesus is coming for a prepared people. ... He will be joined to His bride, the Church, made up of Jews and Gentiles, to live with them forever in the New Jerusalem!"

It took two weeks to complete the course, and I mailed in my paper on April 1. It was so obvious to me that God had given me favor and fired me up! Now I was poised and ready to begin work on the 70-page thesis.

Finding a topic to research for the thesis was easy, because it was already in my heart. At last I would be able to put on paper my deeply-held conviction that the Jewish people and the nation of Israel have blessed the world more than any other people group. I would document their amazing number of contributions in every field of endeavor. I hoped that whoever read my thesis would be filled with awe and gratitude to the Jewish people for their inventions and discoveries, which today continue to touch almost every person in the world! This, I would prove, was all because of God's promise to Abraham that He would make him a great nation, bless him, cause him to be a blessing, and through his descendants bless all the families of the earth (Gen. 12:2-3).

I chose the title, *Destiny of the Jews*. My thesis was: "The destiny of the Jews is to be a source of blessing for the entire world and to glorify God at the end of time, when they welcome their Messiah and King of the whole earth."

I laid the groundwork for the long list of their contributions with an introductory paragraph, showing how God had preserved the Jewish people for their greatest purpose yet to come. The Jews are virtually indestructible until that time, having lasted 4,000 years. The Guiness Book of Records lists the Jews as the oldest minority in the world. They have survived six alien civilizations.[71] They are one of the smallest people groups, numbering about 13,421,000,[72] which represents one-fifth of one percent of the world's population, and yet they have blessed the world through their accomplishments greatly out of proportion to their numbers! The Jews have survived many attempts to annihilate them, because God is preserving them. The destiny of the Jews and the wrap-up of human history are intertwined.

First, I wrote about the call of Abraham and the formation of the Jewish nation. Next followed the accounts of individual Jews who have blessed the world through the years, first in early America, then in music and entertainment, in science and medicine, in sports, and in business and public service. In the field of religion, I wrote about the contributions of Moses, Yeshua of Nazareth, Paul the Apostle, and of Christianity as expressed in science, music, human freedom, morality, and healthcare. Some of the contributors in literature and linguistics were King Solomon, Flavius Josephus, Anne Frank, and Eliezer Ben-Yehuda, who resurrected Hebrew to be the modern, official language of the reborn nation of Israel.

After writing about individual Jews, I wrote in the next section of my thesis about how the **nation** of Israel has blessed the world. Israel's contributions were shown in agriculture, exports, technologies of health, electronics, security, and communications, in education, and in their humanitarianism concerning Palestinian refugees, the absorption of Jews, the "Good Fence," Hadassah University Medical Center, rescue missions around the world, and Yad Sarah, one of the largest volunteer organizations in the world. This section ended with the blessings of the military, the Israel Defense Force, as evidenced in the destruction of the Iraqi nuclear complex, their humane practices in Jenin, their restraint during the Gulf War, and their assistance during the Gulf War.

It was a delight to write this thesis and prove that the contributions of individual Jews to the world ever since God first called Abraham over 4,000 years ago and the contributions of the modern State of Israel in the last 56 years (at the time I wrote it) have been enormous and without precedent in any people group or nation throughout history. (See Appendix C.)

Finally, in the conclusion I wrote about the "invisible Hand" of God miraculously bringing the Jews back to their ancient homeland and making them a "holy" nation, as shown through their national life, which is connected to Scripture. Israel's emblem is the menorah, the seven-branched candelabra, flanked by two olive branches, a symbol taken from the Bible (Zech. 4:2-3). Their flag is a prayer shawl (Num. 15: 3-40). They strictly enforce the Sabbath in public life. The absence of leavened bread in Jewish stores during Passover week is another reminder that Israel is a set-apart people, whose unique relationship with the God of Israel is evident not only in her history but in her daily life.

Apart from the Bible, the survival of the Jews cannot be explained, and their destiny cannot be understood. The God of Israel has preserved His chosen people for their greatest blessing to the world, which is yet to come. The Jewish people look for their Messiah. Orthodox Jews daily recite this creed, "I believe with complete faith in the coming of the Messiah; and even though he tarry, I will wait for him every coming day." This is their destiny, and their greatest blessing to the world, when the Jews welcome back Yeshua of Nazareth as their Messiah. Part of my purpose as a Mizpah is to witness to the Jews about their Messiah, Yeshua HaMashiach, and thereby enable them to fulfill their destiny.

I started my research for the thesis on April 12, began typing it on April 26, and finished it on May 11. Next I had to type up the reference list, a bibliography, title page, and log of my reading. It was in the mail on May 18, 2004! Truly, God's hand was on me to accomplish this 70-page thesis in such a short time, and, indeed, to complete the three courses preceding it so quickly. It had been only a little over three months since I resumed my studies with AIHLS! My regular life outside the studies was also busy for me those three months, but the Lord gave me the grace to persevere toward my goal. Dr. Moseley read my thesis and liked it. Praise the Lord!

Even more satisfying than Dr. Moseley's approval were the good reports I received from my friend, Betty Fancher, who had moved from Columbus to Texas. She is an outstanding Bible teacher, and she wrote that she was sharing my thesis with the Jewish people she was ministering to in a nursing home in Houston. A Methodist named Mel thought it was great. When a rabbi asked what he was reading, he said it was about "you Jews," a thesis that a "young lady" wrote. Then the Rabbi borrowed it and read it. He said it was good, and he used it in a speech. Betty made copies to share with others in the nursing home. One Jewish lady, a teacher of Hebrew, said it was excellent, and I should get a grade no less than a 90 and also a star! Being in a nursing home does not necessarily mean that an aged person can't keep learning. This lady requested that Betty teach them the gospels after they completed Hebrews. Betty's ministry among those Jewish people was bearing fruit, and I was happy to have a part in it. Just what I hoped would be the result of my thesis had happened. Jews were reading it and being blessed.

I determined I would attend the formal graduation ceremony at the American (changed from "Arkansas") Institute of Holy Land Studies on August 7, 2004. What a surprise to learn that our daughter, Susan Petrey, would also be graduating on that exact date from the University of North Texas. I immediately knew what we must do, and Curtis agreed to it. He would fly out to Texas and see Susan get her Master of Education in Curriculum and Instruction. I would invite my friend and ministry partner, Janice Bell, to drive with me to Sherwood, Arkansas. I was disappointed not to be at our daughter's graduation, but at the same time I was excited about getting my degree, a Master of Religious Education in Middle East History.

The Commencement Exercises were a part of their annual Jerusalem Conference. Janice and I had a marvelous time, meeting people of like mind, and hearing first-class speakers. Jim Fleming especially blessed us. His list of titles was so long, but a few of them were: Director of the Biblical Resources Study Center in

Jerusalem, having lived and worked in Israel since 1974, teacher at Hebrew University and American Institute, tour leader to Israel, cartography consultant for Israeli photographs, and on the Advisory Board for Biblical Archaeology Review. (Today he has developed the Explorations in Antiquity Museum in LaGrange, Georgia.)

Dr. Brad Young was another outstanding speaker. Janice was especially interested in his talk, "Historical Context for the Passion of Christ," which explored the controversy surrounding Mel Gibson's film. We enjoyed Dr. Moseley's addresses, which were sprinkled with a lot of humor. An Israeli teacher of Hebrew, Yaffa McPherson, showed Jesus in the Hebrew alphabet. Dr. Fleming spoke about the Twelve Apostles. These are just a few of the speakers' topics, but they all could be described as "meaty" and some of them as entertaining.

When I saw the graduation program I was shocked! Out of nine graduates present for the graduation ceremony, I was the only one receiving a Master's Degree, but, even more surprising, I was graduating Summa Cum Laude (Highest Praise). That meant all my grades were As! Not having received a report card, this was new information to me. To God be the glory!

God didn't let me get the "big head." As they say, "He has His ways," and something funny happened when we rehearsed the graduation. Dressed in my black robe and mortarboard (square academic hat), I reached out to shake Dr. Moseley's hand as he handed me the diploma in my other hand. I don't know if it was because of shaking Dr. Moseley's hand or a bump on the platform, but my mortarboard fell off as I took the diploma! Everyone looking on got a big laugh, and I also laughed at myself. "Pomp and circumstance" were interrupted by a flying mortarboard! Argh! Dignity is no fun anyway.

On January 1, 2004, I had noted in my journal that 2004 was the year that God would **"open the door"** to ministry for me. On January 4 in church that year, I thought God was calling me to preach. This led to my studying for a Master's Degree, which I now had obtained! This year was the **44**th year of our marriage,

and on June 28, 2004, it was the fourth anniversary of our move
back to Petrey. Our address is **44** Community House Road. The
number 4 and the number 44 have been important clues from God
in our lives. Truly, important milestones were achieved in our lives
in 2004. God did "open the door in 2004" in many ways. As I

Nancy receiving Master's Degree from Dr. Ron Moseley at
Arkansas Institute for Holy Land Studies – August 2004

was looking at the new AIHLS catalog, I noticed that the page number for the Master's Degree requirements was page **44**! This was another one of God's little clues to me that I was in the center of His will, and I rejoiced.

Well, my goal was finally achieved. I had my Master's Degree, and I was ready to put it to use, teaching in a junior college. However, I had already had the great privilege and blessing of teaching in a Bible school years before I had my degree.

22

You Have to Knock

It was the summer of 1999 after we had moved to Northport. I was out at the pool one day and got in a conversation with a lady whose last name was Schatzline. I asked her if that name was Jewish, and she said yes. That piqued my interest in her, so we continued to talk. It so happened that her father was pastor of a church close by, DayStar Assembly of God. The wheels started rolling in my head with thoughts of teaching his church about our Jewish roots. But perhaps Pastor Schatzline was already doing that. On July 31 that summer, I met Scott Wimberly, the new associate pastor of DayStar, and his wife. They were moving into an apartment below us. As we talked, I learned that my professor, Dr. Ron Moseley, was coming to speak at DayStar. What were the odds of that happening? It was clearly another one of God's clues that He was directing me. Yes, DayStar was drawing my attention.

On New Years' Day, 2000, I asked the Lord for a verse for the new year. He gave me Matthew 7:7 – "Ask, and it will be given to you; seek, and you will find; knock, and it will be opened to you." Not long after that I began to be distracted about the possibility of becoming a piano teacher. I felt guilty about not using my ability and training to teach others how to play the piano. This guilt was disturbing my sleep. Finally, I asked the Lord specifically, "Should I teach piano lessons?" I opened my Bible at random, and my eye fell on Jeremiah 40:8 – "Then they came to Gedaliah at MIZPAH." That could not have been a co-incidence! I knew I had an answer and was reassured that the Lord wanted me to continue as a Mizpah for Israel. This was my primary calling, and I refused to stay on a guilt trip about not teaching piano. I would continue working toward my Master's Degree in Middle East History, so that God could use me as a Mizpah more effectively.

Remembering my verse for the year, I trusted God to open the doors for ministry. As I pondered God's Word, I thought I heard Him say, "You have to **knock** on some doors for them to open." With new boldness, I acted on what I heard and invited Scott and Melissa, our downstairs neighbors, to lunch! What an interesting conversation we had. I found out that Scott was not only the new Associate Pastor at DayStar Assembly of God, but he was also Administrator for the ORU school beginning at DayStar Bible Institute! We talked about the possibility of my teaching Jewish studies in the school. Scott said he would talk to Pastor Schatzline about it and to get my resume ready.

Lunch with Scott and Melissa was on January 11, and by February 2, I had an answer. Scott said that Pastor Schatzline and the church board wanted me to teach the ORU Pentateuch course at DayStar Bible Institute, and the students had already signed up and were excited! The classes would meet for 12 weeks on Friday nights, beginning at the end of May. Scott was apologetic about their not being able to pay me, but I gladly welcomed this opportunity and knew the Lord would "pay" me far better than they could. Curtis said he had to pray about it, because he knew we would be moving to Petrey by summer time. Two days later I had Curtis' answer. He said yes!

I went into high gear as soon as I received an ORU syllabus of the course. It took some reworking in order to include more explicit Jewish roots elements, which was quite a challenge. My brain was bulging with information from the textbooks as well as material I designed myself. I had six students. After the third class one of my students said to me, "A man from ORU came by and saw your course. He said, 'That's an advanced course. We don't have that yet at ORU, but we're working toward it.'" What a shot in the arm! I had been so worried about presenting this very difficult course and doing it justice. I went into Scott's office to talk. He said, "Your students love you, but don't work so hard. I want you to teach next semester. I don't want you to burn out." When I told Curtis what Scott said, Curtis responded, "You absolutely cannot commute from Petrey to teach the next term." I wouldn't think that far ahead. I knew the Lord had my future in His hands.

I administered the first test in the Pentateuch class, and all the students made As. I was thrilled with the results of all my hard work and theirs. Each class was three hours long with a short break in the middle. I stood on my feet to teach and loved every minute of it. We rarely stopped short of the three hours, and the students seemed fully engaged the whole time. My prayer was that the Lord would help me impart to the students the vision He had given me as a Mizpah for Israel, and it was happening!

The way the Lord orchestrated my teaching in conjunction with moving to Petrey was quite amazing. We moved to Petrey in two phases, the first phase on June 28. On our way back to Northport on June 30 for the rest of our belongings, phase two of the move, we stopped at the **Rest** Stop. We were on two vehicles. The car odometer read 77777777 – eight "sevens." If one seven is the number of completion and rest, then what could eight sevens mean? Since the number eight means "new beginnings," I would say that moving to Petrey represented much rest and a new beginning! I looked forward to what God would do in our lives there.

We were out of the apartment in Northport and had passed inspection by 3:30 that afternoon. Curtis took the loaded van back to Petrey. I went to DayStar to copy my Study Questions for the class that night, studied, went to The Diner for supper, then back to the church to teach my class. It was the best class I had taught thus far.

Chris, one of my students, told me he had heard Lars Enarson speak at their church that week. (I had made the arrangements for Lars to come, but, sadly, we moved the very day he came.) Chris said he could fully understand everything Lars taught because of what he had been learning in my class. He told others what it all meant, and they were amazed he knew so much. Chris was saying back to me what I had taught in the class!

I was really praising the Lord after class as I drove to my friend Karen's house to spend the night. She was the bonus blessing of our short residence in Northport. (See Chapter 4.) The next day I drove to Petrey with my car loaded. The move had been like "clock-work." It had God's fingerprints all over it. By July 1, we were completely moved in.

Looking back on our one-and-a-half-year stay in Northport, I rejoiced that God had used me as a Mizpah for Israel, not only in my teaching at DayStar Bible Institute, but also in having Lars Enarson to speak at our newly-formed church, Christ Church, in downtown Tuscaloosa in July of 1999. How appropriate that the tiny church building was a former synagogue! It was packed the night Lars spoke, and they really grabbed on to the Jewish roots message and the importance of supporting and praying for Israel. Besides music ministry at Christ Church, I also taught a series on the Feasts of the Lord in the home of Polly Dubose and conducted three Passover Seders.

I had to commute from Petrey to Northport to finish the last six classes of the Pentateuch, requiring that I stay overnight each time. Karen was my willing hostess. Our fellowship was a big highlight of each weekend.

Driving home the next morning after the final class, I felt very downhearted, because neither Scott nor Pastor Schatzline had thanked me for my voluntary teaching. I always got good feedback from the students, and I felt good about my teaching and their learning, but I was missing a simple word of thanks from the administration after the course was completed. I put in a Ray Bolz tape as I drove. Listening to the beautiful song, "Thank You," hit a responsive chord in my heart, and I began to cry. While I was sobbing, I seemed to hear the Lord say to me, "I saw all you did, and I thank You. I know you did it for Me, and I appreciate it." I continued to cry happy tears as song after song on the tape went straight to the deepest part of my heart. God's love more than made up for any recognition or approval I had needed from others. I began to sing and praise the Lord for His goodness to me in allowing me to teach His precious Word and to influence His people. The whole trip home was saturated with the presence of God. What a glorious experience!

You can imagine my surprise when I got a call six months later from Scott! He was calling to ask if I would teach the Pentateuch at DayStar again in the fall. Since I had not heard from him or the pastor, I had assumed they did not accept my teaching. Also, I never heard any more from the students and, likewise, thought they may not have fully agreed with my teaching. In spite of my wrong assumptions, God was clearly giving me favor at DayStar. Scott said they would be willing to pay me "whatever it takes." He insisted that I was the only one who could best teach that course, that they really wanted me. I was bowled over! I was even more shocked when Curtis agreed for me to commute to Northport once a week!

Scott asked me to teach an additional course, Hebrew Prophets. I would be teaching Hebrew Prophets on Friday nights and the Pentateuch on Saturday mornings. A student would video tape me for each class, so they could use the videos for future classes. I set about my task joyfully, reading the text book for Hebrew Prophets and the Bible, praying, and compiling a hefty notebook of lesson plans and ideas.

I would be commuting a lot. The first class was on September 6, 2001, and the last one was on December 20. The Lord worked out my overnight lodging through Curtis' brother Joe and another friend, Betty Cole. The classes were very fulfilling. As usual, the teacher learns so much more than the students.

The trip from Petrey to the parking lot of the DayStar Bible Institute was exactly 144 miles. I learned that the number 144 is very significant. It indicates a Spirit Guided life![73] What more affirmation from the Lord could I receive? Every time I made that long trip from Petrey to Northport in the fall of 2001, I was reminded that the Holy Spirit was guiding my life. He guided me to knock on the door that day to ask for a teaching position, and God opened the door!

23

God Opened the Door in Two Thousand and Four!

Seven months before I received my Master's Degree, the ball was already rolling for me to teach in a college, Lurleen B. Wallace Community College (LBW), which had a campus in Luverne. Knowing I would be finishing my degree at AIHLS, I called LBW in Greenville to speak to Dr. Jean Thompson, a former high school friend. She referred me to Dr. Mike Daniels, who said I could possibly teach World Religions when I got my degree. Also, he said, I could teach Continuing Education courses, such as History of the Old Testament or History of the New Testament. I could even design my own course. That certainly appealed to me and would allow me to integrate the Jewish roots angle. By March I was hired! I did not yet have the degree, but, evidently, Dr. Thompson vouched for me. I wrote in my journal, "God is truly OPENING THE DOOR IN 2004!" I had learned how to knock on the door four years before, just as the Lord taught me, when I asked to teach at DayStar Bible Institute.

Eight days before I mailed my thesis in, Dr. Daniels met with me to discuss my teaching History of World Religions as an adjunct professor at LBW. He also wanted me to teach a Continuing Education course on **Genesis**. This all sounded wonderful to me. Earning money made me feel more "official," but it really mattered very little to me. What was important was that I would be holding up God's Word and proclaiming truth! I obtained the text book for World Religions and began studying diligently.

A week after my graduation, I had good news and bad news. Unfortunately, the World Religions class did not "make" (not enough signed up). Here is what I wrote in my journal about this disappointment: "Dear Lord, You control my life for which I am grateful. I love You, I praise You, I trust You. I did all I could do to advertise my class, and I had many praying. I studied and prepared, but I really wanted Your perfect will. So it appears that Your will was not for me to teach this world religions class. Maybe You were protecting me. After all, the subject matter was grisly and even demonic in most of the chapters. I'm glad to know what the false religions are like, and I know this information will be useful. Also, I learned more about the history of the Church and Judaism. That is important."

The good news was that seven people signed up for the Genesis class. They were all Christians. I had hoped to disseminate God's truth in the secular arena, but it was not to be. I used the material I had developed in the Pentateuch course but added so much more. This was really an exciting study.

I had fabulous resource books. One was *The Genesis Record* by Henry Morris and was a verse-by-verse literal interpretation of Genesis. Dr. Morris, now deceased, was president of the Institute for Creation Research and professor of hydrology in the institute's division of graduate study and research. He was highly respected and considered the "father of creationism."

How enriching it was to read Morris' proofs in the biblical text that Genesis is made up of eyewitness accounts, including that of Adam. These accounts were passed on through Abraham to Moses who compiled the records into the Book of Genesis. Moses and the eyewitnesses wrote their accounts through the inspiration of the Holy Spirit. Morris commented on Genesis 5:1 - "This is the **book** of the generations of Adam. ... The record was thus *written*, not just transmitted orally. Quite possibly, Adam himself wrote the section (chapters 2, 3, 4) which concludes with this statement and signature of Adam. Similarly, Noah (note Gen. 6:9) was probably the original author of Genesis 5:1b – 6:9a."[74]

Morris also exploded the false theory of evolution which requires that the earth be millions of years old. He explained how Satan has made inroads into the Church through these pseudo-scientific beliefs. Since Genesis is the foundation of the entire Bible, it has been a target for Satan to undermine faith in all of God's Word. I welcomed this opportunity to shed light on the subjects of creation and Noah's flood, both of which Jesus alluded to several times as real people and real events.

Another excellent resource I used to support the story of Adam and Eve in the Garden of Eden as literal and the story of the worldwide flood as literal was *Eternity in Their Hearts*[75] by Don Richardson. In his book it was interesting to read about a man by the name of Dr. Wilhelm Schmidt, an Austrian, who set out in the 1920s to compile what researchers had discovered around the world about native beliefs in God. It took six volumes totaling 4,500 pages to detail them all. Schmidt found that 90 percent or more of the folk religions on the planet contain clear acknowledgment of one Supreme God! They often called this Being, the "Sky God." It was almost intellectual suicide to oppose the doctrine of evolution and its high priests when Schmidt published his book in 1934. Unfortunately, this data was suppressed, because it contradicted the theory of evolution. Evolution taught that religion had evolved just as human life forms had evolved, and there was no divine intervention at a point in time.

Richardson wrote about the Karen people in Burma as an example of a people's religious beliefs being rooted in the creation story. Tribesmen were looking for a certain "white brother" whom they had been expecting from time immemorial. He would bring them a book, a book just like one their forefathers lost long ago. The author of the book was Y'wa, the Supreme God, they said. When the white brother would give them the book, they would be set free from all who oppressed them. The Karen story of man's falling away from God in their "Book of Y'wa" contains stunning parallels to Genesis chapters 1-3:

Y'wa formed the world originally. He appointed food
and drink. He appointed the "fruit of trial."

He gave detailed orders. Mu-kaw-lee deceived two per-
sons. He caused them to eat the fruit of the tree of trial. They
obeyed not; they believed not Y'wa.... When they ate the fruit
of trial, They became subject to sickness, aging, and death....[76]

King Solomon said it best: "God has also set eternity in the
hearts of men!" (Eccles. 3:11). Even the most primitive of men
have a longing in their hearts to know the eternal God. Paul wrote
to the Romans that evil men who deny the truth have no excuse,
because "the truth about God is known to them instinctively; God
has put this knowledge in their hearts. Since earliest times men
have seen the earth and sky and all God made, and have known of
his existence and great eternal power ..." (Rom. 1: 19-20, Living
Bible).

Another resource I used for the Genesis course was *The
Discovery of Genesis*[77] by C. Kang and Ethel R. Nelson. The
authors showed how the truths of Genesis were found hidden in
the Chinese language. This is an astounding discovery, because
Chinese characters are used by more people than any other script,
and the Chinese have the oldest culture on earth. In their picture
language is a record of earth's beginnings. Their word for "creation"
pictures Adam as the first live man made of dust! The word for
"to covet" is composed of two trees and a woman. The word for
"boat" is a vessel of eight people. Noah escaped the flood in the Ark
(a boat) with his wife, three sons, and their wives, a total of eight
people! These are only a few examples. Yes, the ancient Chinese
characters, like fossils, have been preserved to be a supporting
witness to the Hebrew Scriptures.

It was a delight to bring all this extra-biblical material into the
study of Genesis, and it made for a deeply satisfying experience for
all of us. The course was completed by November 4, 2004.

The following January, I began a course on **Exodus**. A
small number signed up, only six. As I continued to teach these
Continuing Education courses with LBW, the numbers grew

slowly, but, best of all, many students would continue on with me. Quite a few took all the courses I would teach, which totaled ten by the end of 2010.

My third class was **History of Christian Anti-Semitism** in the fall of 2005. The classes were held at two locations, LBW in Greenville and LBW in Luverne. That was quite a challenge for me to drive to Greenville and back at night, but it was a great experience, meeting new people. Dr. Thompson took the course, which made me look good! I had five students in Greenville and ten students in Luverne. At this time I began to use booklets written by Richard Booker. They were all excellent, short, and to the point. For this course we used "How the Cross Became a Sword."[78] We covered the events that separated Christianity from its Jewish roots in the first three centuries of the Church – how the Church embraced pagan ideas and practices that established anti-Semitism as official Church doctrine, and how Hitler could quote Martin Luther to justify the Holocaust.

The fourth course was **Biblical Feasts and Holidays**, which concluded in March of 2006. I had already taught about the feasts many times, but I continued to learn more as I prepared the lessons. The seven annual feasts are described in Leviticus 23. (See Chapter 18.) They form God's Calendar of Redemption. The first three in the spring – Passover, Unleavened Bread, and Firstfruits – are prophetic of the first coming of Yeshua the Messiah in His death, burial, and resurrection. The fourth one, Pentecost, is prophetic of the coming of the Holy Spirit, as described in Acts 2. The last three in the fall – Trumpets, Atonement, and Tabernacles – are prophetic of the second coming of the Messiah in His arrival on the clouds of the air with believers caught up to meet Him. This will be followed by the national salvation of Israel and the setting up on Yeshua's earthly throne for his reign of a thousand years. Our study also included the weekly Sabbath and the extra-biblical Jewish feasts of Hanukkah and Purim.

In the fall of 2006, I taught my fifth course at a new location, South Luverne Baptist Church (SLBC). By this time, the red tape at Lurleen B. Wallace Community College had grown longer and more complicated. I made the decision to teach under the auspices of SLBC, because I was now a member of the church, and our pastor, Mike Green, was happy to let me use the church facilities. My original goal was to reach unchurched people, but it looked like the Lord had intended me to teach only Christians at this point. I would still advertise each course in the newspaper as a "community" Bible study, hoping to reach a wider audience.

Unlike the other courses, there was no fee for this course, **Islam, Christianity, and Israel**.[79] It was a great success, with 15 students, the most students to date. Dr. Richard Booker's booklet by the same name was the main resource. We learned about the biblical roots of the Arab-Jew conflict, the truth about Islam and Muhammed, the Church's responsibility toward Israel, how to pray for the "peace" of Jerusalem, and understanding how prophecy is being fulfilled in today's events in the Holy Land.

At the conclusion of the course everyone was invited to our home in Petrey for a special prayer meeting. Our prayer guide listed points of prayer for the Church to learn about and appreciate her Jewish roots, to repent of her past history of anti-Semitism and replacement theology, to support Israel and the Jews, and to embrace the Messianic Jews. Other subjects on the guide were prayers against Islam, for breakthroughs in the lives of Muslims, for Christians to reach out to Muslims, and for Muslim converts to win their families to faith in Messiah and be protected from radical Muslims who would kill them. Finally, we prayed for the nation of Israel for government and military leaders to make wise decisions, for the people to cry out to their Messiah to come and save them, for God to send more harvesters into His fields there, and for God to be glorified in Israel, so that all the nations will know that HE IS GOD! All these prayer concerns show that being an intercessor is a hard job!

Each succeeding class grew in enrollment. In the fall of 2007, eighteen students signed up for **The Root and Branches**.[80] This was an especially popular course. There were four male students, including my own husband, Pastor Mike, and the county mission director. I had to be on my toes with these three preachers present!

We used a workbook with the same name as the course, authored by Dr. Richard Booker. The lesson titles were – 1 Why Jewish Roots. 2 The Covenants. 3 The Sabbath. 4 The Feasts. 5 Anti-Semitism. 6 The Rebirth of the State of Israel.

Dr. Booker listed the benefits of learning about our roots – 1 Fuller and clearer understanding of the Bible. 2 Exciting new insights about the teachings of Jesus. 3 Clarification of Paul's writings. 4 Clearer comprehension of God's plan of redemption and prophetic seasons. 5 Become a better follower of Jesus.

This course not only reinforced and amplified what I had already been teaching, but it also gave a concise, overview of my Mizpah message for a person who might take only one course.

The seventh course in the fall of 2008 was **Exploring Hebrew**. This was one of my favorites. The lessons were: 1 Uniqueness of

Jewel Killough, Pastor Mike Green, and Curtis Petrey – students in Nancy's class, "The Root and Branches"

Hebrew, Key to Understanding the Bible. 2 The Hebrew Alphabet Reveals the Messiah. 3 A Dead Language Resurrected. 4 Learning Basic Hebrew Expressions.

I read to the students portions of the book, *Tongue of the Prophets*, by Robert St. John, relating the very adventurous life story of Eliezer Ben Yehuda. God used this single man to revive the dead language of Hebrew and restore it as a modern language and the official language of the nation of Israel. What a miracle! In 1879, Ben Yehuda had a calling from God which came to him in a vision while he was a student at the Sorbonne in Paris. He said:

> Suddenly the sky seemed to open up, a bright light shone in my eyes, and a strong inner voice rang in my ears. "Rebirth of Israel in the land of their forefathers." It was because of this voice, which did not leave me for a moment and kept ringing in my ears day and night, that all my ideas, all of the plans I had for my future life, were shaken and upset. After a soul searching inner struggle, a new idea gained the upper hand and the words which captured all my life were, "Israel in its land and its language."[81]

Ben Yehuda and his wife moved to Israel in 1881, determined to speak only Hebrew and to revive the language to modern use.

His work over 41 years of his life, sometimes laboring 18 or 19 hours a day, suffering from tuberculosis and assailed on all sides, culminated in a Hebrew dictionary of 17 volumes, published after his death. What a miraculous accomplishment! On November 29, 1922, the British Mandate authorities recognized Hebrew as the official language of the Jews in Palestine. Sitting in a synagogue with tears trickling down his face, Ben Yehuda listened to the official pronouncement signifying the end of the longest Jewish exile, in the melodious Hebrew he had fought for and won. A month later he died. Assignment completed. Simply amazing!

Today, every new oleh (immigrant) in Israel is required to go to an ulpan (class for intensive study of Hebrew). I was blessed to have the ulpan lessons myself back in 1995, when Maria Flising taught me Hebrew.

The eighth course was **Sitting at the Feet of Rabbi Jesus,** using the book by the same name, authored by Ann Spangler and Lois Tverberg.[82] It was the fall of 2009. Students from seven different churches enrolled. The study was a careful analysis of ancient sources and recent archaeological discoveries, and it presented a stirring depiction of Jesus as a first-century Jewish teacher. This furthered my purposes as a teacher of Jewish roots probably more than any other course.

The first chapter had an enticing title, "Joining Mary at the Feet of Jesus," and this is how we approached the study. The chapter entitled, "Passover Discovery," painted a very real picture of the Last Supper, followed by Jesus' arrest, trial and crucifixion. The disciples falling asleep just when Jesus needed them made perfect sense as we read Ann and Lois' insights. So many Jewish practices were made plain, and it was easy to see Yeshua as a Jewish rabbi.

In the spring of 2010, I taught my ninth course, **A Rabbi Looks at the Last Days,**[83] based on the book by the same name, authored by Rabbi Jonathan Bernis, President of Jewish Voice Ministries International. This was a very exciting and easy book to read, and everyone enjoyed it greatly. Rabbi Bernis offered a fresh look at end times from a Messianic Jewish point of view.

Curtis and I were blessed to meet Jonathan Bernis at a Bless Israel's Believers Cruise in January of 2004. He officiated at the renewal of wedding vows ceremony on the ship, which Curtis and I participated in. We heard him speak and were very impressed with his testimony. His ministry is multi-faceted – Jewish evangelistic music and dance festivals in various countries, medical and evangelistic outreach to poor Jews in Ethiopia and India, television programs, magazines, books, and more.

Bernis gave six signs to show the last days are near – 1 Satan is increasing his attacks on the Jews. 2 Scattered Jews are returning to Israel in record numbers. 3 Many thousands of Jews are returning to Yeshua. 4 The Gospel is being preached to the nations. 5 The stage is set for Messiah's return. 6 The times of the Gentiles are being fulfilled.

In the chapter, "The Mystery of the Two Messiahs," we read a startling account of Rabbi Kaduri in Israel and the controversy surrounding his death. He supposedly met the Messiah, wrote his name on a note, and requested that the name not be read until

Students in Nancy's class, "A Rabbi Looks at the Last Days"

one year after his death. The note was opened early in 2007, and it contained a sentence of six words, with the first letter of each word spelling out the Messiah's name: YESHUA! Another shocker was that little symbols were drawn all over the late rabbi's hand-written papers, and they looked like crosses! The orthodox Jewish community was in an uproar. You can imagine the debate that was touched off in the Holy Land. Jonathan Bernis' book, as

Curtis and Nancy renewing wedding vows on Bless Israel's
Believers Cruise – January 2004

well as all the other books for my aforementioned courses, I highly
recommend.

To date I have taught ten courses since I received my Master's
Degree. The tenth one was in the fall of 2010 and was entitled
Promised Land taught by Ray Vander Laan on DVDs.[84] I had
viewed these videos that were put out by Focus on the Family back
in the mid-1990s. This would be my easiest course, because my
role was mainly to be the facilitator. The class was the largest of
the ten courses I taught. Seven of the 22 students were new. Seven
churches were represented. Quite a few had taken most all the
courses. I was encouraged, and I enjoyed listening to Vander Laan
and using the workbook. There was a lot of class participation. I
wrote extra material to enhance our study and provided handouts.

The video footage of the land of Israel was so beautiful. I hoped that it would plant in the hearts of the students a yearning to go to Israel and see for themselves. In fact I would soon begin to design a custom tour to Israel and try to enlist these and others to explore our Hebrew heritage in the Promised Land as Joshua did. As it turned out, the tour didn't "make." God knew best, because I would not be writing this book if we had made the tour!

Since God "opened the door in two thousand and four," I have exercised His teaching gift among some eager students and "saw the lights go on" in their faces as we explored our Jewish roots and learned many wonderful things. How rewarding to be a Mizpah for Israel.

24

Give Me Back My Money!

Curtis gave me a surprise birthday party on my 67th birthday, October 28, 2006. Our oldest son Perry, his wife Liv, our youngest son Bert, and our grandson P.J. came. Liv made a huge card from Perry and her with the words, "WORLD'S GREATEST MOM AWARD." The fine print at the bottom of the card read, "This award can be redeemed for **two round trip tickets to anywhere in the world** ..." Even though Perry was a successful businessman, this present was way more than generous. My heart did flip-flops,

Bert, P.J., Liv, Curtis, and Perry Petrey celebrate Nancy's birthday in Petrey. Perry and Liv give Nancy two free round-trip tickets to anywhere in the world!

and I almost turned cartwheels! You can guess what place I chose. Yes, you guessed it – Israel!

This time Janice and Jack would accompany Curtis and me. Jack had never been to Israel. This would be the second trip for Janice, the third trip for Curtis, and my sixth trip. We would be going on Rosh HaShanah of 2007, because that was the time that Janice and Jack could use their frequent flier miles. This would be my third time in the land during this biblical holiday of the Feast of Trumpets, the Jewish New Year.

Of the four of us, I was the veteran, so I set about designing the tour. It was quite a challenge to develop an itinerary, when so many places would be closed for the holidays.

Curtis and I would fly out of Atlanta on Lufthansa on September 10 and return on September 21. Janice and Jack booked their flight out of Dothan, Alabama, on Delta/ El Al. I booked rooms for seven nights at the Allenby 2 Bed & Breakfast in Jerusalem, the same place we had stayed in 1996. I also booked rooms in Jaffa (right next to Tel Aviv) for two nights at the Beit Immanuel Guesthouse. After I made these plans in January we had a long wait until September. Prayer increased as the time drew near. Looking back over my journal during that period of time, I found that there were many important and deeply spiritual events going on in my life and in the lives of my family and church. The opportunities for serving God were many, and the glory of God was increasing. How would God use us in Israel?

We arrived safely in Israel on Tuesday, September 11 (an infamous date), and that night met our friends, Shmuel and Pamela Suran, at Joy Restaurant on Emek Rephaim Street in Jerusalem. After our meal we walked to their ministry house, Chazon Yerushalayim, and visited some more. What a neat experience with these "godparents" of many believers in Israel. Then they drove us back to the Allenby 2. Danny Flax was still the ever gracious host, serving us his standard breakfast the next morning. He had not changed since we stayed with him eleven years before. He was a wealth of tourist information. Danny walked with Curtis and Jack over to the car rental place and helped secure a car for us.

We "hit the ground running" with a full day on Wednesday. It was a stressful day, due to jet lag and a sleepless night for me. As soon as we got to the Old City we got our money changed to shekels ($1= 4 NIS). I got 800 shekels, which was $200.

As we walked through a parking lot, going to the Western Wall, a man came alongside of me and unfolded a long assortment of postcards, trying to make a sale. He brushed hard against me, but I adamantly refused to buy. Curtis and I walked on ahead of Jack and Janice. I looked back at them and saw Janice holding up a small straw purse and talking to Jack. I thought, "I didn't know Janice had a purse like mine." I went to see what it was all about. When I looked at the purse with only a little notebook inside, I cried, "That's MINE! And the shekels are gone!" Jack said the man who tried to sell me postcards had put the purse in his back pocket. He saw the man go into the bushes before coming up to Jack to sell him postcards. Jack felt for his wallet, then found the purse.

I remembered the man pushing against me as he showed me his postcards. That was when the little "weasel" had slipped the straw purse out of the large bag on my shoulder, and I didn't even know it! It made no sense to me why the thief would put the purse in Jack's back pocket. (Much later, I came to the conclusion that the thief wanted it to appear as if Jack was the robber!) I asked Jack if he would help me find the thief. We went back to the parking lot. I prayed, "Lord, please help us find him, and let me get my money back."

We retraced our steps, and Jack spotted the thief! He was plying his trade on some more unsuspecting tourists. I said, "Let's hurry and catch him before he leaves." Praying all the while, we got to him, and he was standing between two men who had probably put him up to it. I stood squarely in front of him, pointed my finger in his face, and said, "You took my money, and you have to give it back!" He tried to deny it, but I said, "Yes you did, and you're gonna give it back to me." He asked me how much it was.

I couldn't think, but anyway he pushed some money in my face. I didn't bother to count it but instinctively knew that wasn't all of it. I shouted, "No, I want it **all** back. In the name of Yeshua, you give it **all** back to me." **He gave me all of it!** He had been saying over and over, "I'll give it back if you don't call the police."

In the meantime, Curtis had been observing the scene and had already called the police. At that moment when I had my money, the police came up and arrested the thief. As he was being taken away, I said to him, "I forgive you, but you need to quit stealing!"

The police said we should go to the Jewish Quarter police station which was very close by. We waited and waited for the chief to come. All the while the thief was sitting outside without handcuffs. When the chief finally came, I said, "That man needs to be handcuffed." He bragged, "I am the Chief of Police, and you don't need to worry." About that time, the thief ran off! Jack, Janice, Curtis, and I had a big laugh.

We were then directed to the main police station at Jaffa Gate, where Jack and I were interrogated at length. I used the occasion to witness about the Lord's answering our prayer to locate the thief and get my money back. "I told the thief he had to give it back in the name of Yeshua. He gave it all back. It was a miracle!" I said. One of the policemen seemed amazed.

We spent a lot of time, giving testimony and waiting. When all was said and done, we didn't press charges. We just wanted to get on with our tour. I had my money back, so I was satisfied, although a little irritated that we had wasted so much time. Then I reminded myself that God had delivered us from trouble. He had answered my prayer that I get my money back! He had also answered our many prayers before the trip that we would be His witnesses. I should be grateful and not complain, but recognize that spiritual warfare "goes with the territory."

The next day, Thursday, we drove our rental car across the beautiful countryside to Nazareth to see Nazareth Village, which was a good tour. Then we drove on through Cana to Tiberias, where we got thoroughly lost. This brought back memories of my excursions with Janice back in 2003, when we set out in a rental car to find Hadassah Hospital. What a frustrating experience then, and it was happening again!

I really got upset when we couldn't find places we had planned to go, and if we did, they were closed for the holidays. Rooms were $190 at Holiday Inn. Finally, we went to Capernaum and saw the restored ruins of a synagogue and Peter's house. This was an enriching experience, but time was running out, and we missed the boat ride on the Sea of Galilee and being baptized at Yardenit. Failing to find lodging, we decided to go on back to Jerusalem. I said, "At least we can stop by and see the ruins at Beit She'an." This is the place where the Philistines hanged the bodies of Saul and his sons on the city wall (I Sam. 31:8-12). Alas! It was closed, too. Then when we got to Jerusalem, we got lost trying to find the Allenby 2. More frustration. At last we made it and went to bed early, exhausted.

Praise the Lord! I slept all night and felt like a new person. I felt so good, I even thought about planning a future trip back to Israel, can you believe it? It was Friday. We drove to Masada beside the Dead Sea. Before we got there I read aloud in the car from the writings of Josephus about the Zealots holding out at Masada. We had an excellent guide, and it was all fascinating. I had been "through the fire" the last two days, but now I was "skiing outside the wake!"

After Masada we went to Ein Gedi. This was the wilderness place where David hid when Saul was chasing him. He had the opportunity to kill Saul in a cave, but he would not touch "God's anointed" (I Sam. 24). Jack and I walked the farthest up the mountain trail. Janice loved cooling her feet in a pool of water, and it was a treat to spot three mountain goats. After this Curtis drove us back to the Allenby 2. I loved the day. Curtis did a perfect job of driving, and Jack was a superb navigator – no wrong turns the whole day. We were finally getting the hang of it. If only we could have stayed another week.

It was Shabbat the next day, and we went back to the Galilee, beginning with a visit to the Mount of Beatitudes. Then we had our 30-minute ride on the Sea of Galilee. The view was absolutely gorgeous. Looking around Tiberias for a place to eat that wasn't closed, we found a delightful Italian restaurant open, and we ordered the famous St. Peter fish, which was delicious.

The next stop was Yardenit (Jordan River) to be baptized. Everything was provided, the white robes, showers, and hair dryers. We found a private place to have our own little baptism service, reading scripture and singing. However, we were soon interrupted by a rude group of people who moved into our area, ignored us, and started their pouring service, talking loudly. After they

Reading Scripture before being baptized in the Jordan River at Yardenit

finished, we went down into the water, and Curtis baptized us. He immersed himself. Tiny fish swarmed around our feet and bit our ankles. It was a funny feeling and very distracting. The place was so commercialized that, all in all, it made for a disappointing experience. I struggled to give myself an attitude adjustment.

On the way back to Jerusalem we stopped at Belvoir ("fine view") Castle, which is a Crusader fortress in an Israel National Park on Mount Tavor, located between Tiberias and Beit She'an. It afforded us a breathtaking view of the Jordan valley, Syria, and all the way to Mt. Hermon. Jack and I explored the extensive fortress ruins. It required lots of walking and climbing on rocks. We seemed to be the only ones agile enough to do it, but it was worth all the effort. We saw some amazing things.

Back at the Allenby 2, we had a wonderful extra hour of sleep because of the time change, but I still felt the effects of jet lag. The Lord revealed to me I had been depending on my own wisdom and strength and had made myself a nervous wreck. I made a decision to take my hands off the itinerary and let the Holy Spirit direct us the rest of the way. It was Sunday, and He was leading Curtis and me to take the day off and rest. We did just that.

Jack and Janice decided to take a taxi to the Old City. They walked down the Mount of Olives to the Garden of Gethsemane. Another taxi took them to the Dung Gate, and they went to the Ophel Archaeological Garden which included the southern steps of the Temple Mount. They had a great time, and came back to the Allenby 2, telling us all about it.

Curtis and I also had a great time in our room, reading the Bible, praying, singing, praising the Lord, and resting. On television we heard Adrian Rogers, a good ole Baptist preacher from Memphis, Tennessee, saying that Jacob was crippled before he was crowned. He was broken before he was blessed. I said, "Lord let it be so with me!" I was hoping I had gone beyond the crippled and broken stage and was now eligible to be crowned and blessed! That Sunday morning was a spiritually rich and restful time. We even found a McDonald's for lunch.

25

Provoke Them to Jealousy

The best part of our trip to Israel was visiting Christian ministries and seeing prophecy fulfilled. Paul said, "Brethren, my heart's desire and prayer to God for Israel is that they may be saved" (Rom. 10:1). He insisted that God had not cast them away, but that He had preserved a remnant (Rom. 11:1, 5). He explained that God was using their fall to bring about the salvation of the Gentiles, which would provoke the Jews to jealousy (Rom. 11:11). We saw several Christian ministries in the land doing just that, provoking the Jews to jealousy, so that they would recognize their Messiah and want Him for themselves.

The highlight of our entire trip was attending the King of Kings Community congregation in downtown Jerusalem on Sunday night. This would be my fourth time to attend the church but the first time to attend in their new building, "The Pavilion." The worship and the singing were the best I had enjoyed in years. Our friend, Roy Kendall, was still serving the Lord on the worship team. Mary Kendall was on the front row with their three new students in the School of Worship (S.O.W.). Afterward, we talked to Roy, and, true to form, he exercised his gift of hospitality and invited us to come to their new house the next night for coffee after we had supper with Lars and Harriet Enarson.

On Monday we walked the short distance from the Allenby 2 to the Christian Friends of Israel Distribution Center. They gave us a tour of four of their ministries in that building – Open Gates (for the immigrants), Doors of Hope (for the poor), Under His Wings (terror victims), and the Bridal Salon.

Jack & Janice under the chuppah at the CFI Bridal Salon

Then we visited Bridges for Peace. Marcus and Rhonda were our hosts. They had us dress in first-century costumes and decorate a sukkah (tabernacle), a three-sided structure, which had just been completed for the upcoming holiday, Sukkot (Feast of Tabernacles). During this time the Israelis remember the wilderness wanderings when their forefathers lived in booths (sukkot). The feast commemorates their dependence on God and His provision. We would miss Sukkot, because our last day in Israel would be September 21, and the Feast would begin September 26. (Janice and I had missed it in 2003, also.) They supplied the decorations of artificial fruit, paper chains, and tree branches. We were the very first people to come decorate the sukkah, and we felt so honored. Sitting on low stools, Marcus taught us a Jewish roots lesson.

Then our hosts took us to their new "Land of the Bible Experience" room, which was an authentic first-century setting. Marcus explained the multi-faceted ministry of Bridges for Peace.

Jack & Janice Bell and Curtis & Nancy Petrey in first century costumes in front of the Bridges for Peace sukkah (tabernacle)

Next was a tour of the big, beautiful office building, which was rented from the Ethiopian church. It was built for the Queen of Sheba's sister who never used it. We got to meet the staff, all wonderful people. One Jewish man told us about an open vision he had of Yeshua!

Rhonda walked us up to the Ben Yehuda Walking Mall. We had some popular Israeli food, falafel and shwarma. Then we went back to the Allenby 2 to rest.

Later we met the Enarsons at Joy Restaurant, the same place we had seen the Surans the first night. It is always a blessing to see our good Swedish friends who have been so faithful in prayer for Israel for decades. They had recently moved from the Golan Heights to Jerusalem and were involved with the orthodox community.

Nancy & Curtis under the decorated sukkah

Lars shared some prophetic insights with us, which made for stimulating conversation. It was good to hear about their family, too. Their younger daughter Johanna and husband Ron, as well as their son John, were also living in Jerusalem.

Lars and Harriet Enarson

Leaving the Enarsons, we got a cab to Roy and Mary's gorgeous four-story house, where they have their School of Worship. This is right in the place where David played the harp and drove the evil

Mary & Roy Kendall on their balcony in Jerusalem

Roy Kendall leading us in worship, playing his 7 foot 2 inch grand piano!

spirits from King Saul! They took us on a tour of the house and told us how God had given them such favor that they could obtain this expensive home. Mary had recently turned 50, and to celebrate her birthday they invited 100 Christian friends from all over Israel. On another occasion they invited 150 volunteers from the Feast of Tabernacles over for dinner. That was easy for Roy and Mary, because they were using God's gift of hospitality and being good stewards with the spacious house God had blessed them with.

We enjoyed fellowship and refreshments with them and their three students. I was greatly blessed to play Roy's big grand piano, seven feet, two inches long, a bonafide concert grand piano! Then Roy skillfully played and led us in worship, singing "Great is Thy Faithfulness." It was heavenly.

Mary told us the story of how they got the Kawai grand piano and were able to pay $7,000 for it, including shipping from the U.S. and the customs tax. It was truly a miracle story. What a glorious evening. We felt highly honored to be friends of the Kendalls and enjoyed visiting them on our final night in Jerusalem.

On Tuesday, Curtis and Jack drove the rental car, loaded with our luggage, straight to Beit Immanuel Guesthouse in Jaffa. Janice and I arrived thirty minutes later, having taken the sherut to Tel Aviv and a bus from there for a total of merely 20 NIS. If only we had known how the bus schedules worked, all this time we could have saved a lot of money by using buses instead of taxis. The taxi drivers had been ripping us off, right and left.

Later that day we drove the car to look around and just happened to find the Old Jaffa Port. I'm sure it was no co-incidence though, because I had turned our itinerary over to the Holy Spirit a long time before. I wish I had adjectives to describe the exotic ambience of that place. We walked down 98 polished, cobblestone steps to the sea side. The sun had already gone down, and the lights of nearby Tel Aviv were glistening on the water. It was so romantic. We walked back up the 98 steps and then walked up about 50 more steps to a plaza with historic sites, including St. Peter's church and monastery and Simon the Tanner's house. It was too bad we didn't have a guide to explain things, because we had stumbled onto something great!

We returned the next day to go to the Visitor's Center on the plaza (Kikar Kedummim) and got quite an education from the exhibits and film. We saw the walls of excavated houses thousands of years old and life-size figures in them. What we had viewed the night before at the port was the place where Jonah set sail and got swallowed by a whale. We learned that Jaffa was first settled by Noah's son Japheth. Hey, Gentiles, he is our ancestor! All parts of the Holy Land are brimming over with Bible history.

Beit Immanuel (House of "God with us") has a fantastic history. It is called the Baron's Palace, because in 1878 the Russian-born Baron Plato Von Ustinov (who had become a Bible believing protestant Christian) purchased the building. He made it into a palace. Baron Ustinov was the grandfather of someone we knew, actor Peter Ustinov.

The earliest history was connected with a movement dedicated to the return of the Jewish people to the land of Israel and the restoration and proclamation in the 1800s of the Messianic Jewish hope in Yeshua.

The Israeli army took it over in the War for Independence. In 1954 they returned the building to the Anglican Church (the British CMJ - "Church's Ministry Among Jewish People"), which also has a guest house in Jerusalem at Christ Church in the Old City. That was the place I stayed on the Passover Prayer Tour in 2002. Messianic Jews and Arabs started worshiping at Beit Immanuel in the 1970s.

Both places of our lodging have an important history. The Allenby 2 Bed & Breakfast in Jerusalem is located at Allenby Square, where there is a memorial to the defeat of the Turks by the British at the end of World War I after a 400 years rule of the Ottoman Empire. The Battle for Jerusalem, led by a Christian, General Edmund Allenby, was won on December 9, 1917. Although an accomplished horseman, Allenby refused to ride triumphally into

Curtis at the Allenby Memorial to fallen British soldiers in
the defeat of the Turks, ending their 400-year rule of the
Holy Land on December 9, 1917

the city. He entered on foot out of his great respect for the Holy
City, becoming the first Christian to control the city in centuries.

Beit Immanuel in Jaffa had only one T.V. and no elevators.
We had to walk up four flights of stairs to the second floor, but our
rooms were very nice. The place had a great atmosphere. I had a
financial reason as well as a spiritual motive for choosing the place,
because the rent was only $75 a night. The Allenby 2 was $55 a
night. You can't beat that in Israel. Besides, we were surrounded
by Christians at both places. At Beit Immanuel there were many
young people there for an art school. The first morning Janice and
I took off our shoes and walked into their prayer service. They were
singing "Above All," which drew us in, and we worshiped with
them. What a blessed experience.

On our last full day in Israel, we visited the Dugit ("little
boat") Outreach Center in Tel Aviv. What a joy to again see Avi
Mizrachi, the director of the ministry. I first met him and his wife
Chaya at Dugit at the conclusion of the Passover Prayer Tour in

Avi Mizrachi with the Bells and the Petreys at Dugit Outreach Center in Tel Aviv

2002. Then Curtis and I saw them on the Bless Israel's Believers Cruise in 2004. At that time Chaya gave us an exciting report of her going with a "prayer swat team" excursion into Iraq and being detained at the border, because she had an Israeli passport. Her eyes got big as she related the dangerous situation and how God got her safely to Iraq and back with the team. They saw the mighty works of God in Iraq and encouraged the believers there. We were blessed to hear news you don't hear on T.V., good news, and it was "hot off the wire."

At Dugit after introductions, a devotional, singing, worship, and prayer, Avi showed us a video of their ministry and gave us a DVD. Avi told us there were 150 Messianic Jewish congregations in Israel and about 10,000 to 15,000 Jewish believers. He also inspired us with his account of going to visit believers in Nagaland. When he and Chaya arrived, there were over 1,000 people waiting for them. A prophetess looked at Avi and said, "This is the man I saw in a vision 20 years ago who would come here!" The church had been praying earnestly for Israel and loved the Jews. Avi had more miracle stories for us. What a man of God.

He was born in Tel Aviv-Jaffa in a Jewish home. After serving in the Israeli Air Force, he decided to visit his sister in America. His intention was to go to Las Vegas and get rich. His sister was a believer in Yeshua. To satisfy his curiosity, Avi attended church with her. He was shocked that the people loved God, loved Israel, and loved the Jewish people. His heart was touched, and **he was provoked to jealousy**. Later, alone in his room, he gave his life to Yeshua and accepted him

Avi & Chaya Mizrachi

as Messiah and Lord! That same year he also met and married his wife Chaya, and they returned to Israel together.

In 1985, God opened the door for them to study at Christ for the Nations Institute in Dallas, the same place God had impacted me with His love for Israel and the Jews. Avi and Chaya returned to Israel in 1987 and have been in full-time ministry ever since. In 1993, they opened Dugit as an Outreach Center in the heart of Tel Aviv, offering free coffee, literature and a listening ear to any visitors.

Avi is a recognized leader in the land of Israel and an international conference speaker. He is an evangelist, leading street ministry as well as humanitarian outreach. He disciples Israeli believers to become strong in the Word of God. He also pastors Adonai Roi (The Lord is My Shepherd), a Messianic Hebrew-speaking congregation in Tel Aviv.

The newest part of the Dugit Minisry is their VIP Prayer Tower, a room dedicated solely to prayer and worshiping the Lord.

Congregations and ministries in Israel and abroad are invited to come and hold sessions. They hope to have a meeting in the Tower every night in the near future.

Looking back on our trip to Israel, I realized how many wonderful things happened that we did not even plan. God probably had so much more to give us that we didn't receive. He showed me this in an object lesson involving my camera film. I was very conservative with my picture taking, because I didn't want to give out of film prematurely. I missed some great photo ops because of this. Later I realized that my box of film contained five rolls, not three, as I had thought. It was as if the Lord was saying, "I have so much in store for you. Don't be afraid. Reach out and take **all** my blessings."

I had given too much attention to negative things, such as jet lag, lack of sleep, taxi drivers overcharging, making wrong turns in the car, and places being closed for the holidays. The Lord revealed to me that the frustration and disappointment were coming from satanic attacks, because Jerusalem is a headquarters for strong religious spirits, a place of great conflict.

I needed to give more attention to the positive aspects of the trip. There was so much to praise the Lord for. For starters, Janice and Jack had both been sick right before the trip, but the Lord healed them just in time. Another good thing was that I was able to sleep on an airplane for the first time. On the first day of touring Janice and I had prayed at the Western Wall and had a moving experience. We did not have an accident in all our travels in the land. No one became sick. We visited precious friends – the Surans, the Enarsons, and the Kendalls – doing important ministry in Jerusalem. We walked where Jesus walked. We were surrounded by Christians both at the Allenby 2 and at Beit Immanuel. I recovered my stolen money, a miracle, something unheard of! We were privileged to make donations to all the people in ministry we visited.

I praised the Lord for our son Perry's gift of free airfare to Israel! Besides blessing his mom and dad, his generosity resulted in a huge blessing for Jack and Janice. They were able to connect with Jewish believers and ministries and their biblical inheritance in the "Land of Milk and Honey." I praised God for the privilege of worshiping at King of Kings Community in Jerusalem and with Avi at Dugit, for decorating the sukkah, walking beside the Mediterranean Sea in Jaffa, going up to Masada, visiting Ein Gedi, riding a boat on the Sea of Galilee, seeing Belvoir Castle, and driving throughout the mountainous and flourishing land of Israel. These, plus more, were all priceless experiences.

To sum up this trip to Israel in 2007, it truly was chock full of blessings. I believe God accomplished something through us. He blessed us and made us a blessing. By our simply making the effort to go to Israel, show love, and give offerings to God's work there, we were able to "provoke the Jews to jealousy." I remembered what happened to Avi. Once he saw the devotion of Christians to their Jewish Messiah and their love for Israel and the Jews, the next step was his salvation! Paul gives us God's promise: "Blindness has happened to Israel until the fullness [maturity] of the Gentiles has come in, and so [in this way, or through the agency of the Gentiles] **all Israel will be saved**..." (Rom. 11:25b-26a).

26

Wild Rides and Confrontations

Taxi drivers in Israel are highly skilled and have nerves of steel. They can squeeze through the narrowest of openings in traffic without batting an eye. Once you have tried to drive a rental car in Jerusalem, you definitely appreciate a taxi as a gift from God. However, you have to be "wise as a serpent and harmless as a dove" in dealing with some of them. Tourists are fair game, and when they collect, you may never know what hit you.

Curtis had a run-in with one Arab taxi-driver who tried to collect an outrageous fee. He only took us a short distance, just around the outside of the Old City from one side to the other. Curtis protested that his fee was the equivalent of a trip to the airport and refused to pay it. The driver complained to a man walking by, "This American tourist won't pay his taxi fare!" The man asked Curtis why he wouldn't pay. Curtis said, "I pay by the meter, and the meter was never turned on, so I owe nothing!" The argument went on, and I got alarmed that a real fight might break out. Finally, Curtis paid him, but it was about half of what the driver charged. Whew! We made it out alive. That was my main concern.

I'll never forget the confrontation Curtis had with an Arab vendor in the Old City on our first trip. A friend back home had asked Curtis to get him an Israeli flag, and this was the last day of our tour. Curtis walked into an Arab shop and asked the owner if he had an Israeli flag. The Arab vendor was irate and answered, "Why would I carry the flag of Satan?" Curtis then asked if he had an American flag, to which he replied, "If I don't carry the flag of Satan, why would I carry the flag of the **Great** Satan?" Right then

Curtis took a $20 bill out of his wallet, held it up, and said, "Do you take these?" He responded, "Of course, I do." Curtis said to him, "If you won't carry the **flag** of the Great Satan, why would you take the **money** of the Great Satan? Brother, you don't love Allah. You love the dollar. If you ever have to choose between the two, you will choose the dollar!"

I guess the moral of these stories is, "Don't mess with my husband!"

The last taxi ride I had in Israel was one I will never forget. A taxi picked us up at Beit Immanuel to go to the airport at 1:00 a.m. The taxi driver drove like a maniac all the way to the airport. Raw fear gripped me. It felt like I was going to "lose my stomach." This had to have been the most terrifying experience of my life, and that is saying a lot. In my mind, I had convinced myself that this man was trying to kill us! Why, I didn't know. We weren't running late. We had allowed plenty of time to get to the airport. Maybe he was a race driver and forgot where he was. There was only one good thing about it – it certainly did improve my prayer life. The driver got us there with breakneck speed in only 20 minutes. Never have I been so grateful to get out of a car. I thought for sure we would crash and die. The driver charged us 155 NIS. That was almost $40, but Curtis paid him. He had told the driver when he picked us up, "No meter, no pay!"

In Jerusalem in 1996, five of our team of six had a wild ride in a taxi one night. We were leaving Mt. Zion Hotel where we had served our three-hour assignment of praise and worship before the Lord, and we were ready to go back to the Allenby 2. Our Arab taxi driver, Ronnie, had other ideas. He "kidnapped" us! We allowed it, because he promised a lower fare of 30 shekels, if we would let him take us to Bethlehem to "Johnny's Souvenir Store." He played on our sympathies by telling us the store owner would pay him $20 for a load of customers. However, he was already driving in that direction before we agreed to the deal. I recognized the store. It was the same one our tour group visited in 1994. Only two of us bought anything, because the prices were so high.

Our ride back to the Allenby 2 was harrowing, including crossing the IDF checkpoint. We hoped it wouldn't cause a problem that we were piled in on top of each other. We made it past and decided to have a good time with the driver, Ronnie. We sang praise songs to the top of our lungs, then asked Ronnie to sing. He obliged us. We found out he was a Palestinian Christian. We prayed for him that he would find a better job, a nice wife, have kids, be productive, be happy, and know the Lord better. When we got "home," we were feeling pretty high, and we were grateful for that wild ride.

Of all the wild rides I had in Israel, none was more satisfying than riding camels. Actually, I never really rode the camels. This was the procedure: the camel knelt down; I got on; the camel arose and walked a few feet; the camel knelt down; and I got off. Simple, but satisfying. My first experience was on the Mount of Olives the first time we went to Israel. I was on top of the world. The way the camel ambles along, you feel like you are on a ship that is tossing in the waves, a strange feeling.

Nancy's first camel ride – on the Mount of Olives

The second time I rode a camel was in 2003, with Janice watching. I spotted a camel outside the Jaffa Gate as we were leaving the Old City. It only cost $5 for a "ride," so I made Janice wait for me to have that Middle Eastern experience.

My final camel ride was in 2007, when Curtis, Jack, Janice, and I were on the way to Masada near the Dead Sea. As we came to a snack & gift shop on our right, we noticed a camel sitting down beside it. There was also a camel across the road standing perfectly still. We pulled in on the right, browsed around the gift shop and got a snack. Jack and I walked up to the camel that was sitting down, paid the owners a fee and had that unique camel experience.

When we drove off, we noticed the camel across the road still had not moved an inch. We decided it might be a large stuffed animal. On our way back from Masada we saw that same camel standing exactly where it was hours before. By now we were convinced it was definitely a stuffed animal. Then it moved! Oh, the camel was real after all! We laughed out loud!

Interestingly, the camel's nickname is "ship of the desert." When walking, the camel moves both feet on one side of its body, then both feet on the other. This gait suggests the rolling motion of a boat, explaining the camel's "ship of the desert" nickname. Normal "amble speed" for a camel is three miles per hour. When they gallop, their leg action produces a swaying, rocking motion that makes some riders "seasick."

The hump of a camel is mostly a lump of fat, not a place to store water. If food is scarce, the hump of fat provides energy. The hump shrinks if the camel is starving. He can go five to seven days with little or no food and water and can lose a quarter of his body weight without impairing his normal functions.

A camel's eyes are large, with a soft, doe-like expression. They are protected by a double row of long curly eyelashes that also help keep out sand and dust, while thick bushy eyebrows shield the eyes from the desert sun.

Today camels are not primarily raised for transportation but for milk, meat, racing, and even beauty. The Saudis have camel beauty pageants! Madr, a camel breeder in Riyadh, said, "It's just like judging a beautiful girl. You look for big eyes, long lashes, and a long neck."[85] Mashoufan, a celebrity camel who won a number of beauty pageants, was said to be worth more than $4.5 million! Camel breeding is a multi-million dollar industry in Saudi Arabia. Wealthy Saudi camel owners have parties in the desert to spend time with their favorite camels. The Saudis, as well as all Arabs, love their camels and treat them like family.

Camels are unique creations of God, perfectly suited for their desert environment. One of these days maybe I will have a "wild ride" on a camel and actually cover some ground, not just mount, sit, go a few feet, and dismount. In the meantime I have priceless photos of myself atop camels on three different occasions in Israel, and I look at them admiringly!

27

Colorful Characters

Counterfeit Guide

In my six trips to Israel I have happened upon the same self-appointed guide in the Old City three times. Yes, he was a colorful character. Evidently, he hung around the tourist sites and learned enough facts, listening to the official guides, that he could pose as a real guide himself.

On our first tour of Israel in 1994, Frank, Esther, Curtis, and I were in the Old City. We lagged behind our tour group, because we were busy frequenting the shops in the Arab section bazaar. Curtis and I went on ahead to try to catch up with the tour group. Frank and Esther stayed behind and got lost. When they finally got to us, our group had already seen the Church of the Holy Sepulcher. At that moment, a toothless old Arab man approached us. Without getting our permission, "Mr. Expert Guide" (that's what I'll call him) took my hand and began to lead us all over the church, following another group, and showing us the points of interest. I remember that he urged me to bend down as the others were doing and touch the stone where Jesus' cross supposedly was put in the ground. A worship service was in progress, and Mr. Expert Guide kept referring to the Greeks, the Russians, Coptics, and Catholics and their service times. The Romanians could only come on Saturdays, he said, because the various groups had claimed the other times. I never understood most of what he was saying, because his voice was low. Maybe he wasn't even speaking English! He constantly pulled me by the arm, which made me uncomfortable.

We continued to follow the group ahead of us until it appeared that we had "finished the tour." Then I realized that "Mr. Expert Guide" was expecting a tip. What else could we do but tip him? So we did, but we felt cheated that we did not have a "real" guide.

Would you believe that on the Passover Prayer Tour I attended in 2002, "Mr. Expert Guide" presented himself again? Five of us entered the site of the Upper Room, and there he was. Without being asked, he proceeded to "guide" us in that area. It took a while for me to realize that it was "Mr. Expert Guide!" He wanted to show us more, but I gave him a small tip and signaled to my friends to move on.

On our 2007 tour, Janice, Jack, Curtis, and I went to the Old City and walked around to Zion Gate. Curtis found a bench and waited for us, while I showed Jack and Janice the Upper Room. We had asked a man for directions. Lo and behold, it was "Mr. Expert Guide," even though he now sported a ball cap! He was still up to his old tricks. He asked us for 20 NIS each. What a ripoff. He only showed us one more thing, David's tomb, and then we escaped from him!

Paul

I already related my encounter in 1998 with a colorful character, Daniel, in Amsterdam, who accompanied me to Corrie ten Boom's house. (See Chapter 2.) I met another colorful character – an ordinary Jew, but colorful to me – on the flight from Amsterdam to Israel. He was an orthodox Jew from Beth Shemesh. He didn't want to talk, but I prayed that God would give me an open door, and He did. I asked if he was hungry, and he said he had not eaten all day. Then he asked why I was going to Israel. I told him I'd be doing volunteer work, giving out clothes to immigrants. He didn't know about Christian Friends of Israel or Bridges for Peace. He asked what they do. My answer included an apology for all the terrible things Christians had done to Jews, and I wanted to try to help make up for it.

I talked about Corrie ten Boom's house and about how she forgave the Nazis. He said, "In Judaism you can't forgive the Nazis." I replied, "You may need to be forgiven one day. We might have done the same thing if we had been born in that place and time." (Can you believe I said that?)

I told the story of Corrie meeting the Nazi guard who had become a believer and how she hated him. But as she shook his hand, God melted her heart. Then I talked about Jesus forgiving because "they know not what they do." I explained that we believe that Jesus was sinless and that he could be a sacrifice for our sins. (Can you believe he continued to listen?)

The conversation flowed. He asked about my family, and I found out about his and about his work with computers. He had been to trade shows in Europe. He finally smiled. We talked about the dietary laws. I said I thought God gave the dietary laws to preserve the Jewish people, so He could send the Messiah. "We believe He has already come, but Jews believe He is yet to come," I added. I also said that Satan had tried to annihilate the Jews through Pharaoh and Hitler, that the hatred for Jews could only be explained as Satanic.

He said that Gentiles only were required to keep six Noahide laws, such as don't steal, don't murder, no idolatry, and no blasphemy. He had a hard time remembering them all. I said that God has a plan for the Church and for the Jews, and ultimately we will become one. Later I explained I didn't mean the Jews would be assimilated but would retain their identity as Jews.

For a good while the conversation had flowed, but then it seemed the door was closed. The man took out his Talmud. I waited a long time, then asked him if he was studying, meditating, or memorizing. He said he wasn't meditating. He had four more pages to read. I wondered if he was having to do "penance" for talking to a Gentile woman! I asked God if there was anything more He wanted me to say. Time went by. I had the idea of asking him if I could pray for him. When he was taking my bag out of the overhead compartment, I asked his name and if he had a prayer request. He wouldn't tell me his name, but he said to just pray for the Jews.

When we deplaned in Israel and walked to the shuttle, Daniel came up. I introduced him to my seat mate and said, "Daniel is making aliyah" (so had this man years before, I had learned). The man was very interested and struck up a conversation with Daniel. He told Daniel his name was Paul. Aha! Now I knew his name and would be praying and believing that God would turn him into a powerful believer like the Apostle Paul. Hallelujah! I thanked him again for his kindness in helping me with my suitcase and said goodbye.

What an experience! I knew the church back home was certainly praying for me, or all those things I said to Paul would never have come out of my mouth. I then prayed, "Lord, give me ten more Pauls to talk to." What fun!

John Vest

On that same trip in 1998, my host, Mary Kendall, and her daughter Marianne took me to Shabbat worship at Narkiss Street Congregation, also called The Baptist House. Several churches used the facilities. We went to a Pentecostal international service. In 1982, the Orthodox Jews had burned the building down! It was built back, and a banner with an appropriate scripture hung on the wall – "Beauty for Ashes" (Isa. 61:3). I met several interesting people, but the most interesting one was John Vest.

John was one of those who took the offering, and he sat directly in front of me. When the time came to greet people during the service, John turned around and extended his hand. He was a nice-looking young man, and I found out he was attending Hebrew University, having transferred from Rice University in Texas. As we talked, I was so surprised to learn that his mother, Sherry Shirley, grew up in Glenwood, Alabama, which was only a few miles from my hometown of Luverne. Not only that, but her best friend was Gwen Smith, who was the sister of my best friends, Sybil and Sylvia

Smith of Glenwood! They were twins. We went to high school together, and they were in our wedding.

Here was another God-incidence, but the connection extended even further. Years later I found out that a high school friend, Jack Thomas, was John's school counselor in Niceville, Florida. Jack told me that John had mentioned that he met me in Jerusalem. The familiar saying, "It's a small world" certainly fits this encounter! When I met John, it was just one more confirmation that God was in charge of my life even in the smallest details, and he was "watching" me, just as He does every sparrow that falls.

Other Encounters

God always let me know His hand was on me. I met an interesting person on the sherut, going from Ben Gurion Airport to Jerusalem in 2002. He was a young Jewish man from New York. In our conversation I found out he had come back from visiting a friend in Opelika, Alabama. When Curtis drove me to Atlanta to get the plane, we stopped for lunch at Wendy's in Opelika! What are the odds of meeting someone the next day who had just flown in from Opelika? I thanked God for again "watching" me.

Another encounter happened on the prayer tour in 2002. When we were in the northern part of Israel, we stopped for lunch and took our food outside to eat along the rocky banks of a rushing stream. There were some IDF soldiers there, and I took the occasion to practice my Hebrew and talk to them. Amodz and Nir talked to me a lot. I gave Nir my card, and he joked about coming to see me! I told them we would pray for them. What a good feeling to meet some brave young Israelis who were laying their lives on the line for Israel. This wasn't the first time I had talked to soldiers and told them we were praying for them and supported them.

Brenda Mackay

When Curtis and I checked into the Allenby 2 in September, 2007, we met Brenda Mackay. Jack and Janice got there later than we did. We introduced them to Brenda. She was from New Zealand and was there to do volunteer work at Christian Friends of Israel until the end of December. She introduced us to Ann who was also from New Zealand. Brenda and Ann had never met before, until they wound up in rooms with an adjoining bathroom at the Allenby 2. The amazing thing was that they both were a part of H.I.T. – Helping Israeli Tourists. God had brought them together in the same lodging place in Jerusalem!

Brenda Mackay (center), volunteer at CFI Distribution Center in Jerusalem

Israeli young people are required to serve in the army. After their stint in the IDF and before college, most of them go on "the big trip," backpacking abroad, usually in the Far East. Brenda and

Ann had been opening up their homes to provide lodging for these Israeli youth who were passing through. H.I.T. gave Brenda and Ann the opportunity to not only "bless Israel" but to witness to these young people about their Messiah.

Brenda told me recently that in the ten years she has been hosting Israeli backpackers, 700 of them have been guests in her home. She said, "Some have open hearts to hear about their Messiah. Others are just indifferent at this time. Praise the Lord that He will reveal Himself when the time comes."

Janice was inspired to try the same thing back home on their farm in Elba, Alabama, but it never happened. Alabama did not beckon to adventurous Israeli youth like the Far East did!

Brenda and I had interesting spiritual conversations in the kitchen. She was quite a devoted follower of Yeshua. Curtis and I gave her a donation, but she passed it on to someone who needed it more.

Nancy and Mee Ling in the Negev on the Passover Prayer Tour, 2002

Mee Ling

I was blessed to meet Mee Ling, a wonderful Malaysian girl, on the 2002 Passover Prayer Tour. What a dedicated young woman she was. She was so kind and respectful to me, always smiling. Throughout the tour she would touch my arm and "take care of me." It seemed she had adopted me as her responsibility. I really appreciated her thoughtful care.

She and her friend Hooi were great prayer warriors. Mee Ling wrote me an e-mail shortly after we got home. She said, "On arrival, and leaving the KLIA airport, the banner showed Malaysia as host of the foreign ministers conference on **terrorism**. We prayed and asked for God's forgiveness for words spoken against God's chosen nation." It was easy to see that God had placed Mee Ling and Hooi in this dark place to be a light for Him.

We stayed in touch, and in June of 2004, Mee Ling and her friend Sheila came to visit us in Petrey, Alabama! It was a wonderful time. They attended my little prayer group, and we took them to see the Alabama State Capitol and other places in Montgomery. What an enriching experience, getting to know people from as far

Sheila and Mee Ling from Malaysia visit the Petreys in Petrey, Alabama

away as Malaysia. By e-mails, we have continued to support each other in prayer.

Morris*

I met many outstanding Christians on the 2002 Passover Prayer Tour, but Morris was the most colorful character of all. A highlight of the fellowship with tour members was sitting together with Morris at the breakfast table near the end of the tour. He told story after story about planting churches in different countries. He was such a humble guy, but I could tell God had called him to be an **apostle**! God spoke to him in dreams and visions.

I wrote about Morris in my journal. He told us some mind-boggling things. I couldn't remember all the details to put in my journal, but this is the gist of what he told us: Once he was in Siberia, and he got the word "October 25th." There was an earthquake tremor that day. Then God told him there would be an earthquake north of the city on November 6 at 2:08 p.m. (not exact time). It would be 6.2 on the Richter scale, God said, and he must warn the people. Morris asked for a sign that it was really God. He was told there would be a tremor on November 2 (not exact date). Sure enough, there was! Morris knew he had to warn the people. Through a succession of open doors he was able to go on national T.V. and warn the people, telling them to call on Jesus Christ to be saved from it. People heeded his warning, came out of their houses into the street and called on Jesus! The earthquake did not come to the city, but there was a severe shaking north of the city. Many became Christians. Morris said he was writing a book, and I was eager to read it.

Being around Morris during the tour was very edifying. It was obvious he was a genuine man of God. And he was quite a colorful character, too. I had a little money left for blessing Israel. The Holy Spirit led me to give it to Morris for His purposes.

---

* Morris - Name changed, because I was unable to contact him for approval of this story.

28

Spreading the Word

My Jewish roots journey has been full of exciting people and places. Ever since my call to be a Mizpah for Israel, I have striven to enlist more people for the journey. My own pastor, Mike Green, fell in love with Israel when he went on his first trip there some time after I became a member of South Luverne Baptist Church. Others from the church went with him. Brother Mike went back a second time. He invited an Israeli singer who operated a Galilee boat business to come to our church for a concert. So, it was an easy thing to get permission from Brother Mike to bring in my ministry friends from Israel to light a fire in the hearts of the church for our Jewish roots and God's end-time redemption plans for the Jews.

Lars Enarson and Surans spread the Word

In September of 2003, Lars Enarson came and spoke at our church, as well as Janice's church, Ino Baptist, and a very large church in Montgomery, Frazer Memorial United Methodist Church. Eyes were opened for the first time to see that God had not revoked His calling on the Jewish people, but that it was the job of the Church to provoke them to jealousy, so they would "look upon Him whom they pierced," repent, and be saved.

In July of 2004, Shmuel and Pamela Suran came from Jerusalem and spoke to our church and at Ino Baptist. Pamela displayed her beautiful scriptural paintings of the Holy Land. Shmuel gave a powerful testimony of his salvation. He was a typical New York Jew, but after Yeshua stole his heart, he made aliyah to Israel and soon became active in ministry.

Shmuel & Pamela Suran come to USA and speak at Nancy's
and Janice's churches

Janice and Jack hosted them for a week and formed a close
friendship. During that time Shmuel read my thesis, *Destiny of
the Jews*, and was thrilled with it. I was greatly encouraged by his
affirmation.

Susie Sandager spreads the Word

A big event in our church was a portrayal of Corrie ten
Boom by Susie Sandager on November 4, 2007. She spoke to
our combined adult classes, and they were moved by her message.
She spoke again that Sunday afternoon, and we had an unusually
large attendance. The offering to Bridges for Peace, Susie's sponsor,
was outstanding. Then she went on to Ino Baptist to give another
presentation.

Through her series of one-woman shows, Susie's presentations
bring to life the legendary Corrie ten Boom. "Corrie Remembers"
is the drama she brought to our church. She developed this drama

based on her study of the ten Boom family, interviews of those who knew Corrie ten Boom, as well as Miss ten Boom's own books and recorded messages. It was amazing to me how authentic Susie's Dutch accent sounded, and it was quite a surprise for our church to realize that the 80-year-old woman they saw on stage was really a much younger Susie.

Susie Sandager as Corrie ten Boom alongside the real Corrie

Susie has presented her dramas all over the world, including Israel. In 2011, Susie was recognized by the Knesset in Israel for her work with Holocaust survivors. She also has produced a narration of Corrie's autobiography, *The Hiding Place*, on audio CD. Listening to it, I thought I was hearing the actual voice of Corrie ten Boom! I recommend it to everyone.

When Susie came to South Luverne Baptist Church, I was very blessed to host her in our home in Petrey. We invited our pastor and his wife, Mike and Lisa Green, as well as Janice and Jack, to have dinner with Curtis and me and to meet Susie.

Lisa Green and Susie Sandager (impersonator of Corrie ten Boom) at the Petreys' house

Susie and I had a great time talking and singing together. We found out we had a common love of playing the piano and singing (as did Corrie ten Boom). Susie liked my *Hatikva* CD, and I gladly gave her one.

Something she said stuck with me. Interestingly, Susie's love for the Jews was birthed at the same time she committed her heart to Christ. Being a good Baptist, she was discouraged that although she possessed a great love for the Jewish people, she had not been able to lead a single Jew to Christ. After much prayer about the matter she finally heard from the Lord. Not audibly, but "quotably," He clearly said, "You love, I'll save." Ever since that time she and her husband John have followed that mandate, to just love the Jewish people.

Together they founded a project called Yad b' Yad (Hebrew for "hand in hand"), bringing together Christians and Jews in their community. God gave them great favor with the Jewish community in Albuquerque. Over the years their honors from the Anti-Defamation League, Israel Bonds, the Jewish Federation, and others are too numerous to list. Just imagine, in 1996, Susie, a Christian, was named "woman of the year" by the local chapter of Hadassah, the largest women's Zionist organization in the world! John, also a Christian, served two terms as treasurer of their local Jewish Community Center. They have earned the trust of Jews everywhere, because they have no agenda or ulterior motive, only love for the Jewish people.

Their ministry is called *Sandager Presentations.* John, a Christian attorney and excellent Bible teacher, makes a strong case for Christian support of Israel, and Susie gives voice to the legacy of the beloved Corrie ten Boom. They present to audiences of Christians and Jews in churches, synagogues, and theaters, inspiring understanding and friendship between our faith communities. Happily for me, Susie accepted our invitation to come to L.A. (lower Alabama) and help us spread God's word about His beloved chosen people.

Christians at the Feast in Jerusalem Spread the Word

As I was writing the last pages of this book, I read a news story on the internet that gives a perfect picture of my Mizpah message, that Christians should love and support Israel and the Jewish people:

On October 17, 2011, over 6,000 Christians from more than 80 nations paraded through the streets of Jerusalem in a solidarity march with Israel that culminated their celebration of the Feast of Tabernacles, sponsored by the International Christian Embassy Jerusalem (ICEJ). This march coincided with the release of a captured Israeli soldier, Gilad Shalit, who was kidnapped and imprisoned by the Hamas terrorist group in Gaza for over five years. Israelis danced in the streets as they welcomed this brave soldier home. A number of marchers held signs saying, "Welcome home Gilad" and "Israel is not alone."

Jerusalem Mayor Nir Barkat was among tens of thousands of Israelis lining the streets to greet Feast pilgrims. Enjoying his role as parade marshal, Barkat dived into the waves of Christian pilgrims to shake hands and embrace visitors from around the globe. Seated on the official viewing stand, when the lead banner of the ICEJ passed by, he jumped to his feet again and marched alongside it to the roaring approval of Christians and Israelis alike.

An attendee at the feast, Shay Kasper of Los Angeles, who had attended the annual Feast gathering every year since 1981, said, "We are so grateful about Gilad Shalit's release! It's been a prayer that has been going on for a long time and we are so thankful ... All the Jerusalem marches have been wonderful. We see more and more love going from both sides, from the Christians and the Israelis together."[86]

On the last night of the week-long Feast, Israel's Deputy Foreign Minister Daniel Ayalon spoke. He said, "There is a great awakening here in Israel and around the world of the need for the 'coming together' of Jews and Christians to keep God's commandments. God is sending you home as **watchmen** of Israel, so that His purpose will be fulfilled."[87]

Using the words "watchmen" and "purpose," Ayalon spoke the Word of God. Yea, and amen! I took up the challenge in 1995 to be a **watchman** (Mizpah) for Israel. My prayer while writing this book is that more and more Christians will do the same. We carry out God's **purpose** by loving the Jews, because Yeshua said, "Inasmuch as you did it to one of the least of **these my brethren**, you did it to **Me**" (Matt. 25:40).

Hannah May spreads the Word

In June of 2010, our friend Ben, a lay supply preacher in the Alabama-West Florida Conference of the United Methodist Church, came by to visit. He had just attended the annual conference in Montgomery, and he brought the 2010 Brochure of Reports for us to read.

He knew we would be interested in it, because Curtis was a Methodist pastor for 15 years before he stepped out and started an independent church. I looked through the book, and two resolutions caught my eye, "Resolution Regarding Israel and Replacement Theology" and "Resolution Regarding the Jewish People and Anti-Semitism."

As I read them, big "amens" rose up in my soul! The author's name was Hannah May, Director of East River Ministries. Her e-mail address was listed, so I wrote her an e-mail and thanked her for writing the resolutions. We began to correspond. The conference did not pass the resolutions, but she tried again at the 2011 conference, and they passed!

She had kept me updated prior to the last conference, so I prayed earnestly that the resolutions would pass. In checking out her web page I learned other things about Hannah. I could see we had a kindred spirit, and I rejoiced that God had planted her in the denomination I had grown up in and loved so much. Both Curtis and I had been pro-active in trying to move the Methodist Church back to her Wesley roots. We believed God had led us out only after we completed what He gave us to do.

Hannah has a similar ministry to mine. After I read her book, *Operation Olive Branch, A Collection of Mysteries Uncovered by a Spiritual Sleuth*,[88] my soul rose up again and said, "Amen and Amen!" I found that besides our love for Israel and the Jews, we also share a love for music. She is a violinist, and I am a pianist and singer. Reading about her prayer assignments from God that took her on some very exciting adventures really thrilled me. I also identified with her Nancy Drew theme of getting "clues" from the Holy Spirit in pursuit of her assignments. I was surprised that I knew many of the people in ministry that she mentioned in her book.

Also, finding out that John and Charles Wesley, the founders of Methodism, were ardent Zionists was great cause for rejoicing. Hannah even included in her book the words of two Zionist hymns written by Charles and edited by John Wesley in 1762. In those days there were very few people who espoused the return of the Jews to their ancient homeland, but the Wesley brothers could see it clearly in the Scriptures.

The inspiration I received from Hannah's book planted in me a desire to write my own story, which led to the book you are holding in your hands now. Hannah read my graduate thesis and loved it. She wrote the editor of her book and recommended me as a writer. This was before she knew that I had already contacted him about the possibility of publishing my book!

At this point in time we have never seen each other in person, but our correspondence has become that of old friends and confidantes. We belong to a "mutual admiration society." Hannah May has been a wonderful instrument of God for spreading His Word, and because of her influence, I myself can be more effective in spreading His Word.

Janice Horowitz Bell spreads the Word

After returning from our trip to Israel in 2003, my Jewish friend and ministry partner, Janice Bell, wrote an online devotional for her church page on October 19. Her words capture the heart message of my Mizpah ministry. Hopefully, when you read this, your heart will be moved to action on behalf of God's beloved Jewish people with whom His covenants are still in effect:

HIS CALMING PRESENCE

Today's Scripture: "So shall my word be that goeth forth out of my mouth: it shall not return unto me void, but it shall prosper in the thing whereto I sent it." (Isaiah 55:11)

"Whereunto I am appointed a preacher, and an apostle, and a teacher of the Gentiles." (2 Timothy 1:11)

During our visit to Jerusalem, Nancy and I had become acquainted with a young man who said that the Lord had told him to come to Israel for Yom Kippur. He was a layman who has had opportunity to preach in many different countries of the world. I assumed he had a great love for the Jewish people. Why else would the Lord have told him to come? He had to fly stand-by, and it took him three tries before he was able to get a flight. He made the same flight that we were on and took the same taxi that we did to Jerusalem. I really liked him, and we had some very good conversations. We did discover that he really did NOT understand the Jewish Roots of Christianity. Nor did he understand how the Jews and the Church became separate. Nancy, having a head full of knowledge and scripture, proceeded to attempt to teach him. He really seemed to be open and appreciative of the truths she was sharing with him.

We did not see him for several days, and then one evening I had the urge to go to the WALL to pray. He accompanied us, so we wouldn't have to go alone. I had a very emotional experience with the Lord while at the WALL. We took a cab to McDonald's on Ben Yehuda Street. (We had had all the vegetables that this fast food junkie could stand.) During our conversations I began to sense that he had quite a disdain for the Jews. "After all," he said, "they rejected and killed their Messiah." I was sort of shocked! Why was he here? What was his purpose? I decided that the Lord had sent him to Jerusalem at his own expense, I might add, just to meet Nancy and me. He needed compassion and love for the family that he had been adopted into. My heart just ached. Was meeting him the Lord's purpose for sending us? Was he our DIVINE APPOINTMENT? I probably will never know for sure.

We had a rather interesting conversation with him. When we were back at the hotel and continuing our reasoning with him, he made the remark, "The Jews got what they deserved!" He was referring to the **Crusades, the Spanish Inquisition, the Holocaust, the pogroms, etc., etc**. Needless to say, I was mortified. I could not speak and did not say anything else to him. Nancy continued for a few minutes, but I remained mute. On parting, I simply made a cordial goodbye. My heart was crushed, my spirit bruised, my soul was wounded. I could not shake it, and Nancy tried unsuccessfully to cheer me up. I thanked God it was late so I could just crawl under the covers and retreat to the solitude of the night.

Sleep, however, did not come. I tossed and turned and was grieved in my spirit. Here was a precious young man, flying all over the world preaching the gospel. I know the Lord is using him, but when it comes to this subject, he was so far off base. Who knows how many people he was wrongly influencing?

Oh God, why did I have to hear those words? Nancy had gone to sleep, but I was awake for quite a while. I was on my side, eyes closed, and crying. Suddenly, I felt the Lord's hand slip into my hand. I never opened up my eyes, but I felt HIS presence there with me. My hand was no longer in a curved, relaxed position. It was open, and I could feel HIS warmth and love, and HIS calming Spirit. I went right to sleep and slept like a baby.

I'm not sure what this young man will do with the teaching that we gave him. I do know that HIS WORD NEVER returns void. Isaiah 55:11 says, "So shall My word be that goeth forth out of my mouth: it shall not return unto me void, but it shall accomplish that which I please, and it shall prosper in the thing whereto I sent it." I do not profess to be a preacher, but I know that God has called both Nancy and me to teach the message of Jewish Roots to the Gentile Church, as well as to take the Gospel to the Jews. "Whereunto I am appointed a preacher, and an apostle, and a teacher of the Gentiles." (2 Timothy 1:11)

Jesus also heard the words this young man spoke. He, too, was grieved in HIS SPIRIT. Knowing my distress, HE had empathy for me and simply put HIS HAND in mine, calming me as HE whispered to my spirit, "We have a lot of work to do."

TODAY'S CHALLENGE: Won't you join me in prayer for this young man, we'll simply call S.R.? Pray that God will convict Christians who may share this anti-Semitic attitude.

Do Janice's words grab your heart? Will you join me on my Jewish Roots journey? "Many are called, but few are chosen" (Matt. 20:16). If you have read this far, I can confidently say with Peter, "But **you** are a **chosen** generation, a royal priesthood, a holy nation,

His own **special people**, that you may proclaim the praises of Him who called you out of darkness into His marvelous light" (I Pet. 2:9).

If you are a Gentile believer, you are grafted into the Jewish olive tree (Rom. 11:24) and "adopted" (Rom. 8:15) into the Jewish family of God and the "commonwealth of Israel" (Eph. 2:12). As a part of the Church, you have not **replaced** Israel in the promises of God, but you have been "chosen" to be ONE with God's original covenant people.

Echad

Yeshua made the outrageous claim, "I and My Father are one" (John 10:30). It occurred to me one day that the Gospel of Jesus Christ can be summed up in that simple Hebrew word, a compound word, *echad* **(one)**. In Yeshua's high priestly prayer that night in the Garden of Gethsemane, he no doubt prayed in the sacred Hebrew language to the Father. He said, "I do not pray for these [Jewish apostles] alone, but also for those who will believe in me through their word [Jews and Gentiles]; that they all may be **one** [*echad*], as You, Father, are in Me, and I in You; that they also may be **one** [*echad*] in Us, that the world may believe that You sent Me" (John 17:20-21).

From these words of Yeshua, I can see that the unity or oneness (*echad*) of Jewish and Gentile believers is the **key** to world evangelism. On the Day of Pentecost following the ascension of Yeshua into heaven, His disciples were praying **in one accord (unity)** when the gift of the Holy Spirit was poured out on that group of 120. Today, when such unity is demonstrated once again, the final ingathering of souls worldwide will take place ("that the world may believe that you sent Me").

Every day Yeshua recited the Jewish creed God gave His people in the wilderness, which is named for the first word, "Shema," meaning "hear." Faithful Jews recite this creed today, saying that Hebrew word "echad" – "Hear, O Israel, the Lord our God, the Lord is One [echad]" (Deut. 6:4). Yes, the Lord is **One**, and <u>He</u>

wants all believers, Jew and Gentile, to be **one**. May Yeshua's prayer for *echad* (unity), resulting in the greatest revival the world has ever known, be realized in our time!

That is my hope and prayer as a Mizpah for Israel. Shalom!

APPENDIX A

The Hebrew Alphabet

THE HEBREW ALPHABET (SQUARE LETTERS)

Letter	Name	English	Value	Signification
א	Aleph	'	1	Ox
ב	Beth	b	2	House
ג	Gimel	g	3	Camel
ד	Daleth	d	4	Door
ה	He	h	5	Latticewindow
ו	Vav	v	6	Hook
ז	Zayin	z	7	Weapon
ח	Cheth	ch	8	Fence
ט	Tet	t	9	Snake
י	Yod	y	10	Hand
כ	Kaph	k	20	Bent Hand
ל	Lamed	l	30	Ox-Goad
מ	Mem	m	40	Water
נ	Num	n	50	Fish
ס	Samech	s	60	Prop
ע	Ayin	·	70	Eye
פ	Pe	p	80	Mouth
צ	Tsade	ts	90	Fish Hook
ק	Qoph	q	100	Back of Head
ר	Resh	r	200	Head
שׂ	Sin	s	300	Tooth
שׁ	Shin	sh	—	··
ת	Tav	th	400	Cross

Al Novak, Hebrew Honey (Houston: J. Countryman Publishers, 1987), p. 307

TALLIT (Prayer Shawl) - Interesting Facts

1. Jesus wore a tallit. It was His "prayer closet." The woman who touched the hem of his garment touched the tassel (Hebrew word tzitzit). She and others were healed by touching the tzitzit of Jesus' tallit (Matt. 9:20; 14:36).

2. The Pharisees took pride in their long tassels (Matt. 23:5).

3. God commanded the Israelites to make tassels with a blue thread on the four corners of their garments in order to remember His commandments (Num. 15:37-41; Deut. 22:12). Religious Jewish men wear these prayer shawls at all times (as an undergarment).

4. The tallit was used in proposing marriage (Ruth 3:9; Ezek. 16:8). Today Jewish couples stand under a stretched out tallit (canopy) in the wedding ceremony. Sometimes they are wrapped together in a tallit.

5. Sometimes the tallit on one's outstretched arms is spoken of as wings (Mal. 4:2; Ps. 91:4). This "overshadowing" is also seen in Genesis 1:2, Deuteronomy 32:11, Luke 1:35 and 9:34, and Acts 5:15.

6. The tallit represents the 613 commandments contained in the Tanakh (Old Testament). It is figured thus: the numerical value

of the Hebrew letters of *tzitzit* is 600. Each tassel has 8 strands. and 5 double knots: 600 + 8 + 5 = 613. There are 365 "thou shalt nots" and 248 "thou shalts." In modern times 135 negative laws and 33 positive laws are applicable. The laws relating to the Temple cannot be observed today, since the Temple was destroyed in A.D. 70. The perfect sacrifice of Yeshua, once and for all, removed the necessity for keeping the laws regarding animal sacrifice.

7. Jews use a *tallit* at all major occasions – circumcisions, bar mitzvahs, weddings, and burials. A *tallit* protects the Torah scrolls when they are moved. Damaged Torah scrolls are buried in a tallit.

8. When the nation of Israel was born in 1948, three people (separately) came up with the idea of using a tallit for the Israeli flag with the Star of David in the center.

9. The *tallit* is a "little tent," a private sanctuary like the Tent of Meeting in the wilderness wanderings. (Paul may actually have made *tallits* instead of large tents we normally think of.) The tassels represent the cords that hold down the Tabernacle.

10. The top hem of the *tallit* is called the "crown" (*atarah*) and always hangs the same way like the tent walls of the Tabernacle. The Hebrew words are a blessing: "Blessed art Thou, O Lord our God, King of the Universe, Who has sanctified us by His commandments and commanded us to wrap ourselves in the *tzitzit*."

11. Elijah's mantle was likely a *tallit*. Read II Kings 2:11-14.

APPENDIX C

Blessings to the Nations
By Individual Jews & the Nation of Israel

The worldwide population of the Jews is approximately 13.3 million. There are almost six million Jews in Israel. Israel is the 100th smallest country (roughly half the size of Lake Michigan) with less than 1/1000th of the world's population. In view of the size of this tiny people group, please consider the following facts, and give glory to the God of Israel who promised to make the descendants of Abraham, Isaac, and Jacob (Israel) a blessing to the world!

I   JEWS IN THE MEDICAL AND LIFE SCIENCES (www.jinfo.org)

In the late Middle Ages, Jews were only 1% of Europe, but half the physicians were Jews. Kings, queens, and other rulers of Europe had Jewish personal physicians. Many Popes and every monastery had Jewish physicians. Jews have accounted for some 40% of U.S. Nobel Prizes in medicine and constitute over one-third of the combined membership of the life sciences divisions of the U.S. National Academy of Sciences and its Institute of Medicine.

The contributions of individual Jews are:
- invention of local anesthesia/ discovery of Novocaine
- discovery of blood groups and RH factor
- founding of modern chemotherapeutic medicine/ first treatment of syphilis
- development of penicillin, streptomycin, cortisone, aspirin, Tylenol, anti-depressants, Coumadin, oral contraceptives, Salk and Sabin polio vaccines, Hepatitis-B vaccine, cancer chemotherapy, radiation oncology, AIDS drugs

- breaking of the genetic code/ opening up field of genetic engineering
    - discovery of the basis of MRI diagnostic imaging technique
    - invention of sonogram
    - invention of flexible endoscope
    - co-invention of LASIK eye surgery
    - invention of cataract surgery
    - invention of the cardiac defibrillator, external pacemaker, and cardiac monitor
    - invention of the Heimlich Maneuver

II JEWS IN LITERATURE

The Bible, the single greatest legacy of the Jews, has been translated, as of May 2011, into 2,572+ languages (out of 6,800+ languages in the world), one of the two Testaments in 1,668 languages, and the full protestant canon of the Bible in 457 languages. (http://en.wikipedia.org/wiki/Bible_translations_by_language). The Bible is the most widely read and influential body of literature in all human history, and it originated with the Jews as the Holy Spirit inspired them.

III JEWS IN MUSIC

(www.jinfo.org)

Of the 100 leading virtuoso performers of the 20th century, Jews account for approximately 2/3 of the violinists, half the cellists, and 40% of the pianists. (www.muzicklijsjes.nl/100players.htm)

The most notable classical composers in history have been Felix Mendelssohn, Jacques Offenbach, Gustav Mahler, Arnold Shoenberg, George Gershwin, and Aaron Copland. Jewish composers in the development of the American Musical Theater and in film music are almost too numerous to mention. Approximately 40% of the membership of the Songwriters Hall of Fame is Jewish (www.jinfo.org).

A short sampling of these outstanding Jewish composers and singers are Irving Berlin, Richard Rodgers, Jerome Kern, Al Jolson,

Bob Dylan, Barbara Streisand, Diana Shore, Leonard Bernstein, and Burt Bacharach.

Jewish recipients of Academy Awards and Tony Awards (composers and lyricists):

- Academy Award for best original song – 51% of recipients (1934-2010)
- Academy Award for best musical scoring of a motion picture – 49% of recipients (1934-2003)
- Tony Award for best musical production – 64% of recipients (1949-2011)
- Tony Award for best original score of a musical – 70% of recipients (1947-2011)

IV ELECTRONICS IN ISRAEL (2010 United With Israel
- http://www.unitedwithisrael.com/pdf/amazing_facts.pdf)

- The cell phone was developed in Israel at Motorola's largest development center.
- Most of the Windows NT and XP operating systems were developed by Microsoft-Israel
- The Intel Pentium chip technology was designed in Israel
- The Pentium microprocessor in your computer was most likely made in Israel. (Israel has the highest number of home computers per capita in the world.)
- Internet voice-mail technology was developed in Israel
- Four young Israelis developed the technology for the AOL Instant Messenger ICQ (1996)
- Checkpoint, world leader in online security, and invention of Firewall by Israeli company
- First PC anti virus software was developed in Israel in 1979, and Israel continues as the world leader in developing anti virus software programs.
- M-Systems company developed the USB-Flash Drives, used for portable storage all over the world.
- IBM, Kodak, Cisco, Hewlett-Packard, Google, and many more have large scale research and development centers in Israel.

V AGRICULTURE (2010 United With Israel)

- In response to serious water shortages, Israeli engineers and agriculturalists developed a revolutionary drip-irrigation system to minimize the amount of water used to grow crops.

- Israel has helped several African farming communities with drip irrigation schemes as well as establishing 1,000 water projects in 500 Romanian villages.

- Israel recycles 75% of its waste water – a world record.

- It will soon be possible to order rain in Israel. A group of Israeli, Belgian and American researchers from Ben Gurion University in the Negev have started "The Geshem Project" (*geshem* = rain in Hebrew), which could reduce world hunger. The system put in place over an area of nine km squared could bring rain to a region measuring 40 to 100 km^2.

- Ben Gurion University of the Negev scientist developed a biological control for mosquitoes and black flies that cause malaria and river blindness, saving the sight and lives of millions of people in Africa and China.

VI RECENT LIFE-SAVING DISCOVERIES AND INVENTIONS (2010 United With Israel)

- Israeli scientists developed the first fully computerized, no-radiation diagnostic instrumentation for breast cancer.

- An Israeli company developed a computerized system for ensuring proper administration of medications, thus removing human error from medical treatment. Every year in U.S. hospitals, 7,000 patients die from treatment mistakes.

- Israel's Givun Imaging developed the first ingestible video camera, so small it fits inside a pill. It can view inside the small intestine to detect cancer and digestive disorders.

- Researchers in Israel developed a new device that directly helps the heart pump blood. It is synchronized with a camera and helps doctors diagnose the heart's functions.

• The ClearLight device, a new acne treatment, causes acne bacteria to self-destruct without damaging surrounding skin or tissue.

• Recently, Vaxil Bio Therapeutics in Israel has broken ground on a cancer vaccine, which could be available in 2017, to help treat cancer and keep 90 per cent of cancers from recurring! (Ynetnews, January 16, 2012)

This list of contributions of the Jewish people and the nation of Israel only scratches the surface of the phenomenal blessings the world has received from God's Chosen People. In my graduate thesis, *Destiny of the Jews*, I attempted to show the varied contributions Jews have made in almost every area of life. Following are a few unique ones:

• In her years of existence as a nation, Israel has come to the aid of over 140 countries despite its own difficulties, even to some countries who refuse diplomatic relations with the Jewish state (internet article, "Israel Remains Committed to Global Relief Efforts, Aug. 19, 2010"). For instance, IDF rescue and medical teams led the world in rendering emergency help for the victims of the Haiti earthquake disaster on January 12, 2010. Israel's long experience in disasters and constant terror attacks has helped them develop advanced systems for search and rescue. In Haiti they rescued a 22-year-old man from the rubble of a three-story building after he was trapped for ten days!

• One of the largest volunteer organizations in the world, Yad Sarah, is located in Israel. They even offer home care services in the U.S. and the former Soviet Union.

• Albert Einstein was Jewish. His theories have profoundly affected the laws of physics and understanding of the universe. His name today is synonymous with the word *genius*.

• Hyman Rickover, a Jewish scientist, developed the first atomic powered submarine.

• Abe Saperstein founded and coached the Harlem Globetrotters Basketball Team, who trotted the globe and became

"America's Number One Goodwill Ambassadors." Two famous Jewish baseball players were Hank Greenberg and Sandy Koufax.

• Most of modern America's giant department stores are outgrowths of the early Jewish peddlers' hard work and ingenuity. An example is Stein Mart. Other Jewish names in merchandising are Levi Stauss, Macy's, Tanger Factory Outlet Stores, Ralph Lauren, Calvin Klein, Sears Roebuck, and Starbucks Coffee.

• The world has been entertained by innumerable Jewish comedians, actors, and film directors. A few are Jerry Lewis, Henry Winkler, Walter Matthau, Milton Berle, Marx Brothers, George Burns, Kirk Douglas, Danny Kaye, Jack Benny, Tony Randall, Ed Asner, Bette Midler, Steven Spielberg, Tony Curtis, Paul Newman, and Michael Landon.

This is by no means an exhaustive list of the contributions that Jewish people have given to the world, but the things listed here are quite astounding. However, the most important contribution that God's Chosen People have made to the world is the Messiah of Israel, who was born to a Jewish girl in Nazareth 2,000 years ago. His name is Jesus Christ or Yeshua HaMashiach, the Jewish Messiah and Savior of the World! The Jews will have their finest hour when they say, "Baruch haba b'Shem Adonai" – "Blessed is He who comes in the name of the Lord" (Matt. 23:39).

Endnotes

1   Shabbat – the Jewish Sabbath, meaning "to cease, to end, to rest."

2   Christian Friends of Israel – an international, nondenominational, Christian Zionist ministry, headquartered in Jerusalem with offices throughout the world, with purposes to (1) educate the church about her Hebrew heritage and Biblical responsibility to the Jewish people, and to (2) work for the welfare of the Jewish nation by blessing Israel according to Gen. 12:2. Founded in 1985 by Ray and Sharon Sanders. www.cfijerusalem.org

3   Corrie ten Boom with John and Elizabeth Sherrill, *The Hiding Place*, (Chosen Books, 1971).

4   Ibid, p. 217.

5   Ibid, p. 238.

6   Ibid.

7   Yad Vashem - "a memorial and a name" in Hebrew, based on Isaiah 56:5. Jerusalem museum in memory of the names of the Holocaust victims.

8   Lydia Prince as told to her husband, Derek Prince, *Appointment in Jerusalem*, (Old Tappan, NJ: Chosen Books, Inc./Derek Prince Publications, distributed by Fleming H. Revell Co., 1975).

9   Ibid, p. 33.

10   Michael L. Brown, *Answering Jewish Objections to Jesus*, five volumes (vols. 1-4, Grand Rapids: Baker Books, 2000-2007; vol. 5, San Francisco: Pomegranate Publications, 2010).

11   Passover Seder – A meal on the first night of an eight-day observance of the Exodus of the enslaved Israelites from Egypt. The story of Exodus 12 tells of the death angel "passing over" the homes of the Israelites because of the blood of the Passover Lamb on their doorposts. "Seder" means "order." The cermonial foods represent aspects of their slavery in Egypt and their miraculous deliverance by the God of Israel. All leaven is removed from their homes for eight days.

12   The Watchman International – world-wide prayer ministry for Israel and the Middle East, founded by Lars and Harriet Enarson. http://thewatchman.org/en/about/

13   James Strong, S.T.D., LL.D., *The Exhaustive Concordance of the Bible* (Nashville: Abingdon, 1890).

14   Dick Mills and David Michael, *Messiah and His Hebrew Alphabet* (Orange, CA: Dick Mills Ministries, 1994).

15   The *tav* in modern Hebrew does not look like a cross. However, from "about 2900 years ago, every example of Hebrew lettering from

scrolls, inscriptions, coins, and stone has the letter tav as a cross shape of some type. The first case of the modern *tav* in which there is no intersection of lines occurred in Palmyra in the third century A.D. (See *Jewish Encyclopedia*, Volume 1, pages 449-453)." The ancient cross-shaped *tav* that had been in use from at least Solomon's time through the beginning of the decline of Rome began to change to the present form. This begs the question, could this change have represented an anti-Christian bias?

16   Mills and Michael, pp. 135-136.

17   Eliezer Tirkel, *Everyday Hebrew* (Lincolnwood, IL: Passport Books, 1995).

18   David Biven and Roy Blizzard, Jr., *Understanding the Difficult Words of Jesus*,(Shippensburg, PA: Destiny Image Publishers, 1994) p. 17.

19   *Tanach* is a Hebrew acronym (TNK) for the three parts of the Old Testament: Torah ("instruction" – first five books), Neviim (Prophets), and Ketuvim (Writings). The books are the same but arranged differently from the Christian Old Testament. Jesus validated this three-fold division of the Scripture in His day (Luke 24:44).

20   Martin Luther, "Table Talk," quoted in Pinchas E. Lapide, *Hebrew in the Church*, trans. Erroll F. Rhodes (Grand Rapids: William B. Eerdmans Publishing Col, 1984).

21   Martin Luther, *Concerning the Jews and Their Lies* (reprinted in Talmage, Disputation and Dialogue, pp. 34-36).

22   *The Roots of Christian Anti-Semitism* (New York: Liberty Press, 1981), p. 27.

23   Luis De Torres, a marano and interpreter for Columbus, set foot on American soil at San Salvador in the Bahamas. He later became the first settler in Cuba.

24   Michael L. Brown, *Our Hands are Stained With Blood* (Shippensburg, PA: Destiny Image, 1992).

25   Arthur D. Morse, *While Six Million Died: A Chronicle of American Apathy* (Overlook TP, 1998). For a three-page summary of this subject, go to http://www.internationalsocialist.org/pdfs/While6MillionDied.pdf.

26   Dr. Duane Weis, "Why We Honor Israel and the Jewish People," Tape recording #9101, Israel in Prophecy Conference – "The Final Countdown," Christ for the Nations, Inc., P.O. Box 769000, Dallas, TX 75376.

27   Shavuot – "weeks" in Hebrew, meaning the Feast of Weeks or Pentecost (50 days or 7 weeks plus one day counted from Passover; Lev. 23: 15-16).

28   Rosh HaShanah – "head of the year" in Hebrew, New Year's Day, also biblical Feast of Trumpets (Lev. 23:24).

29   School of Worship in Jerusalem, Roy and Mary Kendall, http://www.sowij.com.

30   Challah – loaf of yeast-leavened egg bread usually braided and eaten by Jews on the Sabbath and other holy days

31   Falafel – a sandwich of pita bread stuffed with ground spiced chickpeas and vegetables shaped into balls and deep-fried.

32   Text of "Jerusalem Documentary," Barry & Batya Segal, *Sh'ma Yisrael, Messianic Praise* - cassette tape (Jerusalem: Greetings from Jerusalem Ltd., 1994 Kingsway ThankYou Music).

33   Haggadah – "tell" the story (Ex. 13:8) – program book for the Passover Seder meal.

34   Sabra – native born Israeli ("fruit of the cactus" – tzabar – rough on the outside but sweet inside).

35   Bridges for Peace – a Jerusalem-based, Bible-believing Christian organization supporting Israel and building relationships between Christians and Jews worldwide through education and practical deeds expressing God's love and mercy. www.bridgesforpeace.com

36   *Via Dolorosa* – Words and Music by Billy Sprague and Niles Borop, ©1983 Meadowgreen Music Co./Word Music (a division of Word, Inc.).

37   *Hatikva* (The Hope) – 17 songs on CD, piano & voice by Nancy Petrey: *The Lord is Building Jerusalem, Up to Jerusalem, Hevenu Shalom Alecheim, It is Good to Praise the Lord, Hodu L'Adonai Ki Tov, All That I Need (My Only Hope), Shaalu Shalom Yerushalayim, Sabbath Prayer, Hineh Ma Tov, Hava Nagila, The Exodus Song, Sh'ma Yisrael, Hatikva, He that Keepeth Israel, In the Shadow of Your Wings, I Rise Up to Worship (tune: Chariots of Fire)*, and *Kol Dodi*.

38   Aliyah – Hebrew for "going up" as in the Psalms of Ascension, 125-129, pilgrim songs of worshipers going up to Jerusalem; a term now used for Jewish immigration to Israel.

39   In 1727, a Pentecost-type revival came to the Moravian village of Herrnhut, in present-day Germany, and a continuous, 24 hour a day, prayer meeting began which lasted 100 years! (http://en.wikipedia.org/wiki/Moravian_Church) Through Count Nikolaus Ludwig von Zinzendorf, a petition for Israel was added to the Litany in 1740. This was the first time a Western church had made prayer for Israel a regular part of the liturgy (Craig D. Atwood, "Zinzendorf and Judaism").

40   Gustav Scheller with Jonathan Miles, *Operation Exodus* (Kent, England: Sovereign World, 1998) p. 9.

41   Ebenezer Emergency Fund – Operation Exodus, Bournemouth UK, www.operation-exodus.org and Lancaster, NY; http://ebenezerusa.org.

42   Marvin J Rosenthal, "The Peace Before the Storm" from *The Middle East: A History of Searching for Peace*, Zion's Fire Magazine, September-October 1993, p. 26 (out of print).

43   Mitchell Bard, "The Palestinian Refugees" from Jewish Virtual Library, www.jewishvirtuallibrary.org/jsource/History/refugees.html.

44   William Hull, "On Eagles' Wings" in *Christians for Israel Today* newspaper, Special Aliyah Edition, (Manassas, VA) pp. 4, 9. Taken from *Israel, Key to Prophecy*, William Hull (Grand Rapids: Zondervan, 1964).

45   Tom Hess, *Let My People Go!* (Jerusalem: Progressive Vision International, 1997).

46   Torah – First five books of the Old Testament, also called Pentateuch. Torah means "teaching" or "instruction." The Greek word is translated "Law."

47   Menorah – lamp stand. We had 9-branched menorahs, "hanukiahs." In the Temple were 7-branched menorahs.

48   Mezuzah – Hebrew word for "doorposts." The small case contains a rolled-up parchment with Scripture, Deut. 6:4-9 and Deut. 11:13-21. The case is attached at an angle to the right side of the doorway to the house.

49   Diane A. McNeil, *Ruth 3,000 Years of Sleeping Prophecy Awakened*, (Xulon Press, 2009), www.xulonpress.com.

50   Greg Myre and Jennifer Griffin, *This Burning Land* (Hoboken, NJ: John Wiley & Sons, Inc., 2010), pp. 114-118.

51   Chazon Yerushalayim (Vision of Jerusalem) – P.O. Box 29340, Jerusalem 91298, Israel (U.S. Address: World Harvest Now, Inc., P.O. Box 911, Denton, TX 76201) – suran@netvision.net.il/ www.jerusalemvision. com.

52   Pamela Suran, Biblical Artist – www.pamelasuran.com

53   The Southern Stairs," *That the World May Know* – http://www.Followtherabbi.com/Brix?pageID=5015.

54   Torger Thompson and Zola Levitt, *Creation of a Masterpiece*, (Dallas: Biblical Arts Center, 1976), pp. 63-64.

55   Saint James the Lesser – http://www.communityofhopeinc.org/ Prayer%20Pages/Saints/james%20lesser.html.

56   Ner Yaakov, Jerusalem, Newsletter – August, 2011, www.neryaakov.com.

57   Pam Bird, *The Jewish Wedding & the Lord's Return*, Christian Friends of Israel UK, 2005, https://www.cfi.org.uk/shop.

58   The Armenian Genocide – General Information," http://www. agiasofia.com/armenia/armenia1.html.

59   Simon Wiesenthal Center – http://www.wiesenthal.com.
60   Josh McDowell, *More Than a Carpenter* (Tyndalle House, 1977).
61   Nazareth Village, Israel –
www.nazarethvillage.com/twots_feb06.ph.p
62   Arkansas Institute of Holy Land Studies, renamed American
Institute for Advanced Biblical Studies, 3905 N. Hills Blvd, North Little
Rlock, AR 72116, tel. 800-617-6205 – founded by a consortium of
scholars of the Hebrew language, culture, and history, both in Jerusalem
and America, in 1991 as a specialty college in the field of Middle Eastern
history. www.americaninstituteonline.org,
63   Marvin R. Wilson, *Our Father Abraham: Jewish Roots of the
Christian Faith* (Grand Rapids: Eerdmans Publishing Co./ Dayton: Center
of Judaic-Christian Studies, 1989), p. 248.
64   Ibid.
65   Norma Parrish Archbold, *The Mountains of Israel* (A Phoebe's
Song Publication, 1993).
66   Josephus, *The Antiquities of the Jews*, 18.3.3, p. 480.
67   Josephus, *The Life of Flavius Josephus*, 26^k, p. 9.
68   Josephus, *The Wars of the Jews*, 4.10.7, p. 694.
69   Marvin R. Wilson, pp. 169-174.
70   Re-Imagining: Christian Feminist Conference –
http://en.wikipedia.org/wiki/Re-Imagining:_Christian_feminist_conference
71   Max I. Dimont, *Jews, God and History* (New York: Mentor of
Penguin Books USA, Inc., 1994), pp. 18-20.
72   Israel Central Bureau of Statistics – 2010.
73   Ed F. Vallowe, *Biblical Mathematics* (Columbia, SC: The Olive
Press, 1998), p. 211.
74   Henry M. Morris, *The Genesis Record, a Scientific and
Devotional Commentary on the Book of Beginnings* (Grand Rapids: Baker
Book House, 1976), p. 151.
75   Don Richardson, *Eternity in Their Hearts, the Untold Story of
Christianity Among Folk Religions of Ancient People* (Ventura, CA: Regal
Books, 1981), pp. 44, 77.
76   Mrs. Macleod Wylie, *The Gospel in Burma* (London: W.H.
Dalton, Bookseller to the Queen, 1859).
77   C.H. Kang and Ethel R. Nelson, *The Discovery of Genesis* (St.
Louis: Concordia Publishing House, 1979), pp. 41, 9, 57, 95.
78   Richard Booker, *How the Cross Became a Sword* (The
Woodlands, TX: Sounds of the Trumpet, 1994).
79   Richard Booker, *Islam, Christianity, and Israel* (The Woodlands,
TX: Sounds of the Trumpet, Inc., 1994).

80   Richard Booker, *The Root and Branches, An Introduction to the Jewish Roots of Christianity* (The Woodlands, TX: Sounds of the Trumpet, Inc., 2001).
81   Robert St. John, *Tongue of the Prophets* (N. Hollywood, CA: Wilshire Book Co., 1952).
82   Ann Spangler and Lois Tverberg, *Sitting at the Feet of Rabbi Jesus* (Grand Rapids: Zondervan, 2000).
83   Rabbi Jonathan Bernis, *A Rabbi Looks at the Last Days* (Phoenix: Jewish Voice Ministries International Publishing, 2008).
84   Ray Vander Laan, *Promised Land Discovery Guide* (Grand Rapids: Zondervan, 1999, 2008). *That the World May Know* and *Faith Lessons* are trademarks of Focus on the Family.
85   Katherine Zoepf, "To Eye of Saudi Beholders, Camels Make Them Swoon," (http://www.nytimes.com/2008/03/16/world/africa/16iht-journal.4.11147854.html, 2008).
86   ICEJ Staff Writers, "Israel's Deputy Foreign Minister Sees Great Awakening" (Charisma Media, 2011, http://www.charismanews.com/world/32196-israels-deputy-foreign-minister-see-great-awakening).
87   Ibid.
88   Hannah May, *Operation Olive Branch, A Collection of Mysteries Uncovered by a Spiritual Sleuth* (Energion Publications, www.energionpubs.com, 2011).

www.ingramcontent.com/pod-product-compliance
Lightning Source LLC
Chambersburg PA
CBHW022118080426
42734CB00006B/170